Diogenes of Sinope

Even bronze groweth old with time, but thy fame, Diogenes, not all Eternity shall take away. (Diogenes Laertius VI, 78)

Copy of a Roman statue of Diogenes found at Villa Albani

Diogenes of Sinope

The Man in the Tub

LUIS E. NAVIA

Contributions in Philosophy, Number 67

GREENWOOD PRESS
Westport, Connecticut • London

Library of Congress Cataloging-in-Publication Data

Navia, Luis E.
    Diogenes of Sinope : the man in the tub / Luis E. Navia.
       p.   cm.—(Contributions in philosophy, ISSN 0084–926X ; no. 67)
    Includes bibliographical references and indexes.
    ISBN 0–313–30672–9 (alk. paper)
    1. Diogenes, d. ca. 323 B.C. 2. Cynics (Greek philosophy)
I. Title. II. Series.
B305.D44N38 1998
183′.4—dc21   98–15322
[B]

British Library Cataloguing in Publication Data is available.

Copyright © 1998 by Luis E. Navia

All rights reserved. No portion of this book may be reproduced, by any process or technique, without the express written consent of the publisher.

Library of Congress Catalog Card Number: 98–15322
ISBN: 0–313–30672–9
ISSN: 0084–926X

First published in 1998

Greenwood Press, 88 Post Road West, Westport, CT 06881
An imprint of Greenwood Publishing Group, Inc.

Printed in the United States of America

The paper used in this book complies with the
Permanent Paper Standard issued by the National
Information Standards Organization (Z39.48–1984).

P

Copyright Acknowledgment

The author and publisher gratefully acknowledge permission for use of the following material:

Excerpts reprinted by permission of the publishers and the Loeb Classical Library from *Diogenes of Laertius: Lives of Eminent Philosophers*. Volume II, translated by R. D. Hicks, Cambridge, Mass.: Harvard University Press, 1925.

> In order to keep this title in print and available to the academic community, this edition was produced using digital reprint technology in a relatively short print run. This would not have been attainable using traditional methods. Although the cover has been changed from its original appearance, the text remains the same and all materials and methods used still conform to the highest book-making standards.

Contents

Preface	vii
Chapter 1 — **A Biographical Sketch**	1
Chapter 2 — **The Practice of Cynicism**	45
Chapter 3 — **The Making of a Cynic**	73
Chapter 4 — **The Building Blocks of Cynicism**	107
Chapter 5 — **The Legacy of Diogenes**	133
Appendix — Diogenes Laertius: *The Life of Diogenes of Sinope*	153
Bibliography	181
Index of Names	195
Index of Subjects	205

Preface

In the preparation of this critical study of Diogenes of Sinope, my aim has been to present a comprehensive and documented account of his life and his philosophical stance on the basis of the information provided by the sources. The task of constructing the biography of Diogenes is exceedingly difficult, because in his case, possibly more than in those of other ancient philosophers, we must deal not only with the scarcity of reliable sources and testimonies, but also with the mountains of anecdotal and fictional accounts that are responsible for the creation of a veritable literary legend around the Cynic who once lived in a tub. Who or what Diogenes was, what philosophical convictions animated and guided his antics and his behavior, what circumstances led him to assume so uncompromising an attitude of defiance toward his world—these are questions that admit of no simple answers and that, when answered, remain problematical issues that are open to interpretation and are entrenched in scholarly controversy. Still, despite the difficulties generated by the scarcity of reliable information and by the multitude of undocumented attributions, it is possible to reconstruct, even if only in outline, the portrait of the famous man who has managed to remain alive in the imagination of many even after the twenty-three centuries since his death.

From this portrait we can draw important philosophical conclusions that are of relevance and value for us, who, despite so many years of cultural evolution and despite innumerable advances in science and technology, remain largely as intellectually dense and morally corrupt as the "less-than-human" creatures among whom Diogenes lived, and for whom he reserved some of his most caustic and devastating comments. Neither in the realm of ideas, nor in the moral fabric of society, nor in national or international affairs, nor, in fact, in any area of human concern and activity, have we advanced one inch beyond the Greeks of classical times. We might even say that cultural stagnation is the appropriate way to characterize the course of human history since the time when Diogenes, carrying a lighted lamp in broad daylight, walked backwards through the streets of Athens, searching unsuccessfully for a true human being. Genuine specimens of humanity are today as rare as they were in classical times.

Classical Cynicism, of which Diogenes is undoubtedly the best representative, constitutes a fascinating philosophical and cultural phenomenon of Greek and Roman times. For almost eight hundred years, philosophers, who called themselves Cynics, literally 'dogs' in their language, preached and practiced a set of convictions and a style of life that challenged, often in brutal and astonishing ways, the norms and conventions of their society. From their point of view, the human world was in a state of moral bankruptcy and intellectual vacuity that required a systematic defacing of its values, which is precisely what the Cynics endeavored to do, quite unsuccessfully, we might say, for the world took only a passing notice of them and proceeded to act as if they had never existed. Even their writings, apparently voluminous and varied, perished and were mostly forgotten. But not for this, should the Cynics be set aside or ignored, for their message has relevance in every human context and especially in ours, when, because of the accomplishments in science and the engulfing progress of technology, we may have come to believe that all our affairs, intellectual and moral, are in good order. Every age, wrote D'Alembert in the eighteenth century, needs a Diogenes, and both the necessary courage to withstand his onslaught on its most cherished convictions and the mental clarity to understand his message. And if this was true in the eighteenth century, it is not difficult to see that it is equally true, if not truer, at the end of the second millennium.

I have divided this study of Diogenes into five chapters. In chapter 1, I have reconstructed his biography as much as the sources allow, making abundant references to ancient testimonies and to modern scholarly interpretations. Chapter 2 is devoted to the elucidation of the most distinctive feature of classical Cynicism, namely, the *practice* of Cynicism, specifically as this was exhibited by Diogenes, who communicated and taught his gospel of rebellion always by means of the example of his life. Chapter 3 deals with the process through which Diogenes became a Cynic and the influences, both Greek and non-Greek, that may have contributed to that process. This process—the making of a Cynic—is complex, and may involve various psychological and sociological factors that may have been responsible for the emergence of Cynicism in Diogenes. In chapter 4, I identify what may be referred to as the building blocks of Cynicism, particulary those of relevance to Diogenes' thought. Cynicism, as will be shown, was not a *system* of ideas in which we can identify well-delineated components or a hierarchical scheme of philosophical tenets. Far more than a theoretical stance vis-à-vis the world, Cynicism was a *response*, a *reaction*, to those conditions of human existence that the Cynics, beginning with Diogenes and perhaps with Antisthenes, found unacceptable from the point of view of reason. This response surfaced among them in the form of apophthegms, aphorisms, and diatribal statements, and especially in actions and modes of behavior that were carefully designed to deface or invalidate the νόμισμα, that is, the values and accepted norms, on the basis of which most people then and now structure their lives. Diogenes' response to the world was expressed by him in terms of what has been called the rhetoric of Cynicism, which is a series of gestures, acts, and comments about specific people and situations. Beneath their seemingly amorphous character, however, they are the manifestation of certain philosophical propositions that are clearly identifiable.

Chapter 5 offers, as a concluding set of reflections, comments on the legacy of Diogenes, that is, on his persistent presence in the history of ideas in the Western world. Somehow, the man in the tub has remained alive throughout the twenty-three centuries that have elapsed since his death, and his presence is felt whenever we entertain ideas such as cosmopolitanism, freedom of speech, natural rights, and clarity of mind. I also provide in this chapter comments on the relationship and the difference between classical Cynicism and what is generally known as modern cynicism. The legacy of Diogenes, that is, the meaning of Cynicism in the classical sense, can be best appreciated as one considers the wide gap that separates the example of his life and his ideas from those of modern cynics. Oscar Wilde once said that Cynicism is the art of seeing things as they are instead of as they should be, and in his insistence on defining philosophy as the practice of calling things by their right names, Diogenes stands in agreement with Wilde. If nothing else is worth remembering about Diogenes, we could conjure his ghost from the remote past to remind ourselves that reality is not what the governing oligarchies want ordinary people to accept, or what flows so abundantly from the media, or what those whom we call 'celebrities' peddle in the public light, or what the endemic inertia of the human mind sanctifies, but the truth that things and situations speak out for themselves. Diogenes can teach us to see the human world precisely as it is, without distortions, euphemisms, or deceptions.

An extensively annotated translation of Diogenes Laertius' *Life of Diogenes of Sinope* has been added as an appendix. This work, I believe, captures well the spirit of Diogenes as a philosopher and as a man, and, despite its flaws, remains for us the principal source of information about him. We would be mistaken if we viewed Diogenes Laertius' biography of Diogenes only as a trivial and unsophisticated collection of bits of gossip.

The bibliography includes all the books and articles quoted or mentioned in the text, as well as other significant modern works on Diogenes. References to classical sources are included in the text, and given the multitude of editions and translations of these sources, I have chosen not to include them in the bibliography.

The scholarly and popular literature related to classical Cynicism in general and to Diogenes in particular is quite extensive, and a review of my *The Philosophy of Cynicism: An Annotated Bibliography*, in which I provide abstracts of over six hundred works, may prove to be fruitful.

Although it is undeniable that Diogenes is the most important representative of classical Cynicism, it is equally unquestionable that this philosophical movement included many other significant Cynics. In this book, however, I have dealt with these only in passing and only inasmuch as they can provide for us some assistance in the process of understanding and appreciating Diogenes' philosophical message. Extended discussions of various major Cynic philosophers can be found in my *Classical Cynicism: A Critical Study*, in which I deal at length with the contributions of Antisthenes, Crates, Onesicritus, Bion, Menippus, Cercidas, Meleager, Oenomaus, Demetrius of Rome, and Peregrinus Proteus. The bibliography of this book includes numerous scholarly works related to the Cynics of Hellenistic and Roman times.

I wish to thank my wife Alicia Cadena Navia for her patient reading and critical review of the manuscript. The support of my daughters Monica, Olga Lucia, Melissa, and Soraya Emilia has been invaluable. From all of them, I have learned a great deal about the significance and relevance of Diogenes' legacy.

Chapter 1

A Biographical Sketch

In his biography of Diogenes of Sinope, Diogenes Laertius recounts three curious anecdotes about him that can provide for us the starting point for these reflections on his life and philosophy. Once, when a certain man failed to obtain for him a cottage that he had requested, Diogenes decided to live in a tub near the Athenian marketplace (D.L. VI, 23).[1] In another passage, the biographer tells us that once, to the amazement of others, Diogenes lit a lamp in daylight and went about the marketplace, saying that he was looking for a man (D.L. VI, 41). Still in another passage, the story is recounted that once, when Alexander the Great visited Diogenes in Corinth, the proud emperor, standing in front of Diogenes, said, "I am Alexander the great king," to which Diogenes, disdainfully looking at him, replied, "And I am Diogenes the Dog" (D.L. VI, 60). The man living in a tub, who would walk around carrying a lighted lamp in search of a human being, and who would call himself 'the Dog' is a strange and perplexing figure who appears in countless ancient and modern works of art and literature, and whose name is recognized even by those who have only a passing acquaintance with the history of ideas in the Western world. More than twenty-three centuries have passed since his death, but he still remains a familiar presence in our contemporary world. Hardly anything of substance has survived of the many writings attributed to him, but his ideas and his views about the world have managed to survive until our own time.

Who was Diogenes and what was the impact of his life among his contemporaries and successors? What significance does his philosophical stance have for our own attempts to deal with the world? What could be the meaning of the exhibitionist antics and gestures through which he succeeded in shocking and upsetting his contemporaries? What place does he have in the history of philosophy in the Western world and in the development of Cynicism? It may be true that, as Epictetus informs us (*Discourses* III, xxii, 88), Diogenes would attract the attention of people by the very appearance of his body, especially by the radiant complexion of his face, but it is unquestionable that his thoughts and the example of his life have succeeded in creating for him a great deal of reputation and, we may say, much notoriety in the course of time. Upon his death in Corinth, according to Diogenes Laertius (VI, 78), the Corinthians inscribed the following words on a statue made in his honor: "Even bronze groweth old with time, but thy fame, Diogenes, not all Eternity shall take away."

Possibly more than any other philosopher of antiquity, Diogenes has been the subject of the most diverse and contradictory collection of assessments. The ancient Cynics, as one should expect, idolized and glorified his name, and viewed him as an unequaled paradigm of virtue and as the very embodiment of the philosophical life. The Stoics, particularly Epictetus and Seneca, sang his praises and emphasized the enormous gap that separated him from his late Roman descendants, and Emperor Julian wrote about the excellence of his character and about the pristine example of his life. Among the Fathers of the Church, despite their ambivalence toward the virtues preached and practiced by the Cynics, there are repeated encomia of Diogenes, in whom they occasionally saw a faint and imperfect prelude of the example and the teachings of Jesus.[2] During the Renaissance, it is not rare to find scholars who viewed him as "a revered model of moral rectitude, a wise and witty observer of men and manners, and an unforgettable personality who stood out like a beacon among the dim philosophical shadows of antiquity."[3]

In modern times, too, the list of those who have recognized in Diogenes an important and praiseworthy philosophical figure is long and impressive. While some viewed him as the representative of reason *par excellence*, as with Bayle, others, like Diderot, Wieland, Voltaire, and Goethe, did not fail to discover in him the unmistakable features that reveal a great and lucid philosopher.[4] More recently, he has been called "one of the most original and spiritual human beings who has ever existed,"[5] and has been viewed as "a 'Zen man', eccentric in his ways yet fundamental in his thought, vastly irritable yet suffocatingly funny, magnetic yet repulsive, a regal vagabond who was somehow in charge of the truth."[6]

In the view of Michel Foucault, in whose philosophical outlook it is easy to discern the influence of classical Cynicism, Diogenes set the ultimate example of what philosophy can teach and of what a genuine philosopher ought to be: a parrhesiast, that is, a man solely devoted to the practice of παρρησία (*parrhesia*), that is, the commitment to speak the truth or, more precisely, 'to say it all', consistently and under all circumstances.[7] Bertrand Russell, who drew a sharp distinction between the ancient Cynics and the sort of people known in modern times as 'cynical', recognized in Diogenes a man possessed by a remarkable passion for virtue and moral freedom.[8] An important scholar of the nineteenth century discerned in Diogenes and in his Cynic descendants "an insatiable thirst for freedom, a profound sensitiveness to the ills of life, an unshakable faith in the majesty and all-sufficiency of reason, and a corresponding abysmal contempt for all traditional ideals."[9]

More than in any other philosopher of the Western world, some have discovered in Diogenes the epitome of a long list of praiseworthy personal and intellectual traits and endowments: an absolute commitment to honesty, a remarkable independence of judgment, an unwavering decision to live a simple and unencumbered life, a paradigmatic devotion to self-sufficiency, an unparalleled attachment to freedom of speech, a healthy contempt for human stupidity and obfuscation, an unusual degree of intellectual lucidity, and, above all, a tremendous courage to live in accord with his convictions. From this perspective, Diogenes emerges as a veritable giant in the history of humanity in general and in the history of ideas in particular, and as a man worthy of the highest praise.

There is, however, the other side, in which we are reminded that Diogenes was nothing but a ragpicker and a ragamuffin,[10] a man of no intellectual worth, in whom and through whom Western history took a turn "toward animalism and a retrogression from civilization,"[11] and whose confused ideas are ultimately nothing but "a doctrine of inaction and negation of life."[12] His pessimistic one-sidedness concerning the value of human accomplishments, his contempt for practically all human beings, his unwillingness to recognize in anyone even the faintest trace of honesty and good intentions, his merciless campaign to debunk and undermine social and political institutions, his exaggerated and histrionic behavior, his shamelessness and his pride about his shamelessness, the coarseness of his speech and manners, his reported inability to transcend the realm of the concrete and the particular, and his incapacity to understand and appreciate universal concepts—all these and other alleged uncomplimentary aspects of his life and personality have been emphasized by some scholars, from whose point of view, then, there is nothing worth studying about Diogenes, except perhaps from a psychological or anthropological perspective, as if he were in reality only a curious and unusual phenomenon in the history of ideas. Nothing attractive or substantive, accordingly, can be found in him, certainly not from the point of view of genuine philosophy, and his life, characterized by exhibitionism and exaggeration, contained nothing edifying or worth remembering. We should perhaps dismiss him as a philosophical scandal and as an ideological aberration, for he was, as a historian has noted,

> bitter, brutal, ostentatious, and abstemious; disgracing the title of "the Dog" (for a dog has affection, gratitude, sympathy, and caressing manners), yet growling over his unenvied virtue as a cur growls over his meatless bone, forever snarling and snapping without occasion; an object of universal attention, and from many quarters, of unfeigned admiration.[13]

There are some who see in him the source of the cynical mood that in recent times has permeated all spheres of culture, and has vitiated all human ideals and aspirations. In the opinion of P. Sloterdijk, Diogenes—"a dog-man, a philosopher, a good-for-nothing, a primitive hippie, and the original bohemian"—stands in first place on a long list of cynics[14] who have undermined even the possibility of idealism.[15] With his defiant attitude of negativism, argues Sloterdijk, the man who "pissed against the wind" has become the nihilistic standard bearer of those who promote a style of life, akin to a malaise of culture, in which neither values nor aspirations have any meaning, and in which egoism and gross materialism reign supreme. As the archetype of the cynical man, therefore, Diogenes can be viewed as the source from which all sorts of cultural and ideological ills have sprung since his time.

What truth and validity can there be in these disparate assertions and assessments of those who have either canonized Diogenes as a philosophical saint and extolled his value as a great philosopher, or condemned him as a deranged rascal, a worthless man, and a psychopath, and dismissed him as a pseudo philosopher? We might argue that one's reaction to Diogenes, as happens in all sorts of other situations, depends on one's own frame of mind. As Schopenhauer once remarked, one does not *choose* to appreciate a certain philosopher or a certain philosophical attitude, for the reverse is true: that appreciation is determined by the kind of person one is. It might be possible that in order to understand and appreciate the value of Diogenes as a philosopher and as a stereotype of Cynicism, one may have to be a Cynic oneself or at least have certain inborn Cynic tendencies. How can someone whose psychological predispositions and whose upbringing incline him to accept blindly all social norms and to deify the Establishment and the status quo, and who, as in the case of patriotic enthusiasts and religious zealots, cannot find any fulfillment in life except as part of a group, discover any value and significance in the antics and sayings of a man like Diogenes, who, partly on account of his inborn character and the circumstances of his life, and partly because of certain philosophical influences on him, felt compelled to wage a relentless war against the human world that surrounded him, and found his fulfillment only in the shelter of his self-proclaimed independence? In order to grasp the significance of Diogenes' life and philosophy, it is necessary to have within oneself at least some incipient dosage of Cynicism and have that rare philosophical ability to see behind and around things, to use Nietzsche's phrase. As Diderot pointed out, one does not choose to become a Cynic, for one is born a Cynic. In his view, "one may choose to become an Academic philosopher, or an Eclectic, or a Cyrenaic, or a Pyrrhoist, or a Skeptic; but one must be born a Cynic."[16] As Honoré Daumier would put it in one of his caricatures of Diogenes in the tub, "*Il est un peu dur d'être obligé de loger dans un tonneau quand on n'est pas né pour être cynique*"—it is hard being forced to live in a tub if one is not born to be a Cynic.[17] It would be indeed be a marvelous thing to find someone, who by temperament and by circumstances is fully at peace with the world, endowed with the capacity to understand Cynicism.

There is, however, another circumstance that may also be held responsible for the wide spectrum of interpretations and assessments of Diogenes as a man and as a philosopher. As with other major figures of antiquity, and even more so, one insoluble problem related to our knowledge of Diogenes is the scarcity of reliable sources of information. As noted earlier, many writings were attributed to him in antiquity. Diogenes Laertius, for instance, lists the titles of thirteen dialogues and seven tragedies, and mentions a collection of letters (D.L. VI, 80), and in other sources, still other works are mentioned, although ancient biographers and doxographers admit that some of these works, if not most of them, were occasionally ascribed to other authors. There is also the testimony of Sosicrates of Rhodes and Satyrus of Callias Pontica, who affirm that Diogenes, like Socrates, left no writings and that his teachings were strictly oral and were conveyed by him only through the example of his life. There is, however, nothing impossible in imagining that Diogenes *did* write, and the allegation that "a man as indolent and indifferent as Diogenes would not be likely to undertake the effort of writing a book,"[18] does not have much weight: Diogenes appears to have been indolent and indifferent only in regard to *certain* things and *certain* kinds of activity, but there was in him neither indolence nor indifference about his philosophical convictions.

Still, whether he did write or not, the fact remains that what *we* know about him is confined to testimonies and accounts written by others, some close to his own time and others as late as the end of classical times. Of the alleged writings of Diogenes at any rate, hardly anything genuine seems to have survived. We come upon various fragments of doubtful authenticity that reveal ideas and teachings found abundantly and more clearly in the secondary sources. The letters attributed to him in ancient times, of which fifty-one have survived, are now generally believed to belong to unknown authors of the second and first centuries B.C.,[19] and although they are of great interest as sources of information *about* Diogenes, they must be treated as part of the vast collection of secondary sources that began to grow in extent and complexity probably as early as the third century B.C.

Inevitably, then, we are at the mercy of these sources, many of which appear to be prejudiced in favor of Diogenes, representing him as a man of great character and superb philosophical acumen, as if their intent had been to lend respectability to the Cynic tradition. Others give the impression of wishing to denigrate Diogenes' style of life and character, and to expose the weaknesses of Cynicism as a meaningful philosophical option. Still others confine themselves to repeating mechanically and uncritically, with expansions and embellishments, certain traditional doxographical and anecdotal reports about his life.

The character of Diogenes as a man and as a philosopher appears to have been such that the temptation to exaggerate and distort, and even invent and fabricate reports about him, must have been irresistible on the part of those who wrote about him. A man who proclaimed himself as a 'dog' at war with the world, who daunted and condemned the norms and conventions on the basis of which most people structure their lives, and who stood proudly as the living refutation of his world, challenging in word and in deed even the most sacrosanct values, must have given rise to innumerable anecdotes and tales, most of them probably based on some element of truth, but many of them surely invested with a generous ingredient of literary creativity. For this reason, in the attempt to construct a biographical account of Diogenes, we find ourselves oscillating between fact and fiction, history and legend, and truth and fabrication, seldom able to draw a clear distinction between who Diogenes of Sinope really was and who those who wrote about him wanted him to be. It is undeniable that as one considers the multitude of testimonies and reports about him, one has the distinct impression of the formation of a legend, a legend that grew in time and went through transformations to accommodate the needs and tendencies of ideologists, detractors, and apologists, a circumstance that is neither unique nor surprising. Biographical legends about famous people have always been created, and in the history of philosophy we come upon many of them. There are, for instance, legends about Pythagoras, Socrates, Plato, and other philosophers of antiquity, and if one glances at the history of religious and political ideas, there, the examples of legends abound everywhere. Nevertheless, at least in the case of Diogenes of Sinope, in spite of those who see in him mostly the focal point of legendary accounts of little historical value,[20] it remains possible to sift cautiously through the evidence and develop a portrayal of some historical value. It is really difficult to imagine that beneath the mountains of accounts about Diogenes we cannot find someone, an actual person, "a walking and talking philosopher" in a recognizably Greek tradition,[21] who does not resemble in some way the composite portrayal that *is* possible to extract from the sources.

Undoubtedly, the most important secondary source of information about Diogenes is the biography written by Diogenes Laertius,[22] an author about whom little is known with certainty. He is believed to have lived during the reign of Alexander Severus (A.D. 225-235), and the date of composition of his *Lives and Opinions of Eminent Philosophers* has been tentatively assigned to the early part of the third century A.D. This work includes the biographies of eighty-two Greek philosophers, who are arranged in eight 'successions' (διαδοχαί) or what we might loosely call 'schools' of philosophers. Book VI is devoted to the 'succession' of the Cynic philosophers, from Antisthenes of Athens (late fifth century B.C.) to Menedemus (third century B.C.). In this part of his work, Diogenes Laertius includes short biographies of Monimus, Onesicritus, Crates, Metrocles, Hipparchia, Menippus, and Menedemus, prefaced by two lengthy accounts of the lives and doctrines of Antisthenes and Diogenes.

The importance of Diogenes Laertius' work is twofold: it constitutes the oldest extensive biographical and doxographical account of the Greek philosophers, and it provides for us references to earlier sources, most of which, however, are not extant. One of the most important among the sources used by Diogenes Laertius, especially in his treatment of Diogenes, is Diocles of Magnesia (first century B.C.), who is quoted several times in Book VI. Diocles himself, who wrote a work entitled *Compendium of the History of Philosophy*, seems to have taken special interest in the Cynics, and his friendship with the Cynic poet Meleager of Gadara is indicative of his philosophical leanings. Meleager is said to have dedicated to Diocles his *Garland*, a collection of poetical compositions.[23] The apparent influence of Diocles on Diogenes Laertius led Nietzsche to suspect that a great part of the latter's work was ultimately an embellished rendition of Diocles' *Compendium*.[24] In reality, although this suspicion may not be fully defensible, the fact remains that the biographies of Diogenes Laertius are largely a series of compilations of numerous earlier testimonies related to the lives and ideas of Greek philosophers, compilations that are often poorly joined together and are filled with repetitions and apparently uncritical insertions. Still, despite its flaws, his work is the most valuable source of information about the lives and ideas of many of the philosophers with whom he deals. If critically used, it can furnish us with significant insights about who the early philosophers were and about their contributions.

In the context of his biography of Diogenes of Sinope (VI, 20-81),[25] Diogenes Laertius' information contains an abundance of anecdotes and apophthegms that had been associated with Diogenes even during his own life time and that became in time the body of standard information about him. We find in it a large collection of *chreia* (χρεῖα) or anecdotes that reveal a great deal about Diogenes' character and about his philosophical convictions.[26] It contains, of course, an abundant dosage of gossip and fabrication, but it does not fail to convey an image of the philosopher that, by reference to sources of greater antiquity, may not turn out to be altogether fictitious. The anecdotal style that permeates the work of Diogenes Laertius is often, as a scholar has noted, an impediment to philosophical informativeness, but in the instance of the biography of Diogenes, it enhances our understanding of Diogenes, because his own style of teaching was through anecdotes, examples, and aphorisms.[27] A critical study of Diogenes Laertius' biography of Diogenes and an unprejudiced comparison of its contents with other sources allow us to form a reasonably clear idea of the man and his thought.

Aside from Diogenes Laertius, there are numerous sources that provide information about Diogenes. These include Aristotle (384-322 B.C.), Cercidas of Megalopolis (third century B.C.), Teles of Megara (third century B.C.), Cicero (106-43 B.C.), Seneca (4 B.C.- A.D. 65), Dio Chrysostom (A.D. 40-115), Epictetus (A.D. 55-135), Plutarch (A.D. 50-120), Favorinus (c. 80-150), Juvenal (c. 60-140), Marcus Cornelius Fronto (c. 100-166), Maximus of Tyre (c. 120-180), Aulus Gellius (c. 130-180), Marcus Aurelius (121-180), Lucian of Samosata (c. 120-190),

Saint Clement of Alexandria (c. 150-215), Tertullian (c.155-222), Sextus Empiricus (third century A.D.), Athenaeus of Naucratis (third century A.D.), Aelian (c. 170-235), Eusebius of Caesarea (c. 260-340), Julian (332-363), Themistius (317-390), Saint Jerome (340-420), Saint Augustine (354-430), and Stobaeus (fifth century A.D.).[28] Their testimonies range from a brief mention of Diogenes, as with Aristotle, to lengthy and imaginative narrations, as with Dio Chrysostom, and from serious philosophical accounts, as with Epictetus, to satirical and amusing fictional pieces, as with Lucian. There are also numerous passages in the various anthologies, especially in the *Anthologia Palatina* and in the *Gnomologium Vaticanum* that shed light on diverse aspects of Diogenes' activities and personality. As an example of non-Greek and non-Latin sources, we could also mention several collections of sayings attributed to Diogenes that are contained in Arabic gnomologies compiled by authors such as Hunayn Ibn-Ishaq (d. 873), Ibn-Hindu (d. 1019), and Mubassir Ibn-Fatik (d. 1049).[29] Only in rare instances, however, do we find that what these sources reveal is not found in some form or another in what is already found in the testimony of Diogenes Laertius or in other classical sources. They do, however, lend *some* credibility to the classical reports, for which reason we assume that an element of genuine historical import underlies many of them.

The year of Diogenes' birth cannot be fixed with certainty. Diogenes Laertius (VI, 79) informs us that he was already an aged man (γέρων) in the 113th Olympiad (324/321 B.C.), and elsewhere notes that "he was nearly ninety years old at the time of his death" (VI, 76). The year of his death appears to be reasonably well established as one of the few facts known with some certainty about Diogenes. According to Demetrius of Magnesia (D.L. VI, 79) and Suidas, his death occurred on the same year of Alexander's death in Babylon (423 B.C.), and Plutarch (*Moralia* 717c) calls attention to the even greater coincidence that Diogenes and Alexander died *on the very same day*, which is also reported by Diogenes Laertius (VI, 79). Still, the constant juxtaposition that we encounter in the sources between the defiant Cynic philosopher, a contemptuous man who looked with disdain upon Alexander and upon the enormous political edifice for which he stood, on the one hand, and, on the other, the proud and vain Macedonian emperor, who embodied much of what Diogenes viewed as the source of human ills—this juxtaposition may have justified the necessity of biographers to have them die precisely at the same time.[30] Nevertheless, in the absence of contradictory evidence, it may be reasonable to assign the year 323 B.C. as the year of Diogenes death.

The year of his birth presents certain problems that cannot be satisfactorily solved. If as Diogenes Laertius maintains, he was ninety or nearly ninety at the time of his death, he would have been born around the year 413 B.C. There are, however, reports that speak of him as having been eighty-one years old when he died, as in the testimony of Censorinus (*De die natali* xv, 2), and we read in Suidas that his birth occurred during the reign of the Thirty in Athens, which lasted ten months in the year 404 B.C. The Thirty were a group of Athenian oligarchs who, under the leadership of Critias and with the blessings of the victorious Spartans, assumed power at the end of the Peloponnesian War. We hear reports, however, of Diogenes having been involved in the defacement of coinage in Sinope as early as the fourth decade of the fourth century B.C., and we learn from the *Chronicon Paschale* that he was a well known man before the year 462 B.C., although neither the reason for his fame nor the place where he was famous is mentioned. If this report is historically correct, there should be no reason for not pushing back the time of his birth to the year suggested by Diogenes Laertius, that is, 413 B.C., for then Diogenes would have been a middle-age man when the famous defacement of the coinage might have taken place. An early date for Diogenes' birth, moreover, allows us to consider as more plausible some biographical relationship between Antisthenes and Diogenes. Antisthenes' birth may be placed as early as in the year 455 B.C. and his death around the year 366 B.C. These parameters make possible a reasonable period of association between these two philosophers, an association that is of some significance with respect to the issue of the origins of Cynicism. There is also the possibility, entertained by some scholars,[31] that even *before* his alleged banishment from Sinope, Diogenes could have visited Athens, where surely he would have come across Antisthenes and others among Socrates' associates.

The sources are unanimous in speaking of Sinope as Diogenes' birthplace. In the late fifth century B.C., Sinope was a flourishing Greek town located at the midpoint of the southern coast of the Euxine (the Black Sea) in a region known as Paphlygonia. Legends speak of the Amazons as having founded Sinope and as having named it in honor of Sinova, their queen. Another tradition ascribes its foundation to Autolycus, the companion of Hercules. There are indications that a Milesian colony had been established in Sinope already by the year 756 B.C., and it is unquestionable that by the middle of the seventh century B.C. the presence of the Milesians and other Ionian settlers had shaped the character and the culture of the town. In 444 B.C., the Athenians under Pericles overthrew a local tyrant and established a democratic form of government that would remain in existence until the Persians, led by a satrap named Datames, captured the town around the year 375 B.C. The Persians remained in control of the town until the presence of Alexander's power was felt throughout Asia Minor, when it regained its independence and asserted its ancient Hellenic heritage. It is reasonable to assume that, like many other Sinopeans, Diogenes came from the same Milesian stock from which philosophers like Thales, Anaximander, and Anaximenes came, and that his language and heritage were purely Greek.

During Diogenes' early years, Sinope enjoyed its most prosperous epoch and was the most important Greek settlement on the shores of the Black Sea. Many years after Diogenes, Strabo (xii, 545) would leave for us a description of a happy and affluent Greek town, adorned with temples and fortifications, proud of its gymnasium and marketplace, and filled with fine buildings and comfortable homes —all of which must have been even more impressive in the first decades of the fourth century B.C. At the end of the caravan route that began at the mouth of the Euphrates, Sinope enjoyed enviable commercial and cultural advantages that contributed greatly to its cosmopolitan and liberal political and social life. It is conceivable that merchants from India were a common sight in Sinope and that Diogenes could have become acquainted with certain elements of Indian culture that, as will be seen in a different context, may have contributed to the eventual formation of Cynic ideas in his mind. Sinope's geographical position, moreover, provided for it a wonderful opportunity to be in control of the maritime affairs of the Greeks in the Euxine, a task that its small but agile fleet was ready to accomplish. Its well-minted and beautiful coinage circulated freely throughout the ancient world. Commerce and travel between Sinope and mainland Greece were ordinary and easy, and the roots that linked the Sinopeans and the Athenians were evident in all spheres of public and private life. In the late fifth century B.C., for instance, the Sinopeans welcomed a large contingent of Athenian citizens who had left the arid landscape of Attica to settle in the fertile plain that surrounded Sinope.

The modern town of Sinop, the capital of a northern province in modern Turkey, is a remote descendant of the Greek town where Diogenes was born. With a population of less than 25,000 inhabitants, Sinop still displays today the vestiges of the Hellenic presence of its ancient past. The foundations of the temple of Sarapis,[32] where Diogenes could have become acquainted with the worship of Oriental and Egyptian deities, are among its many archaeological remains. Nevertheless, the modern town is probably only a shadow of the affluent and influential Milesian colony on the shores of the Euxine.

Nothing is known concerning Diogenes' early years and background. There is only one inconclusive reference in classical sources to his mother. To Antipater, the Macedonian general and regent of Macedonia during Alexander's campaigns, who had reportedly written to him a letter containing slanderous remarks about his mother, Diogenes replied, "You fail to understand, Antipater, that one single tear of my mother can wash away all the calumnies that you write about her" (*Flor. Monacense* 157). Concerning his father, his name and occupation are known.[33] Various sources call him 'Hicesias' (e.g., D.L. VI, 20), and he is said to have been a banker or money changer. The Greek word used to describe his occupation is τραπεζίτης, a derivation from the word for 'table' (τράπεζα). In classical times, bankers (τραπεζῖται) would set up their tables at the marketplace and at festivals, and would exchange currency, make loans, test the authenticity of coins, and arranged credit transactions among cities.[34] In smaller cities and towns, where local currency was minted, bankers were sometimes entrusted with the manufacturing and regulating of coinage, and this was, we suspect, what Hicesias was entrusted to do in his native Sinope, as is confirmed by Diocles (D.L. VI, 20). The occupation of Diogenes' father could lead us to conclude that his family enjoyed some prominence in the city and had the necessary means to ensure a sound education for him.

A widespread custom, still in existence in modern times, was for a son to devote himself to the occupation of his father. Thus, it seems that, in his youth, Diogenes himself played some role in the minting of Sinopean coins and in the banking affairs of his father. Various reports concerning this circumstance circulated freely in ancient times, and numerous versions of Diogenes' affair with the currency have come down to us. Diogenes Laertius (VI, 20-21) provides us with a sketch of some of these reports. In one of them, Hicesias is said to have been entrusted with the management of the currency, and to have adulterated or defaced the coins, for which reason he and his son were punished by the State, Hicesias with imprisonment and Diogenes with exile. In another, it was Diogenes himself who undertook the defacement of the currency, for which he was banished from the city. In still another, the young man, after having counterfeited coins and through fear of being detected, voluntarily left the city to avoid being prosecuted. In some versions, various connections are mentioned between Diogenes' illegal activities and an oracular pronouncement either from the Delphic oracle or from a local Apollonian oracle in Sinope.

The nature and the chronological relationship between the currency affair and the oracle vary from source to source. In one of the accounts, we are told that Diogenes was urged by the workers under his supervision to adulterate or deface the currency, and that he then went to the oracle to ask the god what he should do. When told that he should deface the political 'currency', he, having misunderstood the injunction, went back and proceeded to deface the actual coinage. In another account, the oracular pronouncement takes place *after* his illegal activities and *after* his departure from Sinope. Accordingly, the sequence of events was something like this: father and son are arrested for adulterating or defacing the currency. Hicesias is thrown into prison and Diogenes is banished from Sinope and travels to Athens, and from Athens to Delphi, where he poses this question to the Pythia: "What should I do to gain the greatest reputation?" (D.L. VI, 20). To his surprise, the answer came loudly and clearly: Παραχάραττειν τὸ νόμισμα, which literally means, "Adulterate the currency." After this, and with an understanding of the symbolic meaning of the oracular pronouncement, Diogenes returned to Athens, where he began at once to do what Apollo had ordered him to do, that is, to wage a relentless war on the cultural and political 'currency' of his contemporaries.

An examination of the sources and a review of the various reports in the light of well-attested historical and cultural facts of Diogenes' time yield some modicum of clarity and convinces us that although here, no less than in many other similar accounts of ancient times, legend and fact are inextricably intertwined, an element of truth may still be present. Unquestionably, the story fits so well the character of Diogenes as a Cynic that it is difficult to avoid the temptation of seeing in it a literary fabrication created long after Diogenes for the specific purpose of providing a graphic representation of his frame of mind and of his activities as a philosopher. It may be nothing but an instance of myth formation, in which a legend is fabricated to rationalize a series of events and situations that might be otherwise difficult to account for, or for the purpose of shedding light on some aspect of the person's character. In the instance of Socrates, who, like Diogenes, was also the recipient of an oracular pronouncement, we might have a similar situation: a man who spent his mature life questioning and challenging the wisdom of his contemporaries, and who did so posing as a man of little or no wisdom, was declared by the Delphic oracle to be the wisest man in the world (Plato, *Apology* 21a; Xenophon, *Apology* 14), the meaning of the oracle being, as Socrates himself discovered, that he who recognizes his own ignorance and who understands that "real wisdom is the property of God" (Plato, *Apology* 23a) is truly the wisest man in the world. Still other oracular pronouncements, usually emanating from Delphi, are found in the biographies of other philosophers, as in the instances of Thales of Miletus, who, like Socrates was declared to be the wisest man (D.L. I, 28), and Zeno of Citium (D.L. VII, 2). In most of these instances, we come upon the same scenario: the oracle pronounces a pithy statement about the philosopher that ultimately determines the direction of his life and describes succinctly the character of his mission.

Concerning the reports about Diogenes' involvement with the Sinopean currency, opting for an unreasonably critical attitude is unwise, and dismissing *all* the reports related to it is unwarranted, for beneath such reports there appears to subsist some element of historical veracity. We know, for instance, through numismatic research and findings that a certain man named Hicesias was in fact responsible for the minting of Sinopean coins sometime during the first half of the fourth century B.C. The investigations of C. T. Seltman show that large quantities of defaced and counterfeited coins were in circulation in Sinope around the year 350 B.C.[35] H. Bannert, for his part, has called attention to the fact that the name ΙΚΕΣΙΟ appears in many Sinopean coins that can be dated between 370 and 320 B.C.[36] It was the custom then for the engraver to put his name on the reverse side of the coins, while the seal or emblem of the city would appear on the front. The name on the coins corresponds to the name associated with Diogenes' father, and their circulation time suggests that they must have been minted in the first quarter of the fourth century B.C.[37] Furthermore, the coins, both Sinopean and Persian, show clear signs of defacement or intentional damage, which supports that aspect of the reports that allege that Hicesias and possibly his son were indeed engaged in an effort to put large quantities of coins out of circulation.

The reason for the defacement of the currency remains, however, a matter of conjecture. We could surmise that it may have been a matter of profit or currency speculation through which Hicesias and his son hoped to grow richer, or that political considerations may have been the motive. As noted earlier, around the year 375 B.C., a pro-Persian faction seized control of Sinope and paved the way for the Persians under Datames to assume control of the city. Many defaced or damaged coins from that time are of Persian origin, and thus, it is not difficult to imagine that a prominent banker, reportedly in charge of the city's mint, could have sought to weaken the power of the Persians by putting their coinage out of circulation. This idea, defended by Dudley,[38] but severely criticized by Sayre,[39] is not altogether farfetched. Nevertheless, this cannot be more than a supposition, because solid historical knowledge is lacking in this respect.

As for the matter of the punishment inflicted for the defacing of the currency, it might be easier to assume that when it occurred, the government was still in the hands of the Greeks, if, as some sources report, Hicesias was imprisoned and Diogenes banished. Banishment was seldom the kind of penalty for serious crimes preferred by the Persians, and crimes involving currency adulteration and counterfeiting would have been surely punished by death. The Greeks, for their part, used banishment, normally for twenty years, as a convenient way to deal with undesirable people and even with great criminals. It remains, however, possible that Diogenes was *not* banished or exiled, but that, as one of the reports insists (D.L. VI, 20), he simply fled for fear of the consequences.

The truth is that the facts elude us also in this respect. The statement occasionally heard in the sources that Diogenes did not deny that his fellow citizens once banished him (D.L. VI, 49), does not clarify the matter, because a person who abandons his homeland may consider his decision to be a form of self-imposed banishment. The various reports that affirm that Diogenes himself was willing to admit that he adulterated the currency are important to bear in mind. We are told, for instance, that in his non-extant dialogue *Pordalus* he openly acknowledged his deed (D.L. VI, 20), although, as Sayre correctly points out,[40] his confession could be interpreted as an acknowledgment of the fact that he was engaged in the practice of adulterating human conventions and customs.

From Sinope Diogenes is reported to have traveled to Athens, although it is simply impossible to assign a date for his arrival in that city. It could have been immediately after his reported banishment or perhaps several years later. Furthermore, an earlier visit to the city, before the defacement of the Sinopean currency and even before the death of Antisthenes around 366 B.C., cannot be altogether discounted.[41] Athens was then the center of Hellenic life and a city known for its hospitality toward exiles and visitors from all parts of Greece. During the time of Pericles' leadership of the democracy (461-429 B.C.), and in fact for many decades after this, the Athenians took great pride in offering to foreigners a safe haven in which they could continue their lives undisturbed and in freedom. The words attributed by Thucydides to Pericles are revealing in this respect: "We maintain Athens open and accessible to everybody, and we do not turn away those who flee from danger or who come to us moved by curiosity or by a desire to improve themselves" (*Peloponnesian War* II, xxxix).

This atmosphere of freedom and hospitality accounts for the large number of foreigners who came to live in Athens during the last decades of the fifth century B.C. and the first half of the fourth century B.C. The foreigners (μέτικοι) mingled freely with the citizens and were allowed to participate in most of their activities, although they remained politically marginal and socially deprived of some of the privileges enjoyed by the citizens. Despite the openness of Athenian society, it is unquestionable that the Athenians made every effort to insure that they alone were in control of the affairs of the city. We know of other men of Sinope besides Diogenes who came to live in Athens, an example of whom is Diphilus, a younger contemporary of Diogenes, who became a prominent representative of the New Comedy, and who wrote and produced dozens of comedies that are unfortunately non-extant.

The story about the Delphic oracle merits consideration, although, as with other details of Diogenes' life, its historical import is difficult to ascertain, especially in view of the fact that such a story begins to circulate only several centuries after the alleged incident. There is a report that the oracular incident could have involved, not the Delphic oracle, but a local Delian oracle in Sinope. Delian temples where oracles were given did exist in various places throughout the Greek world, and in them, and also at Delphi, it was believed that Apollo spoke through a priestess, who acted as a medium to convey his messages. The prominence of the Delphic oracle and the sequence of events related to Diogenes' involvement with the currency, as well as to his exile, lend *some* historical support to the supposition that it was at Delphi that Diogenes heard the oracular words that would alter the course of his life.

Oracles in general and the Delphic oracle in particular were widely and reverently used in Greek times as sources of divination and guidance. For at least one thousand years, Delphi, believed to be the very center—the navel—of the world,[42] functioned as the spiritual focal point of Greek life and as a fountain of counsel for the thousands of pilgrims that must have entered the temple of Apollo with all sorts of questions and preoccupations. There, at the feet of the Pythia[43] and at certain appointed times, the pilgrims were allowed to ask questions, personal or otherwise, and to receive a short and generally unclear answer couched in a succinct poetical line. However, clear or not, such answers were regarded as revealing the truth, for, after all, they emanated from Apollo himself, a god who, as Socrates reminds us during his trial, could only speak the truth (Plato, *Apology* 21b).[44] The Greeks, as E. D. Dodds observes in the context of Socrates, "took both dreams and oracles very seriously."[45]

Collections of answers given at Delphi have been preserved. We encounter among them, for instance, certain pithy statements and maxims of great antiquity such as 'Know thyself' (Γνῶθι σαυτόν), and occasionally, as in the instance of the oracle given to the Lydian king Croesus (sixth century B.C.), perplexing responses that give the impression that somehow the Pythia knew more than a simple human priestess would have been expected to know. In an endeavor to test the veracity of the oracular answers, Croesus sent messengers to various oracles, including the one at Delphi, with instructions to ask what the king was doing a hundred days after the messengers had been dispatched. He chose something outlandish to do precisely on the appointed day: he killed a large turtle and a lamb, and boiled them together in a brazen caldron, over which he put a cover of brass. The Pythian answer, as reported by Herodotus (I, 47) was this:

> I know the number of sands and the measure of the sea. I understand the dumb and hear him that does not speak. The taste of the hard-shelled tortoise boiled in brass with the flesh of lamb strikes my senses. Brass is laid beneath it and brass is put over it.

When the king received the answer from Delphi, Herodotus adds, he worshiped the oracle, declaring it to be the only genuine source of truth. Henceforth, he spared no efforts in showing his generosity toward the Delphians who kept watch over the oracle.

What could have been the basis of the oracular pronouncements made at Delphi, has been the subject of much controversy, and scholarly and popular opinions are most varied in this regard, ranging from a critical view that recognizes in them nothing but a politically and financially motivated sham, to the idea that perhaps at times the Pythia, either in a psychedelic or intoxicated state caused by inhaling nitrous oxide (the 'mephitic' vapor)[46] or chewing laurel leaves or bay leaves (Apollo's plant), or as a genuine spiritual medium, was able to transcend the limitations of time and space that normally set the parameters of human knowledge.[47] Perhaps there was a little of all sorts of things: commonplace answers, ambiguous pronouncements, lucky guesses, surprising coincidences, knowledge about the pilgrims obtained shortly before their arrival in Delphi, politically motivated responses, and possibly genuinely inspired spiritual messages emanating from a psychedelic or a mystical experience. The temporal and cultural gap that separates us from Delphi and from the age of oracles is too wide for us to be able to reach a definitive answer as to what was the basis of a tradition that lasted more than one thousand years and that provided so much guidance and inspiration for the Greeks. We do know, however, that philosophers were no strangers to the Delphic tradition. Oracles about Thales and Socrates, as was stated earlier, were reportedly pronounced, and we know that these oracles (or at least the legends about them) left a profound and lasting mark on the development of the traditions that became associated with them. Plutarch himself, a prominent philosopher and historian, was the chief priest of the temple of Apollo at Delphi, where the oracles were given, from A.D. 95 until his death in A.D. 127.

It is interesting to observe, however, that among the Cynics who followed in Diogenes' footsteps, there seems to have been a persistent reluctance to attach *any* value to oracles and other forms of divination, and a negative attitude toward traditional religious practices and cults. In Diogenes himself, we notice an unmistakable air of distrust and contempt toward priests and temple keepers, as is evident in his remark when he saw that a man had been caught stealing from a temple and was being led away by the officials of the temple: "The big thieves are leading away the little thief" (D.L. VI, 45). We are also told (D.L. VI, 73) that from his point of view, there was nothing improper in stealing from temples. Concerning oracles, according to Dio Chrysostom (*Or.* X), Diogenes himself condemned any appeal to them. Dio recounts for us a conversation between Diogenes and an acquaintance of his, who tells him that he is on his way to Delphi to consult the god on a personal matter and whose servant has just ran away from him, which elicits from Diogenes this comment: "How stupid can you be! How can you presume to consult a god, when you are not even able to manage your own affairs?" How can he, Diogenes continues, imagine that he can understand the language of the gods, who speak neither Greek nor any other human language? How can anyone claim to understand what they say?

Several hundred years after Diogenes, Oenomaus of Gadara would vent his Cynicism on what he viewed as the absurdity of the belief in oracles and divination. Like Diogenes, he is reported to have visited an Apollonian oracle, the oracle at Colophon, where, as was customary, he asked the god for guidance. "Seek in the land of Thracis the garden of Hercules," he was told, "where nothing is lacking."[48] He thought for a moment that he had understood the symbolic words of the oracle, which he took to mean that wisdom and happiness can only be found by imitating the example of Hercules, that is, in discipline, asceticism, strength of character, and endurance of suffering. He soon learned, however, that the same oracle had been given moments before to a certain businessman from Pontus, who understood the oracle as granting him permission to devote himself to increasing his wealth and seeking pleasure, that is, precisely pursuing a style of life totally different from that of Hercules. How, Oenomaus wondered, could the same oracle lead to opposite conclusions? Why would the god speak so darkly that profoundly different interpretations of his words were possible? Disappointed and frustrated, Oenomaus walked away from the temple, convinced of the nonsensical nature of oracular statements that ultimately mean nothing and are created only to dupe and confuse simple-minded believers. His work Γοήτων φώρα (*The Sorcerers Detected*), which can be partly reconstructed from later sources, mounts a systematic attack on organized religion and religious practices.[49] According to Eusebius' paraphrase of a passage of Oenomaus' work, "the oracles, over which the Greeks live in such a constant state of amazement, have nothing that can be characterized as otherworldly and nothing divine in them. In reality, they are nothing but clever tricks and sophistical deceptions that are manipulated by expert charlatans in order to deceive the masses" (*Præp. Evan.* VI, xxi, 6).

In view of this attitude, so typical among most of the Cynics, it is, therefore, paradoxical that at the beginning of Diogenes' philosophical career there could have been an oracle, precisely the sort of thing that Diogenes and his descendants condemned and ridiculed so consistently. We must also keep in mind that, as mentioned earlier, reports about the oracle given to Diogenes begin to emerge only during the second century A.D., specifically in a passage of Maximus of Tyre (*Diss.* XXXVI), where we hear not only about Apollo's injunction, but about how Zeus himself commended Diogenes for the enterprise that he was about to undertake. Earlier sources remain silent about the matter, which strengthens the suspicion of those who view in the story of the oracular pronouncement about Diogenes nothing but a pious fabrication to transform a shady Sinopean exile into a philosopher of great significance. An oracular pronouncement from Delphi, as it were, had sufficient weight to lend credibility and respectability to a philosopher's mission, and *this*, if indeed the incident was fabricated by various late apologists of Cynicism, was what they sought to effect with respect to Diogenes.

This reported pronouncement was simply Παραχάραττειν τὸ νόμισμα, that is, "Deface or adulterate the currency." The phrase παραχάραττειν τὸ νόμισμα deserves careful consideration. The word παραχάραττειν (*paracharattein*) is an imperative form of the verb παραχάρασσω, which is the verbal form of the rare noun παραχάραξις (*paracharaxis*). This noun is related to the common word χαρακτήρ, from which the English word 'character' is derived and which means 'a mark impressed on a person or a thing' or 'an impression made on an object'. The faces and symbols impressed on coins are examples of 'character' in its Greek sense. The related verb χαράσσω denotes, among other things, the action of impressing or engraving, as when coins were minted in ancient times. The word παρά (*para*), a preposition that appears as a prefix in countless words, conveys the sense of 'alongside' or 'beside', and also has the extended meaning of 'swerving aside' or 'going against'. Thus, παραχάρασσω can be used to describe the act of blundering, as with a chisel, the original impression or 'character' of a coin, that is, adulterating or defacing its genuine stamp, in order to render it valueless. The ordinary word νόμισμα (*nomisma*) has two related meanings: (1) it stands for 'currency' (*nummus* in Latin) in the sense of 'coins', and (2) it denotes 'customs', 'institutions', or 'accepted values'. The verb νομίζω conveys, among other things, the sense of 'recognizing' or 'accepting' customs, laws, and usages. Thus, the phrase παραχάραττειν τὸ νόμισμα simply means 'Deface the currency'.[50]

On the tenuous assumption that the oracular pronouncement occurred *after*

Diogenes' reported defacement of Sinopean and Persian coins, and that such a defacement actually took place, one can easily imagine his surprise. Apollo, he must have thought, was asking him to do once more what he had done before, that is, to deface the currency. But, as noted earlier, νόμισμα means both the physical currency, and the customs and values by which people live. Diogenes disposed then of the former of these meanings and held on to the latter, concluding that the oracular command was directing him to deface or render valueless the values by reference to which people structure their lives. And this is precisely what he began to do at once. Many years later, as Diogenes Laertius reports (VI, 56), he would remark to someone who reminded him that once he had defaced the state currency: "That belongs to another time—when I was as you are now." In this revealing statement, Diogenes makes it plain that there were two stages in his life, one in which he was like most people, greedy, thoughtless, and full of confusion, and the other in which, having effected a break with the world of ordinary values and conventions, he no longer had a need for defacing or counterfeiting the currency that in the form of coins circulates among people.

We must emphasize again that the historical basis for the incident involving the Delphic oracular pronouncement about Diogenes is, as H. Diels has observed about *all* the reports concerning Diogenes, anything but certain.[51] Diels insists that the entire affair is nothing but an allegorical and symbolic way of accounting for Diogenes' philosophical stance, in which we encounter, more than in any other, a systematic endeavor to invalidate the norms and values by which people live. Many scholars have supported this opinion.[52] It has been argued, for instance, that the mere fact that Diogenes' father was a banker or a man in charge of the Sinopean mint, would have been sufficient for the scandal-loving Athenians to have fabricated scandalous stories about Diogenes.[53]

After the incident at Delphi, we can assume that he settled in Athens. In the latter part of his life, the sources affirm that it was in Corinth that he spent most of his time, and that it was there that he died. Dio Chrysostom informs us (*Or.* VI), that the custom of Diogenes was to spend his winters in Athens and his summers in Corinth. Other places are mentioned as having been visited by him: Myndus, on the southwestern coast of Asia Minor, where he ridiculed its inhabitants for the exorbitant size of the city's gates; Olympia, where he would have been a spectator at the Olympic games, and where he would have had the opportunity to pour contempt on the athletes; Sparta, where he claimed to have found men of *some* value, and from where, as we read in his twenty-seventh letter, he was banished at some point; Crete, where he was reportedly taken by pirates to be sold at the marketplace; and other places such as Delos and Aegina. Establishing the precise chronology of Diogenes' journeys and places of residence is simply impossible, because only rarely do the sources suggest definite dates. His encounter with Antisthenes in Athens, about which much will be said subsequently, should be placed early in his mature life, that is, no later then the year 366 B.C., which is the latest date concerning Antisthenes mentioned by the sources. His meeting or meetings with Alexander in Corinth belong to a later year, probably the year 336 B.C., when Alexander succeeded his father and was elected commander-in-chief (ἡγεμὼν αὐτοκράτωρ) of the Greek and Macedonian armies. This 'election' took place in the Isthmus, not far from Corinth, where, they tell us, Diogenes was living at that time. A report from Plutarch also confirms his presence in Corinth in the latter part of his life. According to Plutarch, it was in Corinth that Diogenes met Dionysius II of Syracuse, the tyrant in whose court Plato, Aristippus, and other philosophers of note spent time. As we learn from Plutarch (cf. Diodorus Siculus, XVI), Dionysius was overthrown and was forced to flee from Syracuse and take refuge in Corinth in 343 B.C., where he died a few years later. It was there that Diogenes had the chance to castigate the tyrant for his excesses and debauchery. Plutarch's testimony in this regard deserves to be quoted:

> Diogenes of Sinope, at their first meeting in the street there [in Corinth], saluted him with the ambiguous expression: "O Dionysius, how little you deserve your present life!" Upon which Dionysius stopped and replied, "I thank you, Diogenes, for your condolence." "Condole with you!" remarked Diogenes, "Do you not suppose, on the contrary, that I am indignant that such a slave like you, who, if you had your due, should have been left alone to grow old and die in the state of tyranny, as your father did before you, should now enjoy the ease of private persons, and be here to sport and frolic at freedom in our society?" (*Timoleon* XV)

We can construct a sketchy chronology of Diogenes' life, bearing in mind its tentative and blurry character. He was born in Sinope sometime in the last two decades of the fifth century B.C. Around the year 370 B.C., and allegedly because of some illegal manipulation of the currency, he either was banished from Sinope or voluntarily left his homeland, accompanied, according to Teles of Megara, by a slave. Shortly after this, having passed through Athens, he visited Delphi, where he received the famous oracle about adulterating the 'currency'. Returning to Athens, he lived there perhaps until the year 350 B.C. The contention advanced by D. R. Dudley that Diogenes' arrival in Athens could not have taken place *before* the year 340 B.C. and that, accordingly, his association with Antisthenes must be discounted as fiction, does not carry sufficient weight. It would compel us to dismiss as fictional also many reports about Diogenes, including, for example, his repeated encounters with Plato (who died in 347 B.C.).[54] It is quite true, however, that the date of Diogenes' departure from Sinope remains the subject of much controversy, and is partly contingent on the date assigned for his birth. As we saw earlier, he must have been born sometime between 413 B.C. and 404 B.C., the earlier of these dates being the most probable date. Although there are no indications in the sources concerning his age at the time of his departure from Sinope, the sense that is conveyed is that he was not an old man then, which could be interpreted as meaning that he had not reached yet his fortieth year.[55]

Several years later, on a voyage to Aegina, an island not far from the Athenian port of Piraeus, the ship on which he was traveling was seized by pirates led by a certain man named Scirpalus (D.L. VI, 74) or, according to Cicero (*De natura deorum* III, xxxiv, 83), Harpalus. In the Aegean Sea, piracy was a real source of peril for travelers. Ships were taken to distant ports, and those among the crew and the passengers who were spared were sold as slaves, and this is apparently the fate that befell Diogenes.[56] Taken to Crete, then, he was sold at the marketplace, where he was purchased by a Corinthian named Xeniades, who returned to Corinth with his new acquisition. The story of Diogenes' abduction by pirates, while perfectly plausible, may not be more than a romantic tale about him.

In Corinth, Xeniades is said to have asked Diogenes to oversee the education of his sons and to manage the affairs of his household.[57] After the death of Xeniades, Diogenes is reported to have remained in Corinth, living alone near a gymnasium known as 'the Craneum', outside the city walls, in a cypress grove facing the harbor. In the words of Dio Chrysostom, "Diogenes had no court around himself, great or small, for he lived alone and by himself in the Craneum; he did not have any disciples, nor was there any crowd around him, as we find around sophists, flute players, and choral singers" (*Or.* IV, 14). It was apparently there that his encounter with Alexander the Great took place, and it was there, too, that his friends found him dead in the year 323 B.C.

Of his life in Athens, Corinth, and elsewhere, some details emerge from the sources, particularly the outbursts of Cynicism for which he became so famous —or infamous. On the reasonable assumption that he arrived in Athens before the death of Antisthenes, we can visualize him gravitating naturally toward the Cynosarges, the park and gymnasium in the Athenian vicinity, where Antisthenes is said to have taught, and where foreigners and exiles were welcomed, and where all sorts of marginal people would congregate. There, he would have met Antisthenes, from whom he could have received his first lessons in Cynicism. The austerity of Antisthenes' style of life, his rebelliousness against the social and political world, his ascetic mode of existence, and his contempt for the customs and conventions of ordinary people—these and other aspects and character traits generally associated with the great disciple of Socrates must have made a profound impression on Diogenes. Like him, too, Diogenes chose Cynicism as his path. Undoubtedly, from Antisthenes and from others among Socrates' associates, he must have learned a great deal about Socrates and must have inherited the desire to emulate his example. Plato himself, recognizing the ideological lineage that linked Diogenes and Socrates, albeit distorted and perverted in his eyes, would call

Diogenes a "Socrates-gone-mad" (Σωκράτης μαινόμενος), as we learn from Diogenes Laertius (VI, 54) and from Aelian (*Hist. Var.* XIV, xxxiii).

Besides the influence of Antisthenes, we have no certainty about other *identifiable* and *direct* intellectual influences in his life, although, as will be shown in chapter 3, it is unquestionable that Diogenes' thought must have been shaped by certain intellectual currents present in Athens during his time. No references are found in the sources to his having studied under any teacher other than Antisthenes, and nothing is said about his having frequented lectures or courses of instruction under anyone. In fact, he spoke of Plato's lectures as "a waste of time" (D.L. VI, 24), and did not have kind words for those who study literature, mathematics, astronomy, and similar subjects (D.L. VI, 27). His aversion toward the Sophists and their teachings would have made it impossible for him to profit in any way from the education that they pretended to impart. On occasion, too, we hear that, not unlike Antisthenes, he spoke of the futility and uselessness of reading and writing. Yet, as we have seen, the sources attribute numerous writings to him, which, if genuine, could not have come from an uneducated man.

Furthermore, the sources repeatedly depict him quoting from the poets, especially Homer and the tragedians, and, on occasion, even giving expression to sophisticated ideas that are traceable to earlier philosophers. In his defense of the consumption of human flesh, for instance, he is reported to have expressed himself in terms closely parallel to statements associated with Anaxagoras of Clazomenae (D.L. VI, 73). All things, said Diogenes, contain parts of all other things, for the elements that make up matter are dispersed throughout all existing things, and thus, when we eat a piece of bread or a fruit, we are ingesting particles that at one time or another were found in human flesh. How then could it be wrong to eat a piece of human flesh, if that is what we do when we eat anything else? Statements like these and the many quotations from Homer and other poets with which he embellished his conversations reveal that, if such attributions belonged to him, Diogenes must have been a man of considerable literary and philosophical learning. His lack of formal training in philosophy and the fact that he remained distant and even hostile to the then flourishing schools of philosophy and rhetoric should be counterbalanced with the ease with which any person of leisure living in Athens was able to gain access to learning. Moreover, the position of his family in Sinope might have provided for him the opportunity of acquiring an education as a young man. Even Sayre, always willing to present Diogenes in the worst possible light, had to admit that he must have had the benefit of a literary education—at least for the purpose of *posing* as a wise man.[58] As will be shown in a later chapter, ignorance, in the sense of knowing little or nothing, cannot be attributed to Diogenes.

Several reports speak about where in Athens and in Corinth Diogenes lived, and about how he managed to survive. While in Corinth, he is said to have lived in the house of Xeniades, where he served as the slave-educator of this man's children. But aside from this period of his life, we find him invariably living as a homeless man, either in a tub near the Athenian Metroön (D.L. VI, 23),[59] under the porticos of the temples (D.L. VI, 22), or in a public gymnasium or a bath (D.L. VI, 77). In agreement with numerous other testimonies, Dio Chrysostom tells us that for Diogenes, "the cities themselves were his dwelling, and he spent all his time in the public places and in the temples of the gods, and the whole earth was his abode—the earth that is the abode and source of nourishment for all human beings" (*Or.* IV, 13).

Diogenes' tub has become a legendary symbol both in literature and in the history of painting, and has transformed itself into *the* image of classical Cynicism. We have several variations of the story related to it. In Diogenes Laertius (VI, 23), we are told that Diogenes opted for living in a tub when a man, who had promised to secure for him a cottage, failed to do so. In his sixteenth letter, he tells us that the idea of a tub for his dwelling came to him after observing that snails carry their houses—their shells—on their backs. In some sources, the tub is described as a temporary abode, but according to Saint Jerome, it was his permanent home in Athens:

> His home was the gateways and porticos of the city, and when he would crawl out of his tub, he would joke about what he called his movable house, for it adapted itself to the seasons. When the weather was cold, he would turn the mouth of the tub toward the south, and when it was hot, toward the north, and so in whatever direction the sun happened to be, Diogenes' palace would face it. (*Adv. Jovin.* II, xiv)

The word 'tub' often used to translate the Greek πίθος (*pithos*) should be understood in the sense of a large earthenware barrel, big enough to be used as a cistern. Placed on its side, it could easily accommodate a person and serve as a place of shelter in inclement weather. According to Aristophanes (*Knights* 792), large tubs were sometimes used as a dwelling by refugees and displaced people during the Peloponnesian War. Diogenes Laertius tells us (VI, 43) that once, when a boy threw stones and broke it, the Athenians, after having him flogged, made arrangements for a new tub for Diogenes.

Although Diogenes' tub is generally believed to have been his dwelling while living in Athens, there are also references to it as his home while living in Corinth. Lucian, for instance, left for us an anecdote, possibly one of the most significant of all the stories told about Diogenes, in which he is described living in a tub near the Corinthian Craneum:

> When news came to the Corinthians that Philip and the Macedonians were approaching the city, the entire population became immersed in a flurry of activity, some making their weapons ready, or wheeling stones, or patching the fortifications, or strengthening a battlement,

everyone making himself useful for the protection of the city. Diogenes, who had nothing to do and from whom no one was willing to ask anything, as soon as he noticed the bustle of those surrounding him, began at once to roll his tub up and down the Craneum with great energy. When asked why he did so, his answer was, "Just to make myself look as busy as the rest of you." (*Historia* 3)

In this anecdote, however biographically genuine it may be, we find the Cynic at his best: ironically and sarcastically, he mimics the senseless activities of the human world around him, ridiculing the stupidity of war and nationalism, and, more generally, denouncing through his actions the mindless bustle that characterizes much of human existence. As others prepare themselves for war, he aimlessly rolls his tub, as if saying, "What I do is as senseless as what you do." He could have exclaimed then, as Stobaeus reports of him in another context, "It is not that I am mad; it is only that my head is different from yours" (III, iii, 51).

Such behavior and mode of existence, exhibiting Diogenes' independence and contempt for what people deem the necessities of life, are well in accord with his conception of himself as a citizen of the world, a κοσμοπολίτης, to use the word attributed to him by Diogenes Laertius (VI, 63) and a word apparently coined by Diogenes himself, that is, a man who conceived of himself as belonging to whatever place he chanced to be at any given moment, a citizen of no particular city, neither an Athenian, nor a Corinthian, nor a Sinopean, nor even a Greek, a man pledging allegiance to no country and rejecting even the idea of nationality— just a human being.[60] This independence was derived in part from his condition as an exile forced to lived in foreign soil, and in part from his conviction that the things a person needs to survive are indeed very few: some food and some shelter, and the ability to come and go in absolute freedom, and these he was fortunate enough to find among the Athenians and the Corinthians. There is a small dosage of truth in a comment made by Sayre when he notes that

> the felicity of Diogenes' life, which he seems to have credited to his own wisdom, was largely due to favoring circumstances over which he had no control. Greece has a mild and equable climate which favors life in the open; the governments of Corinth and Athens were liberal to aliens and vagrants, and the Greeks of that period seem to have been generous to beggars.[61]

Diogenes' love of independence and self-sufficiency is well summed by Maximus of Tyre, who gave us the following description of him:

> The man from Sinope in Pontus, after consulting the Apollonian oracle, stripped from himself all unnecessary things, broke asunder all the chains that had previously imprisoned his spirit, and devoted himself to

> a wandering life of freedom, like a bird, unafraid of tyrants and governments, not constrained by any human laws, undisturbed by politics and political events, free from the hindrance of children and a wife, unwilling to work the fruits of the earth in the fields, rejecting even the thought of serving in an army, and contemptuous of the market activities that consume most people. (*Or.* XXXVI, 5)

This description includes the salient characteristics associated with Diogenes: a systematic abandonment of all superfluities, a conscious and unwavering commitment to break asunder the fetters that in the form of conventions and rules tie and incapacitate human beings, an unquenchable thirst for personal freedom, the courage to despise openly rulers and governments and their laws, an indifference toward political affairs, an unwillingness to serve as a pawn in the wars manufactured and managed by the oligarchies, a life unattached to a wife and children, and a disdain for the market and financial preoccupations that entrap practically everybody. *This*, as Maximus reports, is probably what Diogenes was, and *this* is the image of him that remained constant in Cynic traditions.

It is in the context of Diogenes' independence and commitment to self-sufficiency that we should comment at length on two interesting characteristics of his life, concerning which the sources are in agreement: his celibacy and his lack of employment. His celibacy (ἀγαμία) can be regarded as a fact, for nothing in the sources conveys even remotely that he was ever married or that he had any children, or even that he was especially attached to another person. Some of the sources are explicit and emphatic about his views on marriage and procreation. In Diogenes Laertius (VI, 54), for instance, we read that to someone who wanted to know from him what is the right time to marry, he answered, "For a young man, not yet; for an old man, never at all."[62] Again, according to Diogenes Laertius (VI, 72), it is reported that he advocated that men and women should live, if they were so inclined, in communities in which everyone is the spouse of everyone, without the arrangement of marriage, and that children, too, should not belong to their parents, but to the community at large, an idea that is not altogether foreign to Plato, who in the *Republic* (5.449a ff.; see *Laws* 5.739c) expresses himself in similar terms, when he makes Socrates defend the idea that at least in what concerns the guardians of the State, that is, the philosophers, wives are to be held in common and children are not to know who their actual parents are, but should belong to the State.

In Diogenes' forty-seventh letter we come upon a statement that remains valuable regardless of its probable inauthenticity, because it appears to reflect well his inclination: "Whoever trusts us [the Cynics] will remain single; those who do not trust us will rear children. And if the human species should one day cease to exist, there should be as much cause of regret as there should be if flies and wasps should pass away."

This antipathy toward marriage and procreation remained after Diogenes an ingrained Cynic tradition, so that, with the exception of Crates and Hipparchia, no other major Cynics are known to have departed from Diogenes' recommendation.[63] As Epictetus would remind us (*Discourses* III, xxii, 67-76), a married life, with its innumerable distractions and responsibilities, and especially with the arrival of children, cannot be but a source of interference for a Cynic, whose vocation, in Epictetus' view, is to serve as an emissary and scout of God among his generally dense and misguided fellow human beings, for the Cynic is he "who hath charge of the flock and for many a thing must be watchful" (*Iliad* II, 25). Epictetus pondered, however, over the example set by Crates and Hipparchia, and concluded that *there* we have an exceptional marriage, because in marrying Hipparchia, Crates married another Crates, for she was as committed to a Cynic way of life as he was. Had she not been a Cynic, Crates' life would have been immersed in aggravations and his Cynic mission would have been thwarted by the emotional and domestic concerns of married life.

We are also told by Maximus of Tyre (*Or.* III, 9) that Diogenes did not marry because he had heard stories about Xanthippe, Socrates' wife, whose reputation as an impatient and difficult woman is well known and is the subject of countless stories.[64] How could have Diogenes pursued his Cynic mission in the company of an ordinary woman like Xanthippe, who would have been for him a source of daily distractions and aggravations, and who would have impeded his campaign to unsettle the world? He might have asked himself, however, how it was possible for Socrates to remain married to such a woman *and* yet be able to carry on and fulfill *his* philosophical mission. At any rate, Diogenes did not find someone like Hipparchia—another Diogenes—and remained, therefore, alone and childless all his life. In an Arabic source, we are told that when someone asked him why he had avoided the company of women, Diogenes replied that it was because he had not been able to figure out a way to cope with the demands of dependants.

Diogenes' rejection of marriage could be interpreted as a manifestation of misogyny. There are several passages in the sources, principally in Diogenes Laertius, in which we come upon derogatory statements about women. Seeing some women hanged from a tree, for instance, he is reported to have said, "I wish that every tree bore similar fruit" (D.L. VI, 52). Again, observing a woman being carried in a litter, he remarked that "the cage was not in keeping with its contents" (D.L. VI, 51). A graffito found in Herculaneum, which depicts a woman drowning in a river, attributes to Diogenes the statement that women are the evil of evils, that is, the worst thing in the world (τὸ κακὸν ὑπὸ κακοῦ), leading us to assume that so bad a thing as a woman does not deserve to be rescued from the river.[65]

In Arabic gnomologies, we find numerous statements about women attributed to Diogenes that reveal the mind of a confirmed misogynist.[66] "Woman," he said, "is unavoidable distress" (Mubassir, 55). Again, when asked what women were, he replied that they were nothing but sources of deception and misery. Muhtasar Siwan al-hikma (Diogenes 16) reports that once, when a certain Walisa (an otherwise unknown philosopher) was arguing some philosophical point with Diogenes, she remarked to him that his ugliness was so great that nature would not have gone wrong if he had been born with the ears of a donkey. Diogenes calmly replied to her that in the case of men, their physical appearance is not as important and critical as their intelligence, whereas in the case of women, their looks are paramount because of their normal lack of intelligence.

Still on another occasion, according to Ibn-Hindu (Diogenes 67), when he noticed a woman seeking the counsel of other women, he compared her with a snake borrowing poison from other snakes. Also from the same author comes another apophthegm—a cruel one, we might say: once, when he saw a one-eye woman adorning herself, he said "One haft of evil is also evil" (Diogenes 49). There is still another, in which Diogenes stresses a woman's aversion toward work and her love of wine: "He looked at a woman who hated spinning but loved drinking, and said, 'Put on the top of the wine cask a piece of cotton so that she will not approach it'" (Diogenes 58). From Hunayn ibn-Ishak (Diogenes 8), we learn about Diogenes' view of women and education: when he saw a man teaching a girl how to read and write, he advised him not to make a bad thing even worse.

What are we to make of these and similar attributions? It is undeniable that derogatory statements about women abound in classical literature and are a manifestation of an ancient prejudicial view widely accepted in many ancient cultures, including that of the Greeks, and even in modern cultures. Among the Greeks, women occupied a secondary place in social and political affairs, and their virtues and capabilities were seldom recognized as amounting to anything. There were, of course, exceptional occurrences—one can think of Aspasia[67]—and occasional statements from philosophers like Socrates that reveal a different frame of mind about the value of womanhood.[68] Nevertheless, Diogenes' comments about women, assuming that they reflect genuine statements made by him, are well in accord with the cultural and social climate of his time, a circumstance that by no means exonerates him from his prejudicial shortsightedness, which is surprising in someone who, like him, maintained otherwise enlightened ideas about cosmopolitanism, and who claimed to have reached the necessary state of mental lucidity to begin a war against the idiotic social conventions and prejudices that permeated his world.[69] In this respect, then, Diogenes was probably neither worse nor better than his contemporaries. Statements like the one found in the Herculaneum graffito are typical nonsensical platitudes found throughout the literature and history of ancient times.

If we persist in accusing Diogenes of rampant misogyny, however, one extenuating circumstance should be borne in mind: he also had nothing kind to say about *men*, and there is no exaggeration in affirming that nowhere do the sources report him as having said anything positive or complimentary about *anybody*, including his only known philosophical mentor, Antisthenes. If he disliked women and found them worthless, he saw in men equally worthless creatures. According to Muntahab Siwan al-hikma (Diogenes 17), once, when Diogenes was asked if it was true that he hated all people, he replied that he hated evil people for their depravities and good people for their silence in the presence of moral depravity.

We will examine in chapter 2 his attitude toward the species to which he belonged, an attitude that shaped, we think, *his* practice of Cynicism. His preferred recommendation to his contemporaries was, "Hang yourselves!," as we read, for instance, in D.L. VI, 59, and thus, if he had seen *men* hanging from a tree, he might have also said that he wished that every tree bore similar fruit, and if he had seen a *man* drowning in a river, he might have probably walked away. Let us remember the misanthropic statement ascribed to him in his forty-seventh letter: if the human species were to cease to exist, there should be no cause for regret. His celibacy, therefore, was not born out of dislike or contempt toward women in particular, but probably and partly out of his disdain toward all his likes, whether men or women, for which reason we find it difficult to associate him with disciples or even friends. In his search for human beings, as he walked through the streets of Athens, carrying a lighted lamp in broad daylight, he did not find any: scoundrels and creatures-less-than-human, yes; but human beings, no. According to Dio Chrysostom (*Or.* VIII, 4-5), Diogenes abandoned Athens after Antisthenes' death (around 366 B.C.), because he became convinced that there was nobody in Athens worthy of his presence, and that it was then that he moved to Corinth, a city also filled with worthless human creatures, morally and intellectually worse than the Athenians themselves, but precisely because of this, more in need of his services as a philosophical 'physician', that is, a practitioner of Cynicism, who could set them aright and cure them of their immense stupidity and inveterate depravity by means of his caustic medicine—insults, vituperation, and shocking acts. Corinth, as Dio Chrysostom informs us (*Or.* VIII), was, because of its location and varied population, a center of a great deal of activity and moral depravity, where, more than in any other place, Diogenes could practice his Cynic spiritual medicine, and where he went, just as a physician seeks those who are ill and need his services. "It was appropriate," says Dio, "that the wise man should take up residence where the crowd of imbeciles and fools is the largest, in order to lay bare their emptiness and correct their senselessness." We suspect that there, too, amid the Corinthians, he found no true human beings, and that he remained as alone as in Athens, for the contempt with which he looked upon his contemporaries was well reciprocated by most of them. We hear of instances in which he was insulted and even physically attacked by those who were the victims of his Cynicism, as we learn from the twenty-seventh letter and from Diogenes Laertius (VI, 33), as well as from Arabic sources. Ibn-Hindu, for instance, reports (Diogenes 33), that once, when a man insulted him, Diogenes refrained from returning the insult, saying, "It is sufficient abuse for him that he insulted me but I did not." On another occasion the same source reports that he was warned not to enter the narrow alleys of the city, because certain people had planned to beat him.

The insults and blows that Diogenes received from some, and the indifference and contempt with which many must have treated him, were counterbalanced by the respect and sense of awe of the few, very few indeed, who recognized the courage and persistence with which he pursued his mission, and who must have been attracted by the paradox exhibited in his life—a homeless and wandering man, who recognized no country as his own, who paid no homage to the authorities or the laws, who consistently chose a life of hardship and penury, who spoke with unequaled freedom and impunity, who rejected and often broke laws and conventions, and yet a man who claimed to have attained happiness and who remained at peace amid the turmoil of his surrounding world. Such a man, we must assume, must have been a source of curiosity to many and a person to be admired and revered among a few others. Thus, we hear that monarchs and potentates went to see him, as Alexander did, or sought his company, as was the case with Perdiccas of Macedonia, precisely the kind of people for whom Diogenes expressed the greatest contempt. In his eyes, Alexander was not worth even looking at (Plutarch, *Alexander* xiv), Perdiccas was a tarantula (D.L. VI, 44), Philip II of Macedonia and Antipater miserable men (ibid.), Dionysius of Syracuse a despicable slave (Plutarch, *Timoleon* xv), and so on. Lucian (*Menippus, Or the Oracle of the Dead*) describes how, while in Hades, Diogenes' pastime was to go on with his litany of insults at those who, while alive, had been in positions of authority, power, and wealth:

> The great Diogenes resides near Sardanapalus the Assyrian[70] and Midas the Phrygian,[71] and certain other worthies of that sort; and when he hears them lamenting and remeasuring their ancient fortunes, he laughs and is delighted, and, for the most part, he lies upon his back and sings in a harsh and savage voice, drowning their wailing; so that these men are greatly annoyed, and are thinking about moving their quarters, as they cannot put up with Diogenes.

Diogenes' "harsh and savage voice" in Hades was heard even more loudly while he lived in the physical world, and few, as we will see in the following chapter, were able to escape from his attacks.

Those who admired and revered him during his life, and who became in one way or another his disciples or associates, must have been, we can assume, very few. Seldom have philosophers been admired and revered by the multitude, and, as Schopenhauer once perceptively observed, popularity and greatness of mind are often in an inverse ratio: popularity is a sure indication of emptiness of mind and of spiritual vacuity, for the masses normally admire and applaud those who resemble them, and in no way can we say that Diogenes resembled the common man of his time, nor indeed the common man of any other time. Given Diogenes' eccentric and offending style of life, it would have been a most extraordinary thing to find him at the center of a large number of devoted and admiring followers. According to Julian, "one or two, indeed, used to applaud him in his own day, but more than ten times ten thousand had their stomachs turned by nausea and loathing, and went fasting until their attendants revived them with perfumes and myrrh and cakes" (*Or.* VI, 190).

Diogenes Laertius (VI, 36), moreover, tells us that prospective disciples quickly ran away from Diogenes, once they understood the harshness of the Cynic lessons that they had to learn and practice, and, thus, the list of disciples that has come down to us is exceedingly short. It must have been easy to gape at him and even, at least for a few, to admire him, but it must have been exceedingly difficult to follow his example. We hear of Crates of Thebes having been converted to Cynicism through the example and teachings of Diogenes (D.L. VI, 87), and we also hear of Monimus of Syracuse (D.L. VI, 82-83) and of Onesicritus of Astypalaea (D.L. VI, 84), the man who became the chief pilot of Alexander's ship, when the Greeks and Macedonians returned from India to Babylon.[72] References are also found to Onesicritus' sons, as well as to Phocion the Honest and Stilpo of Megara (D.L. VI, 75-76). Diogenes Laertius mentions, aside from these, "many other men of prominence in political affairs" (VI, 76) as having joined Diogenes in his mode of life. We suspect, however, that the biographer might have exaggerated the facts and that the number of Diogenes' genuine disciples must have been very small indeed. A man like Diogenes could not have found familiarity and closeness with others but a source of mental torture or at least a fount of intolerable boredom. In an Arabic gnomology, Sahzazuri tells us that when people asked Diogenes why he would not converse with them, his sarcastic reply was, "Because you are too important for my subtlety and I am too subtle for your importance."

Concerning the means of Diogenes' livelihood, the sources are unanimous in their descriptions of his habit of begging for alms and food. His own characterization of himself as "a homeless exile, to his country dead; a wanderer who begs for his daily bread" (D.L. VI, 38), is in accord with what we learn about him in innumerable passages. Whether he was a man of some means upon his arrival in Athens, as could be inferred from his being accompanied by a slave and from the occupation of his father in Sinope, or a destitute exile, it is clear that his poverty, brought about by his aversion to any sort of remunerated employment, forced him into begging. We hear about his being once "short of money" and of his need to be fed by generous passers-by (D.L. VI, 46), and we find him on occasion even begging from a statue for the purpose of getting used to being rejected and refused (D.L. VI, 49). We detect in him a certain pride in his begging occupation, as when he reminded those from whom he asked for alms or food that he was not asking for undeserved gratuities, but for what was his due (D.L. VI, 46). On occasion, too, we find him reacting angrily when alms or food were not forthcoming. To a man who said to him, "I will give you, but only if you can persuade me," his amazing comment was, "If I could have persuaded you of anything, I would have persuaded you to hang yourself" (D.L. VI, 59).

The supposition that Diogenes' lack of a 'normal' occupation was the result of his "natural indolence and a snobbish disinclination to lose caste,"[73] is probably just an opinion of little value. It surely takes more effort and endurance to choose a homeless life, live in a tub, beg for one's daily bread, and be at the mercy of others for the sake of conveying a harsh philosophical message, than to accept a senseless and mechanical job and work for the enrichment of others, and join thereby the ranks of the 'normal' human beings, who spend their lives working frantically to maintain a certain style of life. A more reasonable explanation for Diogenes' choice of not working for a living could be found in a statement that Diogenes Laertius attributes to Chrysippus, the Stoic philosopher, who was a disciple of Zeno of Citium and a man who had much in common with Diogenes (D.L. VII, 189). In his *On the Means of Livelihood*, Chrysippus is said to have written:

> And yet, what reason is there that he [the wise man] should provide for his living? For if it is for the purpose of maintaining his life, life itself is something inconsequential. If it is to obtain pleasure, pleasure, too, is inconsequential. If it is to acquire virtue, virtue is in itself sufficient to bring about happiness. At any rate, all forms of earning a livelihood are ridiculous. If a king supports him, he will have to keep the king happy; if his friends take care of him, friendship is the sort of thing that can be purchased with money.

Like Chrysippus, then, and indeed like many other philosophers of antiquity, Socrates included, Diogenes remained free from the subjection of work, and, like many of them, lived reasonably well at the expense of others, attaining a ripe old age. Indeed, for a man who wanted and needed so little, whose house was a tub or some temple portico, whose clothing was a ragged cloak, whose diet was made up of lupines, lentils, bread, and water, who had neither a wife nor a family, and who, as he once remarked to a certain tax-collector who wanted money from him, carried all his fabulous riches within his chest, "where you can neither get them nor see them"—for such a man, employment must have had no meaning and money no value. After Diogenes, the tradition of avoiding remunerated work and begging for one's sustenance became established among the Cynics, many of whom followed his example.[74] In late classical times and in medieval times, it survived in one way or another among the members of Christian mendicant orders.

Concerning his physical appearance, we have some information, although its reliability cannot be taken for granted. There are numerous ancient works of art that depict Diogenes as an old man, either as full-body statues or as busts. In all these instances, however, we only have Roman copies of the originals. Their value is biographically negligible, since it is impossible to determine the closeness of the copies to the original pieces, and the accuracy with which the original pieces could have depicted the philosopher. There are, moreover, neither originals nor copies of works of art that belong to Diogenes' own lifetime. In all cases, we are probably in the presence of idealized representations that depict well the *philosophical* aspects of Diogenes' personality, but not necessarily his physical appearance. The image of a typical Cynic philosopher is well captured in such artistic works, giving us a good idea of the Cynic 'uniform'—a torn cloak, a leathern wallet, a wooden staff, and occasionally an accompanying dog.[75]

There are no verbal descriptions of his physical appearance in classical literature, except for two comments of Diogenes Laertius and Epictetus. Diogenes Laertius (VI, 81) tells us that "according to Athenodorus in the eighth book of his *Walks*, Diogenes had a well-groomed appearance, because of his use of unguents."[76] Epictetus, for his part, notes that "Diogenes used to go about with a radiant complexion and would attract the attention of the common people by the very appearance of his body" (*Discourses* III, xxii, 88). The language used by Diogenes Laertius, as well as the one used by Epictetus, convey the idea of 'shining' or 'glittering' that can be associated with a person whose skin is shiny because of the use of oily creams or unguents. Epictetus' observation that Diogenes "would attract the attention of the common people by the very appearance of his body" can be interpreted in various ways, and leaves us in the dark as to whether Diogenes was handsome or ugly, because in either case he might have surely attracted public notice.

In Arabic gnomologies, we come across explicit references to Diogenes' appearance. Muhtasar Siwan al-hikma, for instance, tells us that he was ugly, and Ibn-Hindu (Diogenes 50) recounts how Alexander once sent a magnificent robe to Diogenes, who, declining the gift, said that when someone ugly wears a beautiful robe, its beauty renders him uglier, whereas if he wears something plain and ugly, his own ugliness is hidden and he gives the appearance of being handsome. In a passage of Sahrastani (Diogenes 5), we hear that once a handsome man expressed amazement at Diogenes' remarkable ugliness, which elicited from him the comment that his physical appearance was not something that he had chosen or something within his power to change, for which reason he could not be blamed for it. Neither was the beauty of his interlocutor, he added, something that he had chosen, for which reason he could not be praised for it. Praise and blame belong only to those things that are within our power to change.

This passage is reminiscent of a report about Socrates, who was also reportedly ugly and about whose appearance we have more reliable information. Cicero informs us (*Tusc. disp.* iv, 27; *De fato* iv, 10) that once, when a famous physiognomist named Zopyrus came to Athens, Socrates had him examine his face. In utter amazement at his ugliness, Zopyrus exclaimed, "Sir, you are truly a monster!," to which Socrates replied, "What you see, Zopyrus, is what I *was*." The point is clear: Socrates had transformed his physical ugliness into a glittering and shining manifestation of spiritual beauty, so that, as Alcibiades says in Plato's *Symposium* (215b), beneath his unpleasant physical frame he carried the representations of the gods. Likewise, then, in the instance of Diogenes: beneath the ugliness of his body there lived a world of spiritual beauty, as if he, no less than Socrates, were a reminder that it is not the appearance of things that matters, but their reality. He, too, like Socrates, had succeeded in transforming himself into something that he was not by birth. It should be obvious, however, that what the Arabic sources report about Diogenes' appearance, no less than what *their* own Greek and Roman sources might have said about it, may not be more than edifying stories, the value of which is symbolic more than biographical. Thus, the actual appearance of the Cynic from Sinope remains unknown.

When at last death caught up with him, he was already an old man, as noted earlier, approaching his ninetieth year. The cause of his death is reported differently by various sources, and Diogenes Laertius (VI, 76-77) provides for us a sketch of several versions. Suicide by self-asphyxiation—by holding his breath —was suggested by Cercidas of Megalopolis, who wrote that Diogenes "soared aloft with his lips tightly pressed against his teeth, holding his breath within." According to Antisthenes of Rhodes (second century B.C.), Diogenes' own friends and associates were convinced that such was the manner of his death. Reports about other Cynics and Stoics also attribute their deaths to self-suffocation, as in the cases of Metrocles of Maroneia and Zeno of Citium, but tempting as such reports may be, the truth is that no one can simply die by holding his breath, for it is a physiological impossibility. Perhaps here, as elsewhere, we encounter a legend that provides a graphic description of a philosophical attitude: what better way could there be to leave this world than opting for the most 'natural' way of dying, that is, holding one's breath? What better way to die than by wilfully stopping the process of breathing, especially for someone whom one of the sources describes as exhausted in his battle against the world? From Muhtasar Siwan al-hikma (Diogenes 45), we have a report that underlines Diogenes' state of exhaustion. A certain man once asked him what it was that he was seeking as he moved ceaselessly among people, to which Diogenes replied that the only thing that he was anxious to find was complete rest. He added, however, that he did not expect to find rest as long as he remained in this world. His battle against the world had proven to be an unending undertaking and thus he could not foresee its end.

Self-starvation, also a 'natural' way, is mentioned in the context of the deaths of other philosophers, but nothing is said in this regard about Diogenes' death. Likewise, other forms of suicide are attributed to other Cynics—hanging, as with Menippus of Gadara, and self-burning, as with Peregrinus Proteus. Still, in relation to Diogenes, only self-asphyxiation is mentioned as *his* form of suicide.

Other more reasonable explanations of Diogenes' death surface here and there in the sources. We are told, for example, that he ate a raw octopus and that as a consequence "his belly swelled up and he died" (Athenaeus, VIII, 341). We also hear that he died after having chewed on ox meat, or that, since he did not use fire, he swallowed a raw fish and died. Censorinus (*De die natali* XV, 2) attributes his death to overeating and indigestion. Gluttony, according to Gregory Nazianzen and Tatian, was the cause of death. We are also told by Epictetus (*Discourses* III, xxii, 58) and by Saint Jerome (*Adv. Jovin.* II, xiv) that he died of a fever caught on the eve of his departure to attend the Olympic games. The testimony of Saint Jerome is wonderfully descriptive:

> It is said that, when already an old man, Diogenes was on his way to the Olympic games, where a great multitude of Greeks would assemble to see the contests, when he was overtaken by a fever, for which reason he lay down on the side of the road. When his friends wanted to place him upon a beast or in a carriage, he refused and found his way to the shade under a nearby tree, saying to them, "You go your way, I beg you, and see the games. As for myself, this night will prove me either the conquered or the conqueror. If I conquer the fever, I will go to the games, but if the fever conquers me, then I will go to the world below." Throughout the night he lay gasping for breath, until, as we are told, he did not just die but banish the fever through his death.

There is also a report that attributes his death to the bite of a dog,[77] a most fitting explanation, regardless of its questionable historical basis. The scene itself is colorful: Diogenes, known universally as the Dog and depicted in works of art living in the company of dogs, is about to eat a raw octopus. The surrounding dogs want a piece of the octopus, and while distributing the creature among them, one of the dogs bites the philosopher, which occasions his death. The 'Celestial Dog', as Cercidas would refer to him, dies, bitten by a 'normal' dog. "Tell us, Diogenes," writes Diogenes Laertius (VI, 79), "what fate took you to the world below?" to which Diogenes answers, "The savage tooth of a dog." Here again, we come upon what gives the appearance of a legend created to underline some aspect of Diogenes' character.

A passage from Diogenes Laertius unveils for us how his death was discovered:

> When, as was their custom, his friends came to him in the morning, they found him wrapped in his cloak, and thought that he was asleep,

although they knew that he was by no means a drowsy or somnolent type. When they drew aside the cloak, however, they found that he was dead. They assumed that his death had been a deliberate act on his part to escape the burden of life. (VI, 77)

We are also told that the manner of his burial was to him a matter of no consequence. When asked how he wished to be buried, he left instructions to be thrown outside the city wall and left unburied, so that wild animals could feast on his body; or to be thrown into a ditch and covered with dust; or, better still, to be thrown into the river Ilissus.[78] According to Stobaeus (IV, lx), it was Diogenes' custom to say that whatever happened to his corpse, it would turn out to be a blessing to him: if eaten by dogs, his fate would be like that of the Hyrcanians[79]; if devoured by vultures, his burial would be like those of the Indians; and if abandoned in some barren field, the elements and time would assure that his remains would be well taken care of by the sun and the rain. From Cicero we learn a bit more about Diogenes' indifference about his burial:

> Diogenes shared Socrates' attitude towards death, although was more outspoken, and, as a genuine Cynic, he would insist without ambivalence that his body should just be thrown away without burial. His associates would ask him, "But could it be that you wish that your body be the food of vultures and wild beasts?" "Not at all," he would reply, "as long as you provide me with a stick to chase those creatures away!" "But, then," they would say, "how could you do that, if you will not be aware of anything?" "Ah yes! If in death I cannot be aware of anything, how could the bites of wild creatures hurt me?" (*Tusc. disp.* I, xlii)

Cicero's reference to Socrates is related to the statement in the *Phaedo* (116a), where Socrates reminds his friends, who have expressed concern about what to do with his body when he dies, that they should do whatever they want, for they would be burying, not Socrates, but only his body.

Paradoxically, we learn that Diogenes' disciples and associates became entangled in a violent dispute about how he should be buried and about who had the right to oversee his burial, an anecdote that seems to convey the sense that those who were devoted to him were ultimately unable to learn from him one of the principal lessons of his doctrine, namely, indifference toward the conventions and customs of human beings. At last, a funeral was arranged by the Corinthians, and he was buried outside the city walls, near the western gate and not far from where he spent his last years. A statue of a dog was placed over the grave, bearing the following inscription:

Εἰπέ, κύον, τίνος ἀνδρὸς ἐφεστὼς σῆμα φυλάσσεις;
Τοῦ κυνός. ἀλλὰ τίς ἦν οὗτος ἀνὴρ ὁ Κύων;
Διογένης. γένος εἰπέ. Σινωπεύς. ὃς πίθον ᾤκει;

Καὶ μάλα, νῦν δὲ θανὼν ἀστέρας οἶκον ἔχει.

Tell me, Oh Dog!, who is the man whose monument thou art guarding? He is no one but the Dog Himself! But who could have been this man, the Dog Himself? Diogenes, indeed! And what is his place of origin? He was a man from Sinope. He who used to live in a tub? Yes, indeed, he himself! But now, in his death, he lives among the stars! (*Anthology* I, 285)[80]

Another inscription, found in Diogenes Laertius (VI, 78) and in the *Anthology*, reads as follows:

Even bronze groweth old with time, but thy fame, Diogenes, not all Eternity shall take away. For thou alone didst point out to mortals the lesson of self-sufficiency, and the path for the best and easiest life. (XVI, 334)

Pausanias (second century A.D.) reports having seen Diogenes' tomb:

As you go up to the hill of Corinth there are several tombs on the sides of the road, and at the gate is buried Diogenes of Sinope, whom the Greeks nickname the Dog. (II, ii, 4)

Various other epitaphs have been preserved in the *Anthology*, one of which is particularly revealing:

Oh Ferryman of the Dead [Charon], receive Diogenes the Dog, who laid bare the whole pretentiousness of life. (VII, 63)

Such, then, was the life of Diogenes of Sinope, a life spent for the most part in a Herculean struggle against the innumerable aspects of human existence that, from the point of view of reason, made little or no sense to him. The testimony of the sources may not be altogether reliable in what concerns the details, but is clear and consistent with respect to the overall character of his life. We can now delve a bit deeper into the sources in order to fill with greater substance the content of Diogenes' life between his departure from Sinope and his death in Corinth, and thereby reconstruct the way in which his Cynicism became manifest as a daily practice.

Notes

1. References to ancient sources will be given in the text, while references to modern sources will be included in the endnotes.

2. For a discussion of the ways in which Cynicism in general and the philosophy of Diogenes in particular were received by the Fathers of the Church, see G. Doribal, "L'image des cyniques chez les Pères grecs," in *Le Cynisme ancien et ses prolongements. Actes du Colloque International du CNRS.* Edited by M. O. Goulet-Cazé and R. Goulet (Paris: Presses Universitaires de France, 1993), pp. 419-443. The relationship between Cynicism and Christianity has been extensively explored in scholarly literature. As examples of this literature, see F. G. Downing, "The Social Contexts of Jesus the Teacher." *New Testament Studies* 33 (1987), pp. 439-451, and *Cynics and Christian Origins* (Edinburgh: T. & T. Clark, 1992).

3. J. L. Livsay, "Some Renaissance Views of Diogenes the Cynic," in *Joseph Quincy Adams: Memorial Studies.* Edited by J. G. McManaway, G. E. Dawson, and E. E. Willowghby (Washington, D.C.: The Folger Shakespeare Library, 1948), p. 455.

4. For a review of the reception of Diogenes' ideas during the Enlightenment, see H. Niehues-Pröbsting, "Die Kynismus-Rezeption der Moderne: Diogenes in der Aufklärung," in *Le Cynisme ancien et ses prolongements. Actes du Colloque International du CNRS.* Edited by M.O. Goulet-Cazé and R. Goulet (Paris: Presses Universitaires de France, 1993), pp. 519-555.

5. V. Brochard, "Diogène le Cynique," in *La Grande Encyclopédie. Inventaire Raisonné des Sciences, des Lettres et des Artes* (Paris: Lamirault, n.d.), Vol. 14, p. 601.

6. R. Lipsey, "Diogenes, the Hound." *Parabola* 10 (1989), p. 52.

7. See Appendix, note 106. The concept of παρρησία is fundamental in the philosophy of Cynicism and has enormous relevance for the understanding of Diogenes' philosophical stance. According to Foucault, the practice of παρρησία is a requirement for any sort of philosophical enterprise that endeavors to be authentic. For comments on Foucault's assessment of Cynicism in general and of Diogenes in particular, see T. R. Flynn, "Foucault as Parrhesiast: His Last Course at the Collège de France (1984)," in *The Final Foucault.* Edited by J. Bernauer and D. Ramussen (Cambridge, Mass.: MIT Press, 1991), pp. 102-118.

8. B. Russell, *A History of Western Philosophy* (New York: Simon & Schuster, 1972), pp. 231ff.

9. T. Gomperz, *A History of Ancient Philosophy.* Translated by G. G. Berry (London: John Murray, 1964), Vol. 2, p. 150.

10. For a discussion of the conception of Diogenes as a *Lumpensammler*, that is, as a typical Parisian *chiffonnier* of the nineteenth century, see D. Rieger, *Diogenes als Lumpensammler. Materialen zu einer Gestalt der französischen Literatur des 19. Jahrhunderts* (Munich: Wilhelm Fink Verlag, 1982).

11. F. Sayre, *Diogenes of Sinope: A Study of Greek Cynicism* (Baltimore: J. H. Furst, 1938), p. 1.

12. Ibid., p. 6.

13. G. H. Lewes, *The Biographical History of Philosophy from its Origins in Greece to the Present Time* (New York: D. Appleton and Company, 1883), Vol. 1, p. 184.

14. I have followed the accepted practice of capitalizing the words 'cynic' and 'cynicism' when the ancient Greek and Roman Cynics or their ideas are mentioned. In their ordinary modern sense of 'cynical', 'cynic' and 'cynicism' are not capitalized.

15. P. Sloterdijk, *Kritik der zynischen Vernunft* (Frankfurt am Main: Suhrkamp Verlag, 1983), pp. 300-310.

16. D. Diderot, "Cynique," in *Encyclopédie ou Dictionnaire Raisonné des Sciences, des Artes et des Métiers* (Stuttgart: Frommann, 1966), Vol. 4, p. 599.

17. Quoted in D. Clay, "Picturing Diogenes," in *The Cynic Movement in Antiquity and Its Legacy*. Edited by R. Bracht Branham and M. O. Goulet-Cazé (Berkeley: University of California Press, 1996), p. 374.

18. F. Sayre, *Diogenes of Sinope*, p. 95.

19. Several important works on Diogenes' letters have been published in recent times. Among these, A. J. Malherbe's *The Cynic Epistles: A Study Edition* (Missoula, Mont.: Scholars Press, 1977) is of great value, as is also V. E. Emeljanow, *The Letters of Diogenes* (Ph.D. diss. Stanford University, 1968).

20. The best example of this exaggerated scholarly tendency is F. Sayre, for whom the process of legend formation concerning Diogenes continues even in modern times. See in this regard his *Diogenes of Sinope*, pp. 99-129.

21. A. A. Long, "The Socratic Tradition: Diogenes, Crates, and Hellenistic Ethics," in *The Cynic Movement in Antiquity and Its Legacy*. Edited by R. Bracht Branham and M. O. Goulet-Cazé (Berkeley: University of California Press, 1996), p. 29.

22. An annotated translation of this work is given in the Appendix of this book.

23. The evidence of this literary dedication is reviewed by R. Goulet, "Dioclès de Magnésie," in *Dictionnaire des Philosophes Antiques* (Paris: CNRS Éditions, 1994), Vol. 2, pp. 775-776.

24. F. Nietzsche, *Beitrage zur Quellenkunde und Kritik des Laertius Diogenes* (Basel, 1870).

25. Possibly the most enlightening analysis of Diogenes Laertius' biography of Diogenes is M. O. Goulet-Cazé's "Le livre VI de Diogène Laërce: Analyse de sa structure et réflexions méthodologiques," in *Aufstieg un Niedergang der römischen Welt* (Berlin-New York: W. de Gruyter, 1990), Vol. 2, pp. 3880-4048.

26. The primary meaning of κρεία is 'use' or 'advantage' (Latin, *usus*). In the context of philosophical traditions, such as that of the Cynics, κρεία can be understood in the sense of an anecdotal report about some famous person, recorded and transmitted for the purpose of communicating a philosophical message of ethical significance. As such, then,

a κρεία is a *useful* story that can be memorized and transmitted. An example of a κρεία can be found in the report about Diogenes' reaction to a child who drinks water from his hand: Diogenes throws away his cup, saying that a child has taught him a lesson in how to set aside the unnecessary encumberments of civilized life. For a discussion of the role of the κρεία as a vehicle for the transmission of ideas, see J. F. Kindstrand, "Diogenes Laertius and the *Chreia* Tradition." *Elenchos* 7 (1986), pp. 219-243.

27. Long, "The Socratic Tradition," p. 31.

28. L. Paquet has published an annotated collection of ancient testimonies (in a French translation) related to the Cynics, including Diogenes. See his *Les cyniques grecs: Fragments et témoignages* (Ottawa: Éditions de l'Université d'Ottawa, 1975). The Greek text (with a Latin translation) of fragments and testimonies concerning Diogenes is found in F.G.A. Mullach, *Fragmenta philosophorum græcorum* (Paris: Firmin-Didot, 1857-1865. Darmstadt: Scientia Verlag, 1968), Vol. 2, pp. 261-395.

29. For an English translation and a study of 194 sayings of Diogenes found in Arabic gnomologies, see D. Gutas, "Sayings by Diogenes Preserved in Arabic," in *Le Cynisme ancien. Actes du Colloque International du CNRS*. Edited by M. O. Goulet-Cazé and R. Goulet (Paris: Presses Universitaires de France, 1993), pp. 475-518. Gutas notes that only thirty-eight of those sayings are found also in Greek and Latin sources. For a critical examination of the value of Arabic sources related to Diogenes in the context of our knowledge derived from classical sources, see G. Strohmaier, "Diogenesanekdoten auf Papyrus und in arabischen Gnomologien." *Archiv für Paryrusforschung und verwandte Gebiete* 22-23 (1973-1974), pp. 285-288. Strohmaier concludes that the Arabic sources are sufficiently significant to warrant their being carefully and critically considered as genuine testimonies.

30. The theme of the encounter between Diogenes and Alexander has been abundantly exploited by a variety of authors, both in ancient and in modern times. Dio Chrysostom, writing in the first century A.D., left for us an account of the encounter, in which the major ideas of classical Cynicism are presented in opposition to what we might call the 'worldly' stance of Alexander. The testimonies and traditions related to this encounter are studied by M. Buora, "L'incontro tra Alessandro e Diogenes. Tradizione e significato." *Atti dell'Istituto Veneto di Scienze, Lettere ed Arti* 132 (1973-1974), pp. 247ff. There are also several dramatic reconstructions of the encounter, as exemplified by D. Pinski, *Aleksander un Dyogenes. Veltgeshikhlekhe Tragedye* (Vilne: B. Kletskin, 1930).

31. Long, "The Socratic Tradition," pp. 45.

32. Sarapis (or Serapis) was an Egyptian deity believed to have originated in Memphis. There are, however, reports that allege that the birthplace of the cult of Sarapis was Sinope and that it was from there that the Greeks brought it to Egypt (Tacit, *Hist.* IV, 81; Plutarch, *Mor.* 361f-362e). In Diogenes Laertius (VI, 63), we are told that when the Athenians invested Alexander with the title of 'Dionysus', Diogenes remarked, "They might as well call me 'Sarapis'." Among the Greeks and other ancient nations, Sarapis did not rank far below Dionysus in power and honor. For comments on the Alexander-Dionysus and Diogenes-Sarapis juxtaposition, see J. Servais, "Alexandre-Dionysos et Diogène-Sarapis. À propos de Diogène Laërce, VI, 63." *L'Antiquité Classique* 28 (1958), pp. 98-106.

33. C. W. Goetling is correct in affirming that "we know nothing concerning the life of Diogenes as a youth." See his "Diogenes der Cyniker oder die Philosophie des griechischen Proletariat." *Gesammelte Abhandlungen aus dem classischen Alterthume* (Halle, 1851), p. 251. As in the instance of Jesus, Diogenes becomes 'known' only when he enters the public scene. There is a reference in Arabic sources to Diogenes' mother (Mubassir, 65) that discloses something about her background: "Snubbed by a man of noble descent for the lowly origins of his mother, Diogenes replied, 'In my case, the line of nobility begins with me, whereas in yours it ends with you'."

34. Information about bankers can be gathered from various sources, including, for instance, from a work by Isocrates entitled *Trapeziticus*, where we learn about the activities of a certain banker named Pasion (d. 370 B.C.), who rose from the condition of a slave to become a very wealthy man.

35. C. T. Seltman, "Diogenes of Sinope, Son of the Banker Hikesias." In *Transactions of the International Numismatic Congress 1936* (London, 1938).

36. H. Bannert, "Numismatisches zur Biographie und Lehre des Hundes Diogenes." *Litteræ Numismaticæ Vindobonenses* 1 (1979), pp. 49-63. For comments on various numismatic findings that could shed light on Diogenes' role in the defacement of the currency, see J. Babelon, "Diogène le Cynique." *Revue Numismatique* 18 (1914), pp. 14-19.

37. Sayre (*Diogenes of Sinope*, p. 72) insists that Diogenes' father must have been in charge of the coinage of Sinope *only* after 362 B.C. and that the currency defacement must have occurred after that time. This may be supported by the numismatic research of T. Reinach, summarized in his "Sur le classement chronologique des monnaies de Sinope." *Revue des Études Grecques* 39 (1926), pp. xlv-xlvi.

38. D. R. Dudley, *A History of Cynicism From Diogenes to the 6th Century A.D.* (Cambridge, 1937. Chicago: Ares Publishers, 1980), pp. 21 and 54.

39. Sayre, *Diogenes of Sinope*, p. 72.

40. Ibid., p. 73.

41. See in this respect the suggestion made by Long, "The Socratic Tradition," p. 45.

42. The sacred stone at Delphi known as the Omphalos (ὀμφαλός, literally 'the navel') was believed to be the center of the world.

43. The Pythia was the priestess who, in a state of ecstatic trance, would answer questions. Her title was derived from the name of Python, the legendary dragon who guarded Delphi and who was killed by Apollo.

44. For a balanced and instructive examination of the role played by the Delphic oracle and other oracles among the Greeks, see R. Flacelière, *Devins et Oracles Grecs* (Paris: Presses Universitaires de France, 1961).

45. E. R. Dodds, *The Greeks and the Irrational* (Berkeley: University of California Press, 1951), p. 185.

46. Nitrous oxide (N_2O), otherwise known as dinitrogen monoxide or laughing gas, is one of the several oxides of nitrogen that, when inhaled, produces insensibility to pain, mild hysteria, and occasionally laughter. Known also as 'the metaphysical gas', nitrous oxide is said to have been found in volcanic cracks underneath the ruins of Apollo's temple at Delphi, which has led some to explain the phenomena of oracular divination at Delphi in terms of psychedelic intoxication. William James observes that nitrous oxide "stimulates the mystical consciousness in an extraordinary degree. Depth beyond depth of truth seems revealed to the inhaler." James, who experimented with this gas, notes that

> one conclusion was forced upon my mind at that time, and my impression of its truth have ever since remained unshaken. It is that our normal waking consciousness, rational consciousness as we call it, is but one special type of consciousness, whilst all about it, parted from it by the filmiest of screens, there lie potential forms of consciousness entirely different. We may go through life without suspecting their existence; but apply the requisite stimulus, and at a touch they are there, in all their completeness, definite types of mentality which probably somewhere have their field of application and adaptation. (*The Varieties of Religious Experience: A Study in Human Nature.* New York: The Modern Library, 1929, pp. 378-379)

47. J. B. Bury, for instance, argues in his *A History of Greece* (New York: The Modern Library, n.d.) that

> the Delphic priesthood were skillful enough in adjusting their policy to the changing course of events; but they cannot be suspected of brooding over the mysteries of things to come, or feeling the deeper pulsations of the thoughts of men. (pp. 564-565)

48. Thracis was a city that in mythological accounts was repeatedly associated with Hercules.

49. Abundant information concerning this work of Oenomaus is provided by Eusebius of Caesarea in his *Præparatio Evangelica* (V, xviii-xxxvi). For a critical examination of Oenomaus work, see J. Hammerstädt, Γοήτων φώρα. *Die Orakelkritik des Kyniker Oenomaus* (Frankfurt am Main: Athenaeum, 1988).

50. The scholarly interest in the oracular pronouncement involving Diogenes has been considerable. Two important articles on the subject are I. Bywater and J. G. Milne, "Παραχάραξις." *The Classical Review* 54 (1940), pp. 10-12, and G. B. Donzelli, "Del παραχάραττειν τὸ νόμισμα." *Siculorum Gymnasium* 11 (1958), pp. 96-107.

51. H. Diels, "Aus dem Leben des Kynikers Diogenes." *Archiv für Geschichte der Philosophie* 7 (1894), pp. 313-316.

52. See, for instance, Sayre, *Diogenes of Sinope*, pp. 73ff. R. Bracht Branham has summarized well a prevailing opinion about the historicity of the oracular pronouncement about Diogenes, when he writes that

> the story that Diogenes received an oracle at Delphi instructing him "to

deface the currency" (D.L. VI, 20-21) is a legendary encrustation on the historical kernel of Diogenes' exile. It is clearly modeled on the oracle Plato's Socrates claims in the *Apology* to have received at Delphi.... The idea of Diogenes consulting the oracle to discover his philosophical mission is of course absurd and clearly incompatible with his utterances on traditional religion. ("Diogenes' Rhetoric and the *Invention* of Cynicism," in *Le Cynisme ancien et ses prolongements. Actes du Colloque International du CNRS.* Paris: Presses Universitaires of France, 1993, p. 445)

For an extended discussion of the historical import of the stories involving Diogenes' affair with the currency and the oracle, see H. Niehues-Pröbsting, *Der Kynismus des Diogenes und der Begriff des Zynismus* (Munich: W. Fink, 1979), pp. 43-63, 77-81.

53. P. Gardner, "Diogenes and Delphi." *The Classical Review* 7 (1873), pp. 437-439.

54. Dudley, *A History of Cynicism*, p. 2. Dudley appears to have been overly anxious to dis-associate Antisthenes from the Cynic movement and to enthrone Diogenes as the original founder of this movement.

55. Sayre (*Diogenes of Sinope*, p. 74) places the arrival of Diogenes in Athens around the year 350 B.C., which, of course, renders his association with Antisthenes a myth, no less than his contacts with Plato.

56. The origins of the story about Diogenes' abduction by pirates can be traced to a non-extant work by Menippus of Gadara entitled *The Sale of Diogenes*. K. von Fritz has argued (*Quellenuntersuchungen zum Leben und Philosophie des Diogenes von Sinope*, pp.22-25) that it is reasonable to assume that the story was *invented* by Menippus.

57. The practice of employing slaves as teachers of children (παιδαγωγοί) was common among the ancient Greeks. In Athens and other major cities, a slave (δοῦλος) occupied the position of what we would call a 'servant'. With some exceptions, the brutal form of slavery found in many ancient Oriental cultures and in the New World appears to have been rare among the Greeks.

58. Sayre, *Diogenes of Sinope*, p. 75. Sayre's *Diogenes of Sinope: A Study of Greek Cynicism* is a valuable work for two reasons: it is the only English comprehensive work devoted mostly to a critical study of Diogenes (aside from the present book), and it provides abundant references to the sources. It must be said, however, that Sayre's book appears to have been written with a preconceived notion about classical Cynicism that the author felt compelled to demonstrate, namely, that the Cynics were ultimately worthless philosophers and that their contributions, whatever their historical genuineness, are either minimal or detrimental. For Sayre, Diogenes—the real founder of Cynicism—was a psychopathic character posing as a philosopher. According to Sayre,

> when an individual reaches a conviction that he is always right and that every one else is always wrong, it is regarded as a psychopathic symptom. Diogenes' disinclination to perform any active or useful labor, his lack of moral inhibitions and his indifference to the opinions

of others were also psychopathic symptoms and he appears to have been regarded as insane by many persons in his own time. (p. 97)

Sayre, a man who came rather late in his life to the study of Greek philosophy, made his career as a military man (West Point, U.S. Infantry and Cavalry School, Army War College, etc.). Later, he worked as a parole officer in Massachusetts, and took extension courses in penology, criminology, and criminal law at Harvard University. His book on Diogenes was accepted as a doctoral dissertation at Johns Hopkins University in 1938, when he was seventy-seven years old. Two additional books on Cynicism were published by him about the same time. It is obvious that his stance vis-à-vis Cynicism is thoroughly negative concerning the sources and the meaning of Cynicism. Obviously, his military training and his patriotic pride made it impossible for him to understand what Diogenes and the other Cynics had to say about the world.

59. See Appendix, note 15.

60. Diogenes' idea of cosmopolitanism will be examined in a subsequent chapter.

61. Sayre, *Diogenes of Sinope*, pp. 97-98.

62. A similar comment is attributed by Diogenes Laertius (I, 26) to Thales: "When his mother attempted to force him to marry, he said that it was too soon, and later in his life she tried again, he said that it was already too late."

63. For a discussion of Crates' marriage to Hipparchia, see L. E. Navia, *Classical Cynicism: A Critical Study* (Westport, Conn.: Greenwood Press, 1996, pp. 132ff.), and R. Eisler, "Crates the Cynic, First Advocate of Companionate Marriage." *Search* (October 1932), pp. 309-317.

64. Xanthippe's bad reputation does *not* come from the testimony of Plato, who mentions her only twice (*Phaedo* 60a and 116a) and from whose references nothing can be inferred about her character. In Xenophon's *Symposium* (ii, 10), a short dialogue between Antisthenes and Socrates presents her in an uncomplimentary light. Socrates says that he chose her as his wife, knowing fully well how difficult a person she was, because he knew that if he could cope with her, he would succeed in coping with any other person. In Diogenes Laertius, there are various passages in which her bad temper is depicted. Several attempts have been made to vindicate the much maligned Xanthippe. There is, for instance, F. Mauthner's novel *Mrs. Socrates* (New York: International Publishers, 1926).

65. Various studies have been devoted to the meaning and significance of the graffito at Herculaneum. Among these, three should be consulted: J. Moles, "The Woman and the River: Diogenes' Apophthegm from Herculaneum and Some Popular Misconceptions About Cynicism." *Apeiron* 17 (198), pp. 125-130; G. Giangrande, "Diogenes' Apophthegm from Herculaneum in the Light of Ancient *topoi*." *Museum Philologum Londiniense* 8 (1987), pp. 67-74; and G. Strohmaier, "Τὸ κακὸν ὑπὸ κακοῦ. Zu einem weiberfeindlichen Diogenesspruch aus Herculaneum." *Hermes* 95 (1967), pp. 253-255.

66. The following quotations from Arabic sources appear in D. Gutas, "Sayings by Diogenes Preserved in Arabic." See Note 29.

67. Aspasia, a native of Miletus, was one of the most remarkable women of classical times. As the companion of Pericles for many years, she exercised considerable influence in Athens. She is reported to have established a 'school' for young women, and, on the testimony of Plato (*Menexenus* 235a), it was she who instructed Socrates in the art of rhetoric. Her activities on behalf of women and her relationship with Pericles eventually led to her being accused and tried for impiety in 429 B.C. Although acquitted of this charge through the intervention of Pericles, she remained the subject of slander and ill-intentioned gossip until her death.

68. In Xenophon's *Symposium* (ii, 9), Socrates remarks that, in his view, women are inferior to men only in physical strength, for in intelligence and ability they are on the same level. "So," he adds, "if anyone among you has a wife, let him confidently set about teaching her whatever he would like her to know."

69. Moles has argued that the content of the Herculaneum graffito is fictitious. The statement ascribed to Diogenes, he maintains, "travesties the bizarreness of Cynic behavior to the point of absurdity" ("The Woman and the River," p. 126).

70. Sardanapalus was the last great king of Assyria (seventh century B.C.).

71. King Midas was a legendary figure in Greek mythology.

72. For comments on these three disciples of Diogenes, see Navia, *Classical Cynicism*, pp. 119-151.

73. Sayre, *Diogenes of Sinope*, p. 76.

74. It has been noted by various scholars that the Cynics' appreciation of physical work was more positive than what is found among other Greek philosophers. While there is some justification for accepting this view, especially in the context of some late Cynics, it remains unquestionable that Diogenes himself displayed no appreciation for any kind of remunerated work, physical or otherwise. Two articles that explore the ways in which the Cynics dealt with the value of work are A. C. Bayonas, "Travail manuel et esclavage d'après les Cyniques." *Rendiconti dell' Istituto Lombardo* 100 (1966), pp. 383-388, and H. Schulz-Falkenthal, "Zum Arbeitsethos der Kyniker." *Wissenschaftliche Zeitschrift der Martin Luther Universität* 29 (1980), pp. 91-101.

75. The iconography of Diogenes is among the most extensive in the classical world. For a discussion of some of the works of art that depict Diogenes, see W. Amelung, "Notes on Representations of Socrates and of Diogenes and Other Cynics." *The American Journal of Archaeology* 31 (1927), pp. 281-296. There are also valuable comments on Diogenes' iconography in R. Eisler, "Sur les portraits anciens de Cratès, de Diogène et d'autres philosophes cyniques." *Revue Archéologique* 33 (1931), pp. 1-13. For a discussion of the depiction of Diogenes in Raphael's "School of Athens," see D. O. Bell, "New Identifications in Raphael's School of Athens." *Art Forum* 77 (1995), pp. 4ff.

76. See Appendix, note 124.

77. For a review of various reports concerning Diogenes' death, see E. Livrea, "La morte di Diogene cinico." *Filologia e forme litterarie. Studi offerti a Francesco della Corte.* Edited by S. Boldrine et al. (Urbino: Università degli Studi di Urbino, 1987), Vol. 1, pp. 427-433.

78. See Appendix, note 119.

79. The Hyrcanians inhabited one of the provinces of the Persian empire. They were famous in antiquity for the peculiarity of some of their customs.

80. For a study of this and other epigrams and epitaphs related to Diogenes, see H. Häusle, *Sag mir, o Hund—Wo der Hund begraben liegt. Das Grabepigram für Diogenes von Sinope. Eine komparativ literarisch-epigraphische Studie zu Epigrammen auf theriophore Namenstrager* (Hildesheim: G. Olms, 1989).

Chapter 2

The Practice of Cynicism

Most of the details of Diogenes' life are given to us in the form of typical Cynic *chreia* (χρεία), which, as noted in the previous chapter, can be defined as stories or anecdotes that illustrate a character trait or a philosophical conviction associated with a Cynic philosopher.[1] It is especially in the biography of Diogenes Laertius that we come upon a multitude of such *chreia*, many of which are found in other sources, including sources almost as ancient as Diogenes himself. Their authentic biographical value is perhaps questionable in what concerns the details that they provide, but with respect to the general portrait of Diogenes that emerges from them, they are invaluable, because they allow us to appreciate the character of the man and his philosophical orientation.

There are, for instance, various anecdotes in which Diogenes Laertius introduces the theme of dogs and several references in which Diogenes is described as a dog or is referred to as a dog. We are told (VI, 33) that he described himself as a dog, the kind that everybody praises, but that everybody avoids, the implication being that, *from a distance and vicariously*, the style of life of a Cynic is admired and respected by many, but that few are those who have the courage and clarity of mind necessary to imitate or emulate it. He repeated this comment (VI, 55) when once they asked him what kind of a dog he was: "When hungry, a Maltese; when full, a Molossian—two breeds that most people praise, although for fear of fatigue they do not venture to go hunting with them. Thus, you cannot stand my company, because you are afraid of the discomforts."[2] Occasionally, too, we hear from Diogenes himself that he could well be compared to a dog because of his ability to act as a guardian whose duty was to keep people on the right track.

We also learn (VI, 40) that when Plato called him a dog, Diogenes agreed with him, adding that it was correct because of his habit of staying close to those who had betrayed him. Plato, as we will see later, was viewed by Diogenes as a philosopher who had betrayed the true spirit of philosophy and yet was someone whose company Diogenes sought, if only to 'bark' at him and remind him of his duplicity. Again (VI, 45), when, hurling insults at him, some boys called him a dog, he countered with this comment: "Don't be afraid, boys, dogs don't eat garbage." This is repeated (VI, 61) with some variations: once, when eating at the marketplace (an inappropriate thing to do among the Athenians), people gathered around him, pointing at him and shouting, "Dog! Dog!" "You are," he replied, "the stupid dogs, when you just gather around me to see me eat," and then added, "Don't panic, you fools, dogs don't eat garbage."[3] Here we come upon the clearest manifestation of one of Diogenes' most salient character traits, his enormous and unforgiving contempt for human beings, who, in his mind, were no better than garbage (τεύτλιον, literally, 'beetroot'). On still another occasion, according to Diogenes Laertius (VI, 46), when people began throwing bones at him at a feast, just as they would at a hungry dog, Diogenes did what dogs do whenever and wherever they feel the need—he urinated on them, as if wishing to underline his dog-like character and as if anxious to put into practice his conviction that natural needs must take precedence over conventions and artificial customs and norms.

In various Arabic gnomologies, too, we come across reports and anecdotes involving the designation of Diogenes as a dog. Muntahab Siwan al-hikma, for instance, tells us that when people asked Diogenes why he was called a dog, he replied that it was because of his habit of confronting rascals and bad characters with the truth about themselves, and being friendly toward good people and unfriendly toward the evil. This same source informs us that Diogenes was referred to as a dog because most people showed contempt for him and treated him as if he were in reality nothing but a dog. Mubassir, echoing a comment by Diogenes Laertius (VI, 60), states that when asked why he was known as a dog, Diogenes said that it was because of his custom of barking at ignorant people and showing respect toward the wise.

Diogenes' death, as we saw in the previous chapter, is said to have been caused by the bite of a dog, and on his grave in Corinth, a statue of a dog stood for several centuries. But possibly the most emphatic association of Diogenes with dogs is found in his own statement to Alexander: "I am Alexander the great king," says Alexander to him, to which Diogenes replies, "And I am Diogenes the Dog" (D.L. VI, 60). Diogenes' acceptance of this canine designation is also made manifest in an anecdote found in the *Gnomolium Vaticanum* (194):

> Once, when Polyxenus the dialectician became enraged on hearing that certain people referred to Diogenes as a dog, Diogenes said to him: "You, too, Polyxenus, can call me a dog. To me, 'Diogenes' is only a name that was given to me. In truth, I am really a dog, a dog of high breed, one of those that keep watch over their friends."[4]

The most ancient direct reference to Diogenes comes from Aristotle, who in *Rhetoric* 1411a24 tells us that "Diogenes the Cynic used to call taverns 'the mess-rooms of Attica'." The Greek text omits the name of Diogenes and merely says "ὁ κύων," that is, "the Dog," assuming, quite correctly, that the identification of Diogenes with "the Dog" could be taken for granted, because *that* was precisely how he was known even during Aristotle's time and probably before, for, as noted earlier, Plato himself, according to Diogenes Laertius (VI, 40), referred to him in the same way. After Aristotle and indeed for the rest of classical times, 'Diogenes' and 'the Dog' became interchangeable terms. Here, then, we discern the origins of the name by which Diogenes' ideas and style of life became known—Cynicism.

The modern words 'cynic', 'cynical', and 'cynicism' are derivations from the Greek κυνικός (*kynikos*), which is the adjectival form of the noun κύων ('dog').[5] To be κυνικός means literally to be like a dog, to behave like a dog, or to have characteristics that are reminiscent of those associated with dogs. Through a common linguistic practice, it is not unusual to invest human beings with animal traits, when their behavior or appearance remind us of what we are accustomed to see in animals. Boorish and uncontrolled demeanor can be a temptation to call someone a gorilla, and cunning and sly behavior can lead us to speak about someone as a fox. Certain kinds of politicians are known as weasels, precisely because they behave like weasels, and there are human types whom we call pigs, because their behavior is reminiscent of what we associate with pigs. Many other examples of this habit of calling human beings by animal names can be readily adduced. Diogenes himself called certain people donkeys, and is reported (D.L. VI, 41) to have spoken of Perdiccas of Macedonia as a tarantula, surely because of the brutal and unscrupulous ways of this Macedonian king,[6] and to have referred to gossipy and cunning women as snakes.

In anthropological language, this habit is known as theriomorphism, because metaphorically we see in a person the shape or form (μορφή) of an animal or beast (θηρίον). This is the reverse of anthropomorphism, a process in which we invest non-human things or creatures with human qualities and attributes. Through anthropomorphic transformations, then, we make in our imagination animals speak and behave like people, as happens in traditional children's tales and in cartoons. Through theriomorphism we conceive of human beings as doing what animals do or as resembling animals.[7] In both processes we transfer qualities from one set of living beings to another, and both have ancient roots that extend to primitive times. In theriomorphism, with significant exceptions, the result is to lower the status of a person or a group of persons to the level of animals, a level that is often conceived of as inferior to that of human beings. Calling someone a gorilla, a pig, a fox, a tarantula, or a dog, is generally a way of insulting that person. The exceptions occur when animal behavior and characteristics are believed to be superior to those of human beings, a belief known as theriophily. There are instances when calling someone a lion or an eagle may suggest a form of praise related to the person's courage, vision or some other characteristic.

As we consider the circumstances in which Diogenes became known as a dog, we encounter both theriomorphism and theriophily, the former on the part of those who were reminded by him of a dog, and the latter on Diogenes' own part. For him, despising as he did the customs and behavior of his contemporaries, animals were undoubtedly preferable to human beings. He could have said what Schopenhauer once said: the life of one dog may be worth more than the lives of many human beings. We have a report from Diogenes Laertius (VI, 22), who, on the testimony of Theophrastus, tells us that after observing a mouse running around in the marketplace, unconcerned about luxuries and unafraid of dark places, Diogenes learned one of the fundamental lessons of Cynicism, namely, to dispense with superfluous things and to adapt himself to all sorts of situations. A variation of the story comes to us from Plutarch (*Moralia* 77e-78a; cf. Aelian, *Hist. Var.* XIII, xxvi): the behavior of the mouse eating the crumbs that fall from a piece of pastry that Diogenes is eating makes him feel embarrassed. Reflecting on how the mouse manages to survive with so little, Diogenes says to himself:

> How can this be? Here is a little mouse who enjoys the crumbs that fall from your hands and nourishes himself with them. You, on the other hand, despite your clear mind, complain and suffer for not being able to get drunk and eat fancy food, lying somewhere on a comfortable and embroidered rug.

Mice, he realizes, do not need a *special* place to live and sleep, and eat whatever they happen to find on their path. If mice could speak they could say what, according to an Arabic source, Diogenes once said when asked if he had a house: his house was wherever he could lie down to rest. Neither social distinctions nor elaborate philosophical systems have any significance in their lives. They are not encumbered by artificial and atavistic conventions, nor are they concerned about the past or the future, living always in the present moment and for the present moment. Thus, Diogenes thought, mice live in a *natural* way and are, therefore, happier and more genuine than human beings, for which reason they deserve to be imitated and emulated. Accordingly, mice and other animals should be our models of life and behavior, for they are invariably *better and more authentic* than the embarrassing specimens of humanity that we find everywhere, who have chosen to distance themselves as much as possible from the world of nature, and who have succeeded in constructing for themselves a world in which neither rest nor happiness can be found. Dogs, too, especially street dogs, live in accordance with nature. Independence, simplicity, the ability to adapt themselves to changing circumstances, an absence of inhibition with respect to their feelings and their physical needs, indifference concerning where and how they live and what they eat, absolute honesty, freedom of 'speech'—for they bark whenever they please and at whomever they dislike—these are some among the virtues or strengths that characterize the canine army, and these are precisely the traits that Diogenes and his Cynic descendants admired and found worthy of imitation. Why, then, should he have taken offense when the Athenian rabble, unable to understand his mode of life, chose to call him a dog? His theriophily, that is, his love and respect for animals, converted the insults of the crowd into expressions of praise. Great embarrassment he would have surely felt if they had called him a man, and, worse still, if anyone would had referred to him as a regular or normal person, or a loyal and law-abiding citizen.

From the point of view of the others, however, he was in no way a regular or normal person, and probably not even a man, for wherever he was and whatever he did, he stood invariably as a creature vastly different from those who in astonishment surrounded him. As a modern scholar has described Diogenes, "because he is willing to flout the rules that everyone else must observe, the Cynic is a freak, a monster, like every violator of taboos."[8] His appearance and mode of speech, and his behavior and style of living, particularly his shamelessness (ἀναίδεια), were the sort of thing that then and now would generally elicit expressions of surprise and shock, no less than condemnation and vituperation. Who could have reacted differently on hearing someone suggest that Oedipus could have solved *his* problem by simply legalizing incest in Thebes, as Dio Chrysostom reports that Diogenes suggested (*Or.* X, 30)? If birds, dogs, and asses, no less than the Persians, appear to have no objections against incest, why should the Greeks be different? Who could have not been shocked in the presence of someone who ate raw meat and who reportedly *wrote* in favor of cannibalism? Diogenes' very presence called for an insulting and disapproving reaction, which explains why they called him a dog.

In a scholium to an Aristotelian passage in *Rhetoric* 1411a24, we find an instructive explanation of the theriomorphic process responsible for the name by which Diogenes and his followers became universally known:

> There are four reasons why the Cynics are so named. First because of the indifference of their way of life, for they make a cult of indifference and, like dogs, eat and make love in public, go barefoot, and sleep in tubs and at crossroads. The second reason is that the dog is a shameless animal, and they make a cult of shamelessness, not as being beneath modesty, but as superior to it. The third reason is that the dog is a good guard, and they guard the tenets of their philosophy. The fourth reason is that the dog is a discriminating animal which can distinguish between its friends and enemies. So they recognize as friends those who are suited to philosophy, and receive them kindly, while those unfitted they drive away, like dogs, by barking at them.[9]

In Arabic gnomologies, we find various statements that endeavor to explain the origins of the designation of the Cynics as dogs. Paramount among such explanations is the idea that it was their style of life, especially that of Diogenes, that earned for them their canine appellation. Their scorn for social norms and conventions, the legendary shamelessness with which they challenged the accepted rules of behavior of their contemporaries, their attachment for what the gnomologies view as their sect, their unwillingness to enter into close relationships with strangers or with ordinary people—all these and similar behavioral traits account for the name by which they were universally identified.

A review of the many anecdotes that recount why and how Diogenes was called a dog by his contemporaries shows that their intention was to insult him and call attention to what was in their eyes the grossness of his behavior and the reprehensible character of his conduct. At least on several instances (as in D.L. VI, 61), it is clear that by returning the designation by which he was called, Diogenes sought also to return the insult. It might not be justifiable to agree with A. Monterroso, who interpreted the designation of dog hurled at Diogenes as the greatest insult ("the lowest and most despicable that one can imagine"),[10] but it is certainly correct to assume that, as Dudley insists, "the name was undoubtedly first applied to Diogenes in a hostile sense, owing to his ἀναίδεια [shamelessness], or habit of 'doing everything in public'."[11] That he did 'everything in public', is clear from the testimonies of Diogenes Laertius, Dio Chrysostom and Athenaeus, although in some of the other sources (e.g., Epictetus), nothing is said about *this* aspect of his life. Saint Augustine (*De civitate Dei* XIV, xx) left for us a statement concerning the excesses of shamelessness of which, in his view, Diogenes was guilty, and which, as a manifestation of original sin, tainted his Cynicism:

> Those Canine or Cynic philosophers overlooked the virtue of modesty, when, in violation of the modest instincts of all human beings, they boastfully proclaimed their unclean and shameless opinion, worthy indeed of dogs, that is, that since the matrimonial act is legitimate, no one should be ashamed to perform it openly in the street or in any public place. Instinctive shame, however, has prevailed over this wild fancy. For though it is related that Diogenes once dared to put his opinion in practice, under the impression that his sect would be all the more famous if his egregious shamelessness were deeply impressed in the memory of mankind, yet his example was not followed. Shame had a greater influence on them to make them blush before people than error to make them affect a resemblance to dogs. And possibly even in the case of Diogenes, and those who imitated him, there was only an appearance and pretense of copulation, and not its reality.

Diogenes' reported shamelessness—public sexual behavior—was so extraordinary that Saint Augustine charitably opts for believing that he and his followers only gave the appearance of doing what they were said to have done!

Still, even if only a modicum of truth belongs to the accounts of Diogenes' practice of 'doing everything in public', the theriomorphic image of Diogenes as a dog-like man must have been clear in the eyes of his contemporaries. Allowing for the expected dosage of exaggeration, some truth is probably found in reports that say that he would take care of his physical needs wherever he chanced to be, and even that performing certain acts done only in private was not foreign to him. "It was his custom to do everything in public, even the works of Demeter and those of Aphrodite," tells us the biographer (D.L. VI, 69).[12]

Diogenes' shamelessness knew no bounds, recognized no exceptions, and accepted no prohibitions, just as if he were an untrained street dog, because such a dog does whatever nature calls him to do, indifferent to the restrictions created by human customs and conventions. Indeed, could there have been for him a more visual and graphic way of demonstrating his desire to deface the 'currency' of his contemporaries than by *acting out* his defiance of society in public, in the marketplace, and wherever he was in the public light? No wonder, then, that, as Dio Chrysostom reports, the crowd—composed of individuals who did the same things as Diogenes, but in privacy and secrecy—concluded that he must have been mad. "The act of defecation," as Bracht Branham perceptively notes, "is meant to remind the audience of this fact—the anomalous status of the Cynic—his privileged perspective on a society he is in and not of, whose *doxa* he need no take seriously."[13] There should be, therefore, nothing surprising in the reaction of disgust with which Diogenes' contemporaries responded to his behavior. Cicero, writing several centuries later (*De officis* I, 41), would echo this reaction, when he wrote about Diogenes and his philosophical descendants: "*Cynicorum natio tota ejicienda est; est enim inimica verecundiæ, sine qua nihil rectum esse potest, nihil honestum*" (The whole sect of the Cynics should be rejected, for it represents the enemy of shamefulness, without which there can be nothing either right or honest).

It seems, moreover, that Diogenes welcomed the appellation by which he was called, the Dog, because it captured an important component of his philosophical stance, namely, his defiant shamelessness and his concerted efforts to invalidate or adulterate the conventions and rules that society places upon human beings. What better way could there be to fulfill his mission as the great defacer of human 'currency' than to behave like a dog and to be so recognized by others? Why not eat wherever he felt hungry? Why not urinate whenever his bladder was full? Why not satisfy his sexual longings whenever his physical frame demanded it? Why cater to the desires of others and abide by *their* artificial regulations? If they insisted on calling him a dog, they were correct, for he was a dog (κύων) and behaved like a dog (κυνικός), and if he had been forced to give a name to his style of life and philosophy, he would not have hesitated to call it 'Cynicism', a word widely used in later times, as can be learned from Julian (*Or.* VI). If Diogenes could have seen the statue of a dog placed by the Corinthians over his grave, he would not have been displeased. The Cynics must have congratulated themselves on being compared to dogs on account of the rudeness and grossness of their style of life and their self-imposed marginal place in society.[14]

The designation of Diogenes as a dog (κύων) and the description of him as a Cynic (κυνικός), however, may have a different, yet related origin. In chapter 1, we argued that the date of Diogenes' arrival in Athens could be pushed back as early as the third decade of the fourth century B.C., that is, at a time when Antisthenes was still alive. As will be seen in chapter 3, the direct biographical relationship between Antisthenes and Diogenes has been the subject of much controversy and debate among scholars, some of whom, such as Dudley and Sayre, have argued that the 'succession' Antisthenes-Diogenes is ultimately a convenient fabrication, created for the purpose of linking Diogenes with Socrates, who was indeed Antisthenes' philosophical mentor.[15] Other scholars lend credence to the testimony of those sources that establish without ambiguity a direct relationship between Antisthenes and Diogenes. In Diogenes Laertius, we read that "on reaching Athens, [Diogenes] came under the influence of Antisthenes" (VI, 21), and this is confirmed by Aelian (*Hist. Var.* X, xvi).[16] The issue is itself not altogether inconsequential, because it sheds light on the question concerning the origins of Cynicism and on the philosophical basis on which this movement was established. Still, even if doubts linger about Diogenes' date of his arrival in Athens and about his direct relationship with Antisthenes, the fact remains, as was recognized by Hegel,[17] that we can discern a common ground of ideas and style of life between them.

Two interesting details about Antisthenes should be kept in mind. Diogenes Laertius tells us (VI, 13) that he was in the habit of teaching in an Athenian gymnasium known as the Cynosarges, and that he would call himself 'the absolute Dog' (Ἁπλοκύων). The association of Antisthenes with the Cynosarges is confirmed by Suidas, and although the appellation of 'the Absolute [or true] Dog' is found only in Diogenes Laertius, there are numerous passages in other sources that speak of him as a dog (κύων) and as a Cynic (κυνικός). Cicero (*De orat.* III, 17), Athenaeus (V, 216b), Clement (*Strom.* I, xiv, 63), and Stobaeus (II, xxxi, 34), to mention only a few, describe him as a dog and link him with the origins of Cynicism. Diogenes Laertius, for his part, states that it was his dog-like style of life that gave its name to the school of the Cynics. There were other philosophers, contemporaries of Antisthenes, who have been also called Cynics— one thinks of Zoïlus of Amphipolis, of whom Aelian (*Hist. Var.* XI, x) speaks as "a rhetorical and satirical Cynic," and of Simon the Shoemaker, the friend of Socrates.[18] However, it is traditionally Antisthenes who has been recognized as the first Cynic, that is, the original Dog.

The Cynosarges was a gymnasium and a park situated outside the

Athenian walls, on the eastern side, near the gate Diomea.[19] Its existence is traceable to early Greek times, for Herodotus (V, 63) mentions the tomb of a certain Anchimolius (sixth century B.C.) located near the temple of Hercules in the Cynosarges. Although its temples were destroyed by Philip V of Macedonia in 200 B.C., it managed to survive until at least the time of Pausanias (second century A.D.). Its name is etymologically curious: Pausanias (I, xix) informs us that it meant 'the white or true dog' (ἡ κύων ἡ λευκή), and that "the story of the white dog may be learned by those who have read the oracle." Unfortunately, we have no information about the oracle in question and can only guess as to what its meaning could have been. The word κύων (*cyon→cynos*) stands for 'dog', while the word ἀργός (*argos*) could mean 'white', 'bright', or 'glistening'. Curiously, however, the epitaph πόδας ἀργοί was used to describe swift-footed dogs, because their rapid movements created the impression of a flickering light emanating from them. In *Odyssey* XVII, 292, we find Ulysses calling his dog 'Argos', the same name of the builder of the ship, also named *Argos*, that would take the Argonauts in their search for the Golden Fleece.

Somehow, then, the Cynosarges—the park of the White or Swift Dog—is the place where Antisthenes is said to have taught, just as Plato taught in the Academy, Aristotle in the Lyceum, Epicurus in the Garden, and Zeno of Citium in the Stoa. The Cynosarges is known to have been the site of various temples, the principal among which was dedicated to Hercules, whom, as we will see later, the Cynics regarded as a paradigm of virtue and as their model. We also know that the Cynosarges was mostly frequented by non-citizens and foreigners, specifically, by a certain class of Athenians known as νόθοι (*nothoi*), that is, persons of illegitimate birth or bastards, as we learn from Demosthenes (*Contra Aristocrates* 691). Antisthenes himself, the son of an Athenian citizen and a Thracian slave (D.L. VI, 1), was a bastard in the context of Athenian law. His association with the Cynosarges has been interpreted as a pious fabrication created by ancient biographers and doxographers in an effort to give Cynicism, like other schools of philosophy, a place of origin. Billot speaks of this report as "too beautiful to be credible," although she is willing to concede that there is nothing that renders it improbable.[20] The existence of the Cynosarges, its cult of Hercules, its population of marginal people who would congregate in its groves and use its gymnasium, and the presence of Antisthenes in Athens during the first decades of the fourth century B.C.—these are facts that are unreasonable to dismiss as fictional. Moreover, as we will see in chapter 3, Antisthenes' own austere and ascetic mode of life, his rebelliousness and spirit of revolt, his illegitimate birth, and his alleged habit of calling himself 'the absolute Dog'—these, too, are aspects of his life that are not contradicted by the sources. His gravitation toward the Cynosarges, especially after the execution of Socrates in 399 B.C., is not an unjustified assumption to entertain. Furthermore, we know that other philosophers taught in the Cynosarges, as was the case with Ariston of Chios (c. 250 B.C.), a Stoic philosopher anhbad a direct disciple of Zeno, the founder of Stoicism, and a man of marked Cynic tendencies. Thus, we can say that the Cynics became known as 'dogs' or 'dog-like people', both because of Diogenes' style of life *and* probably because of Antisthenes' association with the Cynosarges and his self-designation as 'the absolute Dog'.

Turning now our attention to Diogenes, our task is to reconstruct, on the basis of the sources, the specific style of life that earned for him the title of 'the Dog' and that sealed, as it were, the name by which the 'school' of philosophy that emerged from him and probably from Antisthenes became known. As one reviews the history of classical Cynicism, however, what we encounter is *not* a school of philosophy in the strict sense of the term. We are more justified in speaking of Platonism, Aristotelianism, and Stoicism as schools of philosophy, because in those cases we come upon a set of convictions and ideas passed with canonical strictness from one generation to another for at least one century. The heads of those schools, the scholarchs, inherited certain philosophical tenets taught to aspiring disciples, who, in their turn, would assure their continuation. Naturally, after some time, even the most firmly held principles of the founders became mingled with other ideas and were dissipated into an atmosphere of eclecticism. Plato's school, established on the basis of intellectual optimism and epistemological absolutism, was headed, only one hundred years after Plato's death in 347 B.C., by Carneades of Cyrene, a philosopher whose skeptical stance made him significantly removed from Plato's frame of mind and from what is traditionally associated with Platonism. Therefore, even in the case of Plato's school—and the same can be said of Aristotelianism and Stoicism—the idea of a dogmatic transmission of ideas is not appropriate, for the very spirit of philosophy would preclude the continuation of dogmas inflexibly accepted, as occurs in the transmission of religious beliefs.

With respect to Cynicism, however, we find ourselves in a more extreme situation, because Diogenes' philosophical ideas, while firmly held and adhered to, lacked the necessary level of development and content that would have allowed them to be integrated into a system, something that Diogenes himself would not have wished for his philosophical stance. Despite the vigor and vibrancy of those ideas, it is easy to detect in them a truncated growth that renders them, albeit valuable and challenging, generally negative and inconclusive in their import. Moreover, and probably because of this circumstance, the way in which Diogenes and in fact many among the other Cynics gave expression to their convictions and principles was highly idiosyncratic, so that, aside from certain common denominators, the styles of life of the many Cynics of ancient times, as well as the ways in which they confined their ideas into writing, were quite varied: we could find them living in a tub, as with Diogenes, or living comfortably in the court of a king, as with Onesicritus of Astypalaea and Bion of Borysthenes; removed from the political world, as with Monimus of Syracuse, or leading an army and framing the constitution of a city, as with Cercidas of Megalopolis; or altogether intransigent in their endeavors to denounce and undermine their social world, or making accommodations with the status quo. Their writings assumed all sorts of forms, and thus we find dialogues, epistles, poetical compositions, dramatic pieces, aphoristic statements, parodies, diatribes,[21] and collections of maxims. Their 'doggishness' rose to the surface in a great variety of ways, sometimes in a harsh manner, biting and snarling like Diogenes, or gently barking and maintaining their contemporaries on the right moral track, like Crates of Thebes, or in gentle and sweet poems, as with Meleager of Gadara.[22] Nevertheless, regardless of the differences among the various Cynic styles of life, the fact is that it was Diogenes who remained, during the more than eight hundred years that classical Cynicism lasted, the paradigm of a Cynic, as if he had been the example that every Cynic felt compelled to imitate. Several hundred years after Diogenes, Epictetus and Julian insisted that Cynicism, that is, genuine Cynicism, was what Diogenes exemplified, all other Cynics being only imperfect replicas of the man from Sinope, who emerges in the sources and in modern literature as the proto-Bohemian, to use Sloterdijk's phrase,[23] perhaps not in the sense of having been the first Cynic, for Antisthenes may have a claim to that honor, but in the sense of having been the most authentic *practitioner* of Cynicism.

The word *practitioner* is well chosen, for Cynicism, especially in the context of Diogenes, is, as has been recognized by many historians and scholars, a practice or a way of life more than a set of ideas. Diogenes Laertius tells us (VI, 11) that according to Antisthenes, the attainment of virtue (ἀρετή) is not a matter of thought or learning, but is something that can be achieved only through deeds and practice, which is precisely what we find in Diogenes. Faithful to the teachings of Diogenes, Crates would insist (*Epist.* XXI) that the path to happiness, which is the goal of philosophy, is found, not in discourse and thought, but in the constant *practice* of virtuous deeds and actions.

Undoubtedly, such a practice must be grounded in certain ideas and convictions, for otherwise it would constitute a senseless concatenation of meaningless acts. But it is the practice of such acts, that is, the actualization of ideas, that gives structure and meaning to Cynicism, especially in the instance of Diogenes. There is in Cynicism, as will be shown in a later chapter, an impatience (not to say animosity) toward theoretical constructs and universal concepts that moves the Cynic inexorably toward the realm of the concrete and the practical. This tendency, seen by some as a sort of anti-intellectualism,[24] is responsible for Diogenes' need to exemplify his ideas by means of *concrete acts* and *actions*. We are told by Diogenes Laertius (VI, 48) that Hegesias, a Cyrenaic philosopher,[25] once asked Diogenes to lend him one of his writings, to which Diogenes replied, in language that is reminiscent of a passage of Plato's *Phaedrus*,[26] "You are a fool, Hegesias, because you choose painted figs to real figs, and pass over true training and opt for written rules." The painted figs represent the speculative and theoretical concepts —the written rules—that are learned in books and lectures, but with *these*, Diogenes had little to do, for his orientation was decidedly toward the world of the concrete and the practical. Once, when Plato was discoursing on the reality of ideal Forms and spoke about the ideal Table and the ideal Cup, Diogenes is reported (D.L. VI, 53) to have said that he never saw such things but only a certain table and a certain cup in the physical world. Plato observed that *his* problem was obviously that his intellect was limited and that he was, therefore, unable to understand and appreciate concepts and pure ideas, having eyes only for visible and tangible things. From this point on, Diogenes spoke about Plato's lectures and mode of philosophizing as a waste of time, because, as we are told by Themistius (Stobaeus III, xiii, 68), only those teachings of philosophers that can awaken people into action and that, like sweet-sour unguents, can irritate human wounds, are worth anything. The rest is empty talk and useless games played by philosophers and intellectuals, whose major preoccupation is to hide their spiritual emptiness. For his part, Diogenes had eyes and ears, and very good ones indeed, only for the concrete and for what could be empirically shown.

Again, once, according to Diogenes Laertius (VI, 40), when Plato defined man as 'a featherless biped', the Cynic plucked a chicken and, showing it to Plato's audience, said, "Behold Plato's man."[27] A concrete featherless chicken was, therefore, *all* that Plato would have needed to define the human species. Words, definitions, and discourses had little significance for Diogenes, for which reason he expressed contempt for all sorts of learning. Music, geometry, and astronomy, the three ancient categories of learning under which most of what we would call today a liberal education could be subsumed, he regarded as useless, if not outright detrimental, as we learn from Diogenes Laertius (VI, 73). The worthiest among human beings, said Diogenes according to Stobaeus (III, lxxxvi, 19), are those who despise learning and prefer a state of ignorance (ἀμαθία), ignorance understood not in the sense of not knowing anything, but in the sense of dispensing with unnecessary learning and acquiring only the knowledge that is sufficient for a good and simple life, which is precisely what he understood to be the meaning and purpose of philosophy.

In an Arabic gnomology, we learn from Sahrastani (Diogenes 3), how Diogenes drew a sharp line between ordinary people and himself. When asked by a group of ignorant people what was the main source of his nourishment, Diogenes replied that it was precisely whatever *they* found repulsive and worthy of rejection, meaning philosophy, and when they inquired what it was that *he* found repulsive and worthy of rejection, he answered that it was what *they* deemed good and desirable. Hunayn (Diogenes 4), for his part, tells us that Diogenes compared the lack of education and learning in a person with a house built without foundations, for without the development of the mind, no human accomplishment is lasting.

Thus, it is not that Diogenes waged war against learning and education, for he understood well that these are the foundations on which a happy and good life can be established, but only if they are oriented in the right direction, and this direction he specified with clarity. Not in the cobwebs and labyrinths of words constructed by philosophers and poets, and neither in the senseless training that goes nowadays by the name of career education and that prepares the youth to enter blindly and obediently the slave marketplace, but in those forms of learning that help people live a simple and natural life—there, Diogenes insisted, true education can be found. Like the Socrates of Xenophon's *Memorabilia*, who said that the only purpose of learning mathematics was allowing us to count change at the marketplace, Diogenes saw no value in education except for the *practical* benefits that it can provide for the right conduct of life. Learning in which language is used as the primary tool and in which words are multiplied *ad infinitum* either to express a simple truth, or to give the appearance of conveying a profound meaning, was, in his view, something to be avoided at all costs. Diogenes Laertius (VI, 26) provides us with an anecdote in which this point is well made:

> Once Diogenes asked Plato for wine and dried figs, upon which Plato sent him a whole jar of wine. "If someone asks you how many two and two make, will you answer," asked Diogenes, "twenty? So it seems that you neither give what you are asked nor answer as you are questioned." Thus he scoffed at him as one who talks without end.[28]

For the right conduct of life, then, the less we speak and the less we write may take us to the desired goal, and Plato and other philosophers were far from this goal, among other reasons because of their habit of being entrenched and entrenching others in idle talk. One cannot but wonder how Diogenes would have reacted if, transported to the late twentieth century, he could have observed how people are consumed by the senseless need to acquire unimaginable amounts of information. Where has the information superhighway taken them?[29]

For this reason, Diogenes said that he had learned the art of living by observing animals, for nature had provided them with all the knowledge that is necessary to live well. Without language and unable to read or write, they are well adapted to their natural world. After observing the behavior of a mouse in the marketplace, says Diogenes Laertius (VI, 22), Diogenes understood how superfluous are most of the things that we learn and seek. Dio Chrysostom (*Or*. IV, 31ff.) notes that he sought to emulate the life of the gods, a simple and peaceful life, and that he insisted that it was the animals that exemplify best how to emulate that life. Why, then, should we complicate ourselves with unnecessary and bothersome learning, with abstruse language, and with speculative ideas and theories, all of which render our lives less natural and increase the already heavy burden of existence under which most people live?

Practice, then, not theory, was the dimension in which Diogenes sought to function, and only those practical concerns that affect human life were paramount in his mind. If the writings ascribed to him were indeed his, we suspect that it was the advantages of that dimension that were extolled in them. He insisted that the most meaningful way to learn and appreciate his philosophical message was not by studying his works, as Hegesias pretended to do, but by observing his behavior, just as he had observed the behavior of a mouse. This circumstance explains why practically all the ancient accounts of Diogenes' philosophy take the path of anecdotal reports and are filled with *chreia* (χρεῖα), in which he is depicted *in action*, saying something specific about a given situation, and undertaking a concrete kind of behavior, because he was convinced of the primacy of practice over theory, and of the concrete over the universal. The roots of this conviction, as we will see in the following chapter, are traceable to Antisthenes, who, like Diogenes, was not preoccupied with anything that transcends the domain of the physical world and was impatient in regard to any kind of discourse that pretends to describe a different world. In the history of the Cynic movement after Diogenes, we encounter repeatedly the same tendency to set aside, as impediments for the attainment of a good and happy life, all concerns that distract the mind from the reality of the here and the now.

This orientation inherent in Diogenes' philosophical stance is responsible for his having been accused of anti-intellectualism, primitivism, and gross materialism, which is partly justified if such terms are understood in a limited sense. His anti-intellectualism can be taken for granted, but only in the context of his campaign against *certain* types of intellectual constructions such as we find exemplified in philosophical and ideological systems, and in the context of his opposition to those intellectual activities that, from his point of view, fill the mind with unnecessary and distracting thoughts and speculations. Likewise, it is clear that a bent toward primitivism is discernible in his sayings and actions. A man who regards animal behavior as a paradigm worthy of imitation, who dispenses with cups and utensils, who eats raw meat, and who, more generally, dismisses as useless the creations and inventions that most people associate with civilized life—such a man, what else can he be but primitive?

His materialism, on the other hand, is more problematic. We can assume that he was not a materialist in the strict philosophical sense of the word, that is, a person who denies, perhaps as Democritus did, the existence of anything that transcends the physical or material world. For Democritus, reality was inexorably limited to the existence of physical atoms, anything else being either unreal or merely the creation of human imagination, which is itself nothing but the result of the movement of certain kinds of atoms inside the human body. *This* sort of philosophical materialism cannot be attributed to Diogenes, for there are no testimonies that support that attribution. On the contrary, there are reports that indicate that, his denunciation of religion notwithstanding, he was not averse to entertaining the possibility of the existence of other dimensions of reality aside from the tangible domain of the physical world. Certain occasional comments of his reveal, albeit indistinctly and in veiled language, a conception of God that transcended the ordinary polytheistic and anthropomorphic religious ideas of his contemporaries, as when, according to Sahrastani (Diogenes 1), he is reported to have said that God is not the source of the evils that permeate human existence, but is the source of all that is good. Furthermore, both in Cynic and Stoic traditions, we come upon the belief that the ideal philosopher must see himself as a messenger, emissary, and scout (σκοπός) of God among his fellow human beings, as we learn from Epictetus (*Discourses* III, xxii, 70). Regardless of the historical value of the story of the Delphic pronouncement about Diogenes, which, as we said in the previous chapter, commanded him to alter and deface human beliefs and conventions, the least we can say is that it sought to ascribe to Diogenes a spiritual or divine mission. His emphatic denunciation of the religious beliefs and practices of his contemporaries does not preclude the profound sense of spirituality that probably animated his peculiar mode of life and his rebellious activities. After all, as Dag Hammarskjöld observed, "the lovers of God have no religion but God alone."[30] Thus, we should hesitate to refer to Diogenes either as a gross materialist, for a true materialist cannot entertain even the possibility of the existence of a nonphysical God, or as an avowed atheist like Theodorus of Cyrene, who, among all the philosophers of classical times, was probably the most atheistic.[31]

Neither can we refer to Diogenes as a materialist in the ordinary sense of the word, that is, someone who values and amasses material things, cherishes and caters to his body, and finds his fulfillment only in the comforts and amenities furnished by the material world. Quite to the contrary, what we find in Diogenes is an abysmal contempt for such things and a conviction that materialism in this sense is the source that feeds the habitual confusion and dissatisfaction in which most people live. With respect to others, we find him sparing no words to condemn their materialistic inclinations and habits, referring to money, possessions, and comforts as the roots of their evil characters. In their world, as well as in ours, and in relation to material things and comforts, *more* is always viewed as better than *less*. But with Diogenes, we find an altogether different frame of mind: *less* is better than *more*. Thus, we encounter him *seeking* poverty and vicissitudes, *welcoming* insults and destitution, cheerfully *embracing* every circumstance that, in his view, could strengthen his moral character, following the footsteps of Hercules, who is said to have augmented his spiritual and physical powers by means of a concerted effort to confront and conquer painful labor—the legendary labors that made him so famous. The labors of Diogenes were certainly not as great as those of Hercules, for he never fought against the Nemean lion or against the many other monsters that brought affliction to humanity. Still, there were labors in his life, and when they were scarce, he would invent them, as when we find him, according to Diogenes Laertius (VI, 23, 34), rolling over hot sand in his tub in the heat of summer, or, during the winter, embracing statues covered with snow, or walking barefoot on snow. His reported admiration for the Spartans was due to their ascetic, simple, and rugged way of life that was vastly removed from the materialism found elsewhere. Diogenes' asceticism (ἄσκησις) and poverty (πενία) worked with him as a sure antidote against vulgar materialism.

In what sense, then, could Diogenes have been a materialist? The answer to this question lies in part in two interrelated aspects of his thought and activities that can be associated with him without hesitation: first, his insistence that all intellectual pursuits that displace the existence of a person as a physical entity to an inconsequential plane of importance are misguided and detrimental, and, second, his commitment to convey his Cynic message in a visual and tangible way. The first of these two aspects is responsible for his polemical stance vis-à-vis speculative philosophy as exemplified, for instance, in Plato's metaphysics and in the contentions of Eleatic philosophers who rejected the reality of motion.[32] We hear in this regard that once, when people were arguing about whether or not motion is real, Diogenes *got up* and *walked away*, as we learn from Diogenes Laertius (VI, 39) and from Sextus Empiricus, who tells us that when a philosopher was defending the thesis that motion is impossible, Diogenes "without uttering a single word, simply got up and began to walk about, showing thereby that motion does in fact exist" (*Hyp. Pyrrh.* III, 66). What practical purpose could there be, he must have thought, in arguing about whether or not things move, if it is not difficult to see and experience their motion? In arguing about the reality of motion, do we not have to move at least our lips and tongues? The phrase of Sextus Empiricus, "without uttering a single word," is important, because it sheds light on the uselessness of language to explain and account for things and circumstances that can be plainly experienced through the senses. Likewise, in a passage quoted earlier, Diogenes attaches far more importance to *this-table-here-now* and to *this-cup-here-now* than to the Platonic ideal Table and ideal Cup, showing thereby his conviction that the material plane of existence is and must remain, not only our point of departure, but our only port of destination in all intellectual pursuits.

Thus, Diogenes' one-sided preoccupation with the physical world in general and with the human body in particular can be interpreted as a form of materialism. We must bear in mind, however, that this preoccupation was rooted in his conviction that the human spirit functions only through the medium of the body and in the context of the material world. When, as happens in the case of materialists who define the worth of human existence in terms of possessions and pleasures, the material world drowns the spirit and engulfs the mind in a cloud of confusion that is responsible for the unhappiness and madness that Diogenes recognized everywhere among his contemporaries, then and only then are we justified in speaking of gross materialism. And, when, as happens with those who are intent on setting aside the physical aspects of human existence and despise anything that is, from their point of view, tainted with materiality, as perhaps in the instance of Plato, then the spirit and the mind become emaciated and distorted, floating in an atmosphere of chimerical expectations and illusions that render human life senseless. Furthermore, the masses, vulgar and gross as they generally are, ignore such pretensions and regard as inconsequential all and every attempt on the part of philosophers and intellectuals to downgrade the value of the physical world. Philosophy itself, then, forsakes every opportunity to have a significant impact on the lives of ordinary people, which is what seems to have occurred in modern times. People and human communities go on living and doing what they have always done as if philosophers had never existed, and opt for a stance of indifferentism toward the cobwebs that speculative philosophers spin out of what they regard as their disembodied minds, as Kant noted.[33]

Diogenes, for his part, despite his contempt for his contemporaries or, rather, for their style of life, appears to have been moved by a missionary spirit that compelled him to communicate his Cynic message to the masses in a way that could have been understood by them.[34] Hence, he chose to address them in their own language, the language of the body, with all the coarseness and vulgarity that insure that the masses would understand and pay attention to him. Here is, then, the root of various outward manifestations of Diogenes' Cynicism and the source of what a modern scholar has aptly called the *rhetoric* of Cynicism.[35]

This rhetoric emerges clearly in the context of the medium through which Diogenes practiced his Cynicism. He presents himself to the world as a performer and as an exhibitionist, and every idea and belief of his takes on the garb of a *physical* gesture or is expressed by him in apophthegms in which the language denotes unmistakably *physical* functions. For this reason, all the sources are filled with anecdotes in which we find him either using his body, especially his hands, or speaking about physical things. We witness him in a series of "performance pieces"[36] that abound with grossness and display a tremendous sense of humor.[37] In every instance, he must instantiate his Cynicism by means of concrete physical gestures and acts. Thus, he insists on eating in the marketplace and in the temples, drinks out of his hand and eats scraps of food from the floor, urinates in the presence of baffled witnesses, does certain other things—"even the works of Demeter and those of Aphrodite," to use the euphemistic phrase of Diogenes Laertius (VI, 69)[38]—that people do only in private, walks backwards through the streets, enters theaters only when people are leaving, embraces statues covered with snow, rolls on sand when the days are hot and walks barefoot in the winter, wears boxing gloves to protect himself from a bully, points to people whom he dislikes with his middle finger, sleeps in a tub or in the porticos of the temples, accepts disciples only if they are willing to carry a large fish or a piece of cheese in public, whistles amid the crowd in order to express his displeasure toward a dull speaker, plucks a chicken to demonstrate the senselessness of Plato's ideas, soils his feet in mud before entering Plato's house, endlessly calls attention to people's physical characteristics—their fatness, their thinness, their height, their baldness, their beauty, their ugliness, their deformities—and to their physical posture, for instance, whether they are lying down or kneeling, carries a wooden stick—his royal scepter —and does not hesitate to use it to strike those who gape at him, folds his ragged cloak to expose his nakedness, and so on and on. The man is undoubtedly a walking riot, a clownish character, a *performer* of the highest caliber, who knows well how to mingle with his sarcasm and diatribal tone an extraordinary amount of humor and joking, mixing a liberal dosage of vulgarity and grossness in his innumerable antics with a great deal of unrelenting moralizing. His outrageous and caustic remarks and acts still make us laugh, as much as they probably did his amused and disbelieving contemporaries, but we would be mistaken, were we to conclude that such behavior was meant only to amuse or to call attention to himself.

An anecdote recounted by Dio Chrysostom (*Or.* VIII) brings to the clearest light all the ingredients that characterized Diogenes' performance and practice of Cynicism.[39] It was his custom, we are told, to attend the Isthmian games,[40] where, as he said to someone who asked him why he went to the games, he saw himself competing side by side with the athletes, but in competitions far more demanding than theirs. For, whereas *they* wrestled and fought among themselves, *he* struggled with dreadful monsters such as gluttony, lust, greed, drunkenness, pride, and other similar foes that threaten humanity. At the games, he would observe as a spy of God the senseless desires and ambitions that moved the crowds of spectators, and would offer his free services as a physician of the mind, who could cure them of their spiritual ailments. Few, however, he noticed, ever came to him for assistance and preferred to be left in peace with their voluminous bellies, their empty heads, and their frolicking celebrations. There, then, amid a huge crowd of spectators, while the Sophists made a display of their pretended wisdom, and while jugglers and clowns entertained the multitude forever thirsty for diversions, Diogenes mounted upon the stage, so to speak, and, addressing the crowd, delivered a long and fervent speech on the need to struggle against the ingrained human need for pleasure and comfort that consumes people, and on the importance of training the spirit in the discipline of conquering unnatural desires and impulses. With a genuine air of seriousness and earnestness, Diogenes evoked the memory of the great Hercules, who struggled against so many monsters in the form of beasts and evil people, and in the form of human vices such as sensuality, ambition, and pride. Even a seducing and enticing Amazon, Diogenes reminded the crowd, Hercules was able to conquer by showing to her that her beauty was not as deserving of his love as his own spiritual possessions. The crowd, observes Dio

Chrysostom, was enjoying enormously Diogenes' eloquent and impassioned speech, especially when he recounted how Hercules, desiring to demonstrate that his victories were not only against frightening monsters, once decided to prove his prowess by cleaning the stables of King Augias that were overflowing with the excrement of several thousand oxen and that had not been cleaned for at least thirty years. At last, with his body covered with dung, the victorious Hercules emerged from the stables as a conquering hero. Now comes the real punch: Diogenes looked intently at the enraptured multitude, whose ears, as could be expected, were well attuned to any talk that involved dung, brought his speech to an abrupt end, lifted his cloak, squatted on the floor, and proceeded to do, according to Dio Chrysostom, "something vulgar." What exactly Diogenes did, can be left to our imagination. Dio Chrysostom merely says "something vulgar or disgraceful" (ἄδοξον).

As Bracht Branham observes, "this might seem a distinctly odd way to conclude a moral homily, but it makes perfect sense in the context of Cynic rhetoric."[41] It does, indeed, because it appears to be a fitting way to bring to a close a moral discourse delivered to the kind of crowd we would expect to find at athletic competitions. Diogenes' squatting on the floor and doing whatever he did was, of course, a vulgar joke, the only kind of joke understood by the masses, and ultimately a joke *about* the masses, who follow blindly all sorts of pointless rules of etiquette and decorum, while neglecting the task of improving themselves and the necessity of living a life 'according to nature' (κατὰ φύσιν ζῆν).[42]

In reality, then, Diogenes' joke was part of a carefully conceived and well-carried out plan that can be understood as part of his commitment to deface and invalidate the values by which people live. Thus, beneath all the joking, and the apparent silliness and vulgarity of his behavior, there lived in him a tremendous intellectual seriousness and an unparalleled moral earnestness that *could have* unsettled the very political and social foundations of his world, but that, in fact, only succeeded in arousing in certain people, his very few disciples and his Cynic descendants, the same spirit of rebelliousness and defiance that animated him, but only for a short time and with diminished intensity. For revolutions, whether political, intellectual, or spiritual, have a peculiar characteristic that accompanies *all* of them—they fail in the end, for soon after the great revolutionary dies, his followers dilute his message and begin either to make embarrassing accommodations with the status quo or to subject the original message to atrocious deformations. For its part, the public tends to remember only the outward manifestations of the message but misunderstands or, more often, ignores its substance. We can remember, for instance, Saint Francis of Assisi as a poor and humble monk on whom birds would come to rest and from whose hands all sorts of animals were fed, but we have neither the understanding nor the courage necessary to maintain his spiritual revolt alive. Again, we are told that Jesus once said, "It is easier for a camel to go through the eye of a needle than for a rich man to enter the kingdom of God" (*Matt.* 19:24). But how could the wealth of the Church be justified, and how could the affluence and opulence of its prelates be made acceptable, except by either ignoring altogether Jesus' disturbing admonition or by distorting it by insisting, for instance, that he extolled 'the poor in spirit' (*Matt.* 5:3; cf. *Luke* 6:20[43]), not simply the poor, and that he condemned, not actual wealth, but some invisible and immaterial kind of wealth? His message, too, had to be adulterated in order to make convenient accommodations with the world, and thus his spiritual revolt was successfully neutralized by his own followers.

The case of Diogenes is not altogether different. His visible gestures remain in the public's consciousness and his reported words continue to be quoted, but their underlying essence soon dissipates itself in the normal and socially compliant atmosphere of people's lives, and we find peace of mind believing either that he was deranged or that he did not mean what he did and said. Surely, Diogenes' squatting on the floor and relieving himself of his intestinal load must have been greeted with much laughter and derision, as Dio Chrysostom notes, and, we can assume, that cries of "Mad!" and "Dog!" must have resounded everywhere, but soon after the act, again as Dio Chrysostom observes, the crowd went back to its usual frolicking activities, while the Sophists resumed their accustomed loud concatenations of platitudes. The distraction passed and the diversion was over, and now it was time to look for some other novelty. For many centuries, it must have been well remembered that the Dog-philosopher once soiled the floor with his own excrement while attending the Isthmian games, but the meaning of his gesture was altogether lost.

However, as a modern scholar asks, "what are the Cynic gestures that have been transmitted to us through legends but parables expressed in action?"[44] This interpretation of Diogenes' practice of Cynicism is correct, for *every* one of his gestures and statements, his mode of dressing, his diet, his living in a tub, his verbal and behavioral responses to what he heard and saw, his shocking antics—all these were parabolic expressions of his philosophical stance. His philosophy, then, became embodied in a series of exhibitionist "performance pieces"—the Cynic *chreia* of which we spoke earlier—that may appear at first enigmatic and irrational, but that ultimately were carefully staged and well performed, because they proceeded, not from the mind of a deranged man, but from the very lucid mind of someone who had a specific message to convey. Seen from the outside and from a superficial point of view, Diogenes was a madman, a fool, but once his purpose is understood, we realize that, his shortcomings notwithstanding, it was those whom he endeavored to shock and awake that were the crazy ones and the fools. When, as we saw in the previous chapter, someone once called him a madman, Diogenes replied, "I am not mad; it is only that my head is different from yours" (Stobaeus, III, iii, 51), by which he meant that his frame of mind and that of most of his contemporaries were separated by an enormous chasm. *Theirs*, not his, was a mind filled with confusion and perversion, befogged by what the Cynics would call τῦφος (*typhos*)—smoke and darkness.[45] Once, according to Aelian (*Hist. Var.* IX, xxxiv), when Diogenes was at Olympia, he noticed a crowd of young athletes from Rhodes wearing fancy robes. "Here," Diogenes said, "I see nothing but smoke." Soon after, he saw a group of Spartan athletes wearing rugged and soiled clothes, upon which Diogenes remarked, "Here again, I only see smoke."

And that is what Diogenes discovered everywhere, smoke in politics, where deception and greed reign supreme, whether in democracies or in tyrannies, and where the only concern of politicians and those who determine the fate of nations is to take advantage of the masses; smoke in religion, where, under the clever manipulation of clerical hierarchies, superstition and obscurantism are distilled systematically and abundantly upon the multitudes of mindless believers and followers who need such things as urgently as the addict needs his drug; smoke in social affairs, where inveterate and atavistic customs and traditions are perpetuated and kept alive under the pressure of the intellectual vacuity and spiritual inertia of ordinary people; smoke in personal and sexual relationships, where opportunism and the craving after pleasure are the hidden forces that guide human behavior; smoke in the world of education, where the ultimate goal in the training of the youth is to prepare them to function as obedient and efficient slaves in the work force; smoke in the world of ideas, where philosophers and ideologues mask their own deceptions in webs of complex concatenations of words and phrases that are altogether unrelated to the real world; smoke, then, just about everywhere, as if it were a vast and engulfing cloud that surrounds the artificial human world created by what goes by the name of civilization. Its permeating existence is assured by what Diogenes perceived as the lack of mind that characterizes practically all aspects and domains of human affairs, from those in which the unthinking masses are led like donkeys into wars,[46] to those in which family relationships are tainted by abuse and neglect. Most people, Diogenes maintained, are mad or nearly mad (D.L. VI, 35), and anybody endowed even with a speck of lucidity can ascertain this to be a fact, whether in the Greek world of Diogenes or in any other human context.

What, then, was the Cynic to do? What were his options in so uninviting a world? He might have opted for killing himself, as some Cynics and Stoics did, as if wishing to seal irretrievably their rupture with the world. Diogenes, however, chose to remain on the stage of human life until an advanced age. He might have taken the path, as is told of Bion of Borysthenes, of "adapting himself to the circumstances, as sails to the wind,"[47] and, could have set aside his Cynicism, joining the world and being an inauthentic participant in the human madness, but, as can be judged from his treatment of men in power, adaptation and accommodation were not part of his program. He might have literally bracketed the world away and retired into solitude, perhaps living as an anchorite in the desert or in a secluded Cynic community, as is reported of the Cynics of Gadara,[48] but he chose to remain in the middle of things, there, as Socrates says in the *Phaedrus* (230d), "in the cities, where men live." He could have also anticipated the behavior of the disciples of Pyrrho of Elis, who lived among people but in absolute silence. In the instance of Diogenes, however, these options were not chosen, and he opted for remaining in the world for the express purpose of challenging its customs and practices, its laws and conventions, by his words and, more so, by his actions. *Practicing* his extreme brand of Cynicism, then, he stood as a veritable refutation of the world and, as the Gospel would say of Saint John the Baptist, as "a voice crying in the wilderness" (*Matt.* 3:3). Unlike those with whom he shared his life and space, he had lucidity, clarity of mind, ἀτυφία (*atyphia*),[49] and, above all, a tremendous store of will that allowed him to practice what he believed in all circumstances and at all times.

Undoubtedly, the bridge that assured for Diogenes the passage between the realm of ideas and the domain of practice was his will to live in accordance with his philosophical stance. This has been recognized by various scholars, who have not failed to emphasize that Cynicism in general and Diogenes' philosophy in particular can be best understood and appreciated as a wilful commitment to live to the fullest extent and to put into practice a set of convictions.[50] What must now be explored is the process by which those convictions became ingrained in Diogenes' mind. How, then, can we account for his having become a Cynic? What circumstances could have led an exile from Sinope to transform himself into a dog? How can we explain the making of a Cynic?

Notes

1. See Chapter 1, note 26.

2. See Appendix, note 84.

3. See Appendix, note 56.

4. No specific information is available about Polyxenus. In Diogenes Laertius (II, 76), he is described conversing with Aristippus.

5. For a discussion of the origins of the word 'cynic', see J. Fellsches, "Zynismus," in *Europäische Enzyklopädie zu Philosophie und Wissenschaft*. Edited by H. J. Sandkühler (Hamburg: Felix Meiner Verlag, 1990), Vol. 4, pp. 1008-1010; and A. Lalande, "Cynisme," in *Vocabulaire technique et critique de la philosophie* (Paris: Presses Universitaires de France, 1972), pp. 200-201.

6. See Appendix, note 54.

7. Theriomorphism and theriophily have been the subject of numerous historical and anthropological studies. Two studies that have special significance for the understanding of classical Cynicism are J. E. Gill, "Theriophily in Antiquity: A Supplementary Account." *The Journal of the History of Ideas* 30 (1969), pp. 401-412; and A. O. Lovejoy and G. Boas, *Primitivism and Related Ideas in Antiquity* (New York: Octagon Books, 1965).

8. R. Bracht Branham, "Diogenes' Rhetoric and the *Invention* of Cynicism," in *Le Cynisme ancien et ses prolongements. Actes du Colloque International du CNRS* (Paris: Presses Universitaires de France, 1993), p.471.

9. Quoted in D. R. Dudley, *A History of Cynicism from Diogenes to the 6th Century A.D.* (Chicago: Aries Press, 1980), p. 5.

10. A. Monterroso, "Diógenes también," in *Cuentos* (Madrid: Alianza Editorial, 1986), pp. 39-50.

11. Dudley, *A History of Cynicism*, p. 5.

12. See Appendix, note 107.

13. Bracht Branham, "Diogenes' Rhetoric and the *Invention* of Cynicism, p. 471.

14. L. Paquet, *Les cyniques grecs: Fragments et témoignages* (Ottawa: Éditions de l'Université d'Ottawa, 1975), p. 41.

15. Ibid., p. 2. Sayre argues that Cynicism can only be traced back to Diogenes, and that Antisthenes should be considered above all a Socratic philosopher. See his "Antisthenes the Socratic." *The Classical Journal* 43 (1948), pp. 237-244.

16. Other confirming testimonies include Saint Jerome (*Adv. Jovin.* II, xiv, 345) and Eusebius (*Præp. evang.* XV, xiii, 7).

17. G.W.F. Hegel, *Lectures on the History of Philosophy*. Translated by E. S. Haldane (London: Routledge and Kegan Paul, 1963), Vol. 1, p. 438.

18. Comments on Zoïlus and Simon will be made in chapter 3.

19. For an account concerning the Cynosarges, see M. F. Billot, "Antisthène et le Cynosarges dans l'Athènes des Ve et IVe siècles," in *Le Cynisme ancien et ses prolongements. Actes du Colloque International du CNRS.* (Paris: Presses Universitaires de France, 1993), pp. 69-116; and "Le Cynosarges: Histoire, mythes et archéologie," in *Dictionnaire des Philosophes Antiques* (Paris: CNRS Éditions, 1994), pp. 917-966.

20. Billot, "Le Cynosarges: Histoire, mythes et archéologie," p. 919.

21. Diatribe (διατριβή) is generally defined as abusive criticism or denunciation. The Cynics, beginning with Diogenes and perhaps even with Antisthenes, made of this form of expression one of their chosen ways to convey their message. The diatribes of Bion of Borysthenes (the *Bionei sermones* imitated by Roman writers, including Horace) are probably the best example of this literary genre. For a discussion of Bion's Cynicism, see L. E. Navia, *Classical Cynicism: A Critical Study* (Westport, Conn.: Greenwood Press, 1996), pp. 151-155.

22. For comments on the poetry of Meleager, see Navia, *Classical Cynicism*, pp. 167-169.

23. P. Sloterdijk, *Kritik des zynischen Vernunft* (Frankfurt: Suhrkamp, 1983), Vol. 1, p. 300.

24. Diogenes' alleged anti-intellectualism is discussed at length in J. M. Meilland, "L'anti-intellectualisme de Diogène le Cynique." *Revue de Théologie et Philosophie* 3 (1983), pp. 233-246. Meilland argues that Diogenes' stance should not be interpreted as a rejection of *all* intellectual achievements and aspirations, but as a dismissal of *certain* aspects of the realm of ideas. Specifically, he contends that Diogenes' seemingly anti-intellectual stance stems from his commitment to make philosophy useful and helpful to as many people as possible, and to rescue it from the possession of 'technicians' of philosophy, who in Diogenes' time, no less than in ours, dominated the world of ideas.

25. See Appendix, note 63.

26. In the *Phaedrus* (275d-e), Socrates says to Phaedrus:

> You know, Phaedrus, that's the strange thing about writing, which makes it analogous to painting. The painter's products stand before us as though they were alive, but if you question them, they maintain a most majestic silence. It is the same with written words; they seem to talk to you as though they were intelligent, but if you ask them anything about what they say, from a desire to be instructed, they go on telling you the same thing forever.

27. Plato's definition of man, found among the definitions attributed to him (415a), is more complex: "Man is a biped animal deprived of wings and with flat nails, and the only animal capable of rational understanding." Needless to say, Diogenes would have found *this* definition even more ludicrous.

28. See Appendix, note 23.

29. Pyrrho of Elis (c. 360 B.C.-272 B.C.), the father of Skepticism, had much in common with Diogenes. Some of his followers opted for giving up language altogether and confined themselves to simple hand signs to convey their thoughts and needs. What else could have they done if their master insisted on the necessity of suspending judgment about everything? For a discussion of the relationship between the skepticism of Pyrrho and the ideas of the early Cynics, see A. Brancacci, "La filosofia de Pirrone e le sue relazioni con il cinismo," in *Lo scetticismo antico. Atti del Convegno organizzato dal Centro di Studi del Pensiero antico del CNR.* Edited by G. Giannantoni (Rome: Bibliopolis, 1981), pp. 213-242.

30. D. Hammarskjöld, *Markings*. Translated by Leif Sjöberg and W. H. Auden (New York: Alfred A. Knopf, 1971), p. 103. Hammarskjöld is quoting a line from Maulana Jajal-uddin Rumi, the most famous Sufic poet (thirteenth century).

31. Theodorus of Cyrene, a contemporary of Socrates and a teacher of Plato, was known for his radical and uncompromising atheism, for which he became known as 'the Atheist" (ὁ Ἄθεος). As M. Winiarczyk has shown, some of the sayings ascribed to Diogenes, especially those related to God and the gods, appear to have originated in reports about Theodorus. See his "Theodorus ὁ Ἄθεος und Diogenes von Sinope." *Eos* 69 (1981), pp. 37-42.

32. The term 'Eleatic' refers to Parmenides of Elea (c. 450 B.C.) and Zeno of Elea (c. 450 B.C.), as well as to the advocates of their doctrines. The Eleatics mounted a campaign to downgrade the value of sense experience as a source of knowledge, arguing that what the senses reveal is only an illusory dimension of reality. They denied the possibility of motion and change, and conceived of Being as a unitary, unchanging, and immaterial reality.

33. In the preface to the first edition of the *Critique of Pure Reason* (A x-xi), Kant complains that "the prevailing mood" toward philosophy in general and metaphysics in particular "is that of weariness and complete *indifferentism*—the mother, in all sciences, of chaos and night." He notes, however, that indifferentism toward philosophy may some-times be "the effect not of levity but of the matured judgement of the age, which refuses to be any longer put off with illusory knowledge" (*Immanuel Kant's Critique of Pure Reason.* Translated by N. K. Smith. London: Macmillan & Co., 1961, pp. 8-9).

34. The missionary spirit that characterized some of the Cynics is one of the most significant features of classical Cynicism. It discloses clearly the gap that separates the ancient Cynics from modern cynics, for whereas the former saw themselves as missionaries whose vocation was to compel people to improve their characters and cleanse their lives of moral pollution, the latter, who live themselves immersed in that pollution, remain indifferent with respect to the condition of their contemporaries. The example of Crates of Thebes illustrates well the missionary spirit of classical Cynicism. This disciple of Diogenes, renowned for his gentleness and kindness, is said to have spent his life literally going from place to place, from house to house, from person to person, seeking to make himself useful as a source of consolation and peacefulness, 'curing' all those who crossed his path of their intellectual and emotional ailments. It is said that as a token of their appreciation for his efforts to help them in their tribulations and sufferings, it was the custom among many Athenians to place a tablet on the door of their houses with the inscription "Crates is welcomed here."

35. R. Bracht Branham, "Diogenes' Rhetoric and the *Invention* of Cynicism."

36. T. McEvilley, "Diogenes of Sinope (c. 410-c. 320 B.C.): Selected Performance Pieces." *Art Forum* 21 (March 1983), pp. 58-59. McEvilley compares Diogenes to those artists who sometimes put *themselves* on exhibition and create out of their own lives an entire performance for the expression of their ideas and sentiments.

37. Diogenes' sense of humor is an element of his style that is discernible in countless anecdotes and apophthegms associated with him, but that has been seldom appreciated by scholars. Sayre, for instance, has no clue concerning Diogenes' humor, for which reason Bracht Branham is correct is referring to him as "the humorless Sayre" ("Diogenes' Rhetoric and the *Invention* of Cynicism," p. 472). If one cannot laugh upon reading the accounts of Diogenes or at least is able to appreciate the humor contained in them, one is constitutionally incapacitated to appreciate his philosophical stance. Braham's appreciation of Diogenes' humor as an integral component of his rhetoric is an important contribution to a balanced understanding of Cynicism.

38. See Appendix, note 107.

39. The biographical and historical reliability of Dio Chrysostom's writings about Diogenes cannot be taken for granted. Writing four hundred years after Diogenes, Dio Chrysostom's aim in reconstructing the portrait of Diogenes was not to leave an accurate account, but to create a rhetorical and convincing image for sophisticated readers in imperial Rome. As we read the four extant orations on Diogenes of Dio Chrysostom, we suspect that we are reading more about their author than about the Cynic of Sinope. Still, there is no point in dismissing as fictional either the general portrayal of Diogenes or *all* the details of his life and ideas as these are presented by Dio Chrysostom. Unquestionably, both the portrayal of Diogenes and many of the anecdotes must have been based on reliable sources available to Dio Chrysostom, but not to us. Whether or not Diogenes did something vulgar or disgraceful at the Isthmian games is inconsequential. We can rest assured, however, that what Dio Chrysostom says that he did, is the sort of thing that Diogenes was probably prone to do and probably did on repeated occasions. For a discussion of the value of Dio Chrysostom's writings on Diogenes, see F. Jouan, "Le Diogène de Dion Chrysostome," in *Le Cynisme ancien et ses prolongements. Actes du Colloque International du CNRS.* (Paris: Presses Universitaires de France, 1993), pp. 381-397. Jouan avoids what he calls *"le scabreux problème"* of the relationship between the historical Diogenes and the Diogenes of Dio Chrysostom, a problem that, he argues, is more complex than the issue of the relationship between historical Socrates and the Socrates created by Plato and Xenophon. For further comments on Dio Chrysostom's testimony about Diogenes, see M. Szarmach, "Les discourses diogéniques de Dion de Pruse." *Eos* 65 (65), pp. 77-90, and G. Giannantoni, "Tradizioni cinici e problemi di datazione nelle orazioni diogeniane di Dione Crisostomo." *Elenchos* 1 (1980), pp. 92-100.

40. The Isthmian games took place in the spring of every other year in the vicinity of Corinth. Large crowds of Athenians are known to have attended these games, in which the amusements were more numerous and more festive than in the other games.

41. Bracht Branham, "Diogenes' Rhetoric and the *Invention* of Cynicism," p. 470.

42. The phrase 'a life lived according to nature' will be discussed in chapter 4.

43. While in Matthew's account of the Sermon on the Mount (5:3), Jesus speaks of "the poor in spirit" (πτωχοὶ τῷ πνεύματι), in Luke's account (6:20), he speaks simply of "the poor" (πτωχοί), that is, the physically destitute and the materially deprived. It does not require much imagination to understand why the former of these versions is more welcomed by the hierarchy of the Church. It is clear that in denouncing wealth, Diogenes and the later Cynics were denouncing *material* wealth, and that in preaching and practicing poverty, they were expressing their attachment to *material* poverty. One can venture to say that Diogenes would have been baffled by the idea that the 'poor in spirit' are the ones who deserve God's blessings and by the corresponding belief that it is possible to live in extravagance and opulence and still be somehow 'poor in spirit'.

44. H. Ner, *Les Paraboles Cyniques* (Paris: Éditions Athéna, 1922), p. viii.

45. The concept of τῦφος is fundamental in classical Cynicism. It will be discussed at length in chapter 5.

46. Crates would refer to generals as donkey drivers (D.L. VI, 92). It is interesting to observe that the Cynics were probably the first people to have assumed a systematic and intransigent position against war. With very few exceptions, the Cynics refused to take part in military activities.

47. For comments on Bion's 'accommodations', see Navia, *Classical Cynicism*, pp. 151ff. At least during part of his life Bion is reported to have been willing to live under the patronage of certain wealthy potentates, exemplifying the type of person whom Diogenes would often refer to as 'parasites'.

48. Gadara (possibly modern Umm Qays) was an ancient Palestinian town on the southeastern shore of the Sea of Galilee (present-day Jordan), where a Cynic community is said to have existed from the third century B.C. until late classical times. For comments on the geographical identification of Gadara, see Navia, *Classical Cynicism*, pp. 166ff.

49. The concept of ἀτυφία will be discussed in a chapter 5. It conveys the idea of clarity of mind or lucidity and represents what the Cynics regarded as the ultimate aim of philosophy.

50. See in this regard A. Comte-Sponville, *Valeur et verité. Études cyniques* (Paris: Presses Universitaires de France, 1994). The author speaks of Diogenes' Cynicism as a philosophy "*occupé seulement à vouloir*" (engaged only with the will), and devotes considerable attention to the elucidation of what he calls "*la volonté cynique*" (the Cynic will). Comte-Sponville recognizes the will as *the* fundamental moving force in the philosophy of Diogenes. Accordingly, he interprets Cynicism, not as an intellectual stance in which we view and understand the world in a certain way, but as a wilful reaction to the world and an impulse to reject certain aspects of the world.

Chapter 3

The Making of a Cynic

If there is anything that can be affirmed about Diogenes of Sinope, it is that his presence is a baffling phenomenon in the history of philosophy that admits of no simple explanation. In him, we come upon an obviously intelligent and learned man, living in the midst of the most refined and sophisticated culture of ancient times, enjoying the greatest social ease and the benefits of the most open and welcoming of any among the nations of classical times, and rubbing elbows with the most superb intellects of the Western world, and yet, a man waging a relentless and merciless war precisely against that world, almost as if his only purpose in life was to undermine its very foundations and reduce its accomplishments to naught, leaving nothing intact, nothing erect. Mubassir (Diogenes 51) tells us that once, when asked why he did not wage this war *also* against himself, his answer was, "If I did, what could possibly remain standing?" Thus, outside of himself, his wish was literally to undertake the demolition of the world with regard to its laws, customs, traditions, and moral norms, because he, too, like Schopenhauer, must have reached at one point or another the dreadful conclusion that "the world on all sides is bankrupt, and that life is a business that does not cover the costs."[1] Had Diogenes been able to read Schopenhauer's pessimistic assessment of the world, he would not have been in disagreement with it, as when Schopenhauer insisted that even if the evil of the world were a hundred times less than it is, its very existence would suffice to convince any person of clear mind that its non-existence would be infinitely preferable to its existence, for it is undoubtedly "something that at bottom ought not to be."[2] Accordingly, those who find the world something worthy of praise, or who congratulate themselves for having been born into the world, are either intellectually blind or morally perverse.

As will be shown in the following chapter, Diogenes' pessimism about the world and the pessimism of Schopenhauer stem, however, from vastly different philosophical roots and disclose two fundamentally different ideological orientations, although, in their outward manifestations, they were equally intense and caustic.[3] Schopenhauer was convinced that "human life must be some kind of a mistake"[4] and, even more, that existence itself had sprung from a source of unfathomable evil, the Will, for which reason it must be rejected and transcended by an escape into absolute nothingness, an escape that he viewed as practically an impossibility.[5] No such dark thoughts, however, can be associated with Diogenes or, in fact, with any of his Cynic descendants. Unlike the great German pessimist, the Cynics still retained an element of the refreshing optimism that one encounters everywhere among the Greek philosophers, and that led many of them to conclude that, regardless of the moral bankruptcy and degeneracy of the human world, it remained possible to move, albeit painfully and gropingly, toward a condition of amelioration and regeneration, the path for this progress being provided by a commitment to reason and lucidity. Such optimism abounds, for instance, among some of the Presocratics, and is clearly discernible in Socrates, Plato, and Aristotle. Even Cercidas of Megalopolis in his darkest moments, as when he said that "there is no one who has glanced for a moment on the character of humanity without cursing humanity,"[6] maintained alive in himself, despite his Cynicism, or, we should rather say, *because* of his Cynicism, the conviction that it is *not* that human life is a mistake, but that it is *we* who have insisted, because of our irrationality and senselessness, in converting it into a mistake. If, indeed, the human world is bankrupt, it is because *we* have brought about this lamentable condition on ourselves. From times immemorial we have simply gone astray.

In Diogenes, too, there is pessimism in his assessment of the human world, as when he concluded that most people are either completely mad or only one finger away from madness, or as when he searched in vain for a true human being, but there is also an undeniable sense that the remedy is there, waiting for us, if only we had the necessary will and mind to make use of it. Thus, contrary to what some historians and scholars have argued, Cynicism is *not* a philosophy of despair, an existential plunge into abandonment (*Verlassensein*, to use Heidegger's term), that promises no redemption and no escape, but is a philosophical stance that correctly diagnoses and perhaps crudely identifies the sorrows and ills that permeate the human condition of this and every other time, and points the way, harsh and brutal as it may be, that can alleviate at least in part those sorrows and ills. Human madness, Diogenes would say, is curable, which explains the missionary zeal with which he and his followers pursued their philosophical mission as physicians of the mind. Schopenhauer could have said, as he often did, "*velle non docere*," which means, "Do not attempt to teach anyone anything," or, from a moral point of view, "Let people drown in their own moral depravity," for human character, individually and collectively, is ultimately unchangeable: it would be easier to force a brick to sing a melody than to make anyone alter his ways. No one can learn to change the course of his life, and no one can be persuaded to transform his innately determined character.[7]

Such a despairing attitude toward human nature, however, is altogether absent from the Cynics. Instead of leaving people alone to sink deeper in their depravities, the Cynics made it their business to pursue them, as hunting dogs, and to assail them wherever they were, imagining and hoping that their barking and biting were not altogether futile. Thus, we find, for instance, according to Philostratus (*Life of Apollonius of Tyana* VI, xxxi), that Demetrius of Rome, a Roman Cynic of the first century A.D.,[8] assumed the responsibility of following Emperor Titus wherever he went, for the express purpose of barking both at him and at other people whenever Demetrius became aware of a breach of justice or an evil deed. Diogenes himself did the same. He followed and pestered his contemporaries, frequenting those places where people would congregate, whether in theaters, temples, gymnasia, or festivals, because it was there that his harsh barking could be heard by large crowds, and where his Cynic medicine would have some effectiveness. In the *Phaedrus* (230d), Socrates compares himself to "a hungry animal that can be driven by dangling a carrot or a bit of green stuff in front of it," and describes his business as one that has to do with *people*. In Xenophon's *Symposium* (viii, 2), he remarks that he cannot name a time in his life when he was not in love with someone. In both statements, Socrates' missionary zeal comes clearly to the surface: the dangling carrot or the bit of green stuff that makes him run desperately as a hungry animal is the possibility of engaging someone in meaningful discourse, not only for the purpose of attaining knowledge, but for the purpose of instilling in others the same passion for virtue that lived in him, for it was the love of others that moved him and gave direction to his activities.

Likewise in the case of Diogenes: his contempt for people notwithstanding, it was his commitment to their moral regeneration that impelled him to practice his Cynicism wherever he was. For him, it remained possible to hate the degeneracy of his contemporaries without abandoning them to wallow in their moral mire. It is for this reason that we find him especially where such degeneracy was rampant, for instance, in Corinth, where wantonness and corruption were found everywhere, as Dio Chrysostom reports (*Or.* VIII), and where Diogenes' services as a physician of the mind were most needed, for, in the words of Dio Chrysostom quoted in chapter 1, "it is preferable that the wise man should set up his residence there where the crowd of imbeciles and fools is the largest." Thus, we expect to find Diogenes in brothels, in taverns, at the marketplace, at athletic competitions, and, literally as a hungry and angry hound, following the scent of the rich, the powerful, and the arrogant, and in frantic pursuit of the throngs that live submerged in stupidity and thoughtlessness. Like the Jesus of the Gospels, who did not hesitate to dine with publicans, tax-collectors, and other forms of low-life (*Matt.* 11:19; *Luke* 7:34), Diogenes, too, found his niche among such people.

For us, however, the pressing question is what could have led Diogenes to his life of Cynicism, that is, what were the conditions and circumstances that can be held responsible for the making of a Cynic? Three kinds of considerations can assist us in this regard, namely, the character and predispositions of Diogenes himself, the specific circumstances and vicissitudes of his life, and the intellectual influences to which he was subjected.

With respect to Diogenes' character *before* his emergence into the Athenian world as a confirmed Cynic, hardly anything can be said, for our knowledge about his background and youth is practically null. We gather from the sources that his family could have been prominent, and his father's occupation as a banker and an officer of the public mint points in that direction. We can also assume, if the story about his defacing the Sinopean currency is trustworthy, that he did not regard abiding by the laws as a sacrosanct duty, for he was willing to break the laws by defacing the currency. A touch of rebelliousness, then, could have been in him even in his early years. To say more than this, however, is mere conjecture and speculation, for the young Diogenes is, no less than the young Socrates or the young Jesus, an altogether unknown entity.

Nevertheless, it may be true, as Diderot insisted, that the acceptance and the practice of Cynicism presuppose a certain psychological predisposition that, when absent, renders a person unable even to understand what Cynicism is.[9] One is born, said Diderot, a Cynic, and those who are not born Cynics are bound to remain foreign to anything that Cynicism can teach or manifest, which explains perhaps why certain scholars, knowledgeable and erudite as they may be in some respects, have approached Diogenes and the Cynics only to walk away either in a state of bafflement or with an understanding of the subject that baffles those who presume to appreciate sympathetically who and what the Cynics were.[10] Still, the idea that Cynicism presupposes an innate predisposition, and that even to understand and appreciate Cynicism one must be somehow predisposed toward Cynicism, is difficult to support empirically, especially in the absence of any knowledge about what a Cynic like Diogenes could have been *before* his accession into Cynicism. Furthermore, it is intellectually dangerous to play the psychologizing game in an effort to explain why and how a certain person comes to embrace a given mode of life or a set of ideas. The psychologizing game, in which we attempt to account for intellectual convictions by appealing to psychological predispositions and conditions, while occasionally useful, is ultimately only a game.

More light, however, can be shed on the issue of the making of a Cynic by considering the external circumstances that could have brought to the surface whatever Cynic predispositions the younger Diogenes might have sheltered within himself. Here, too, however, the conjectures and speculations outnumber the certainties, but, observing Diogenes from an external point of view, we might at least have the impression that some understanding of his Cynicism can be gathered from certain things that are said to have happened *to* him. Unless we are willing to dismiss *all* the sources about Cynicism, we cannot but recognize as a historical fact that in practically all the classical Cynics we encounter some circumstance, some incident, some vicissitude, that appears to have been their turning point toward Cynicism. More often than not, a Cynic seems to have been plunged into Cynicism by some natural or social circumstance that affected him.

We discover this circumstance in a multitude of instances. Antisthenes comes into the world as the bastard son of a Thracian slave and remains throughout his life tainted by the lowly character of his mother's origin and branded as an outsider by the discriminatory character of Athenian society. Crates of Thebes walks into the scene as a lame hunchback. Monimus of Syracuse begins his life as a mistreated slave who eventually forced himself into faked madness in order to secure his freedom. Bion of Borysthenes, one of the harshest Cynics, is the son of a prostitute and a dissolute father, who ends up being sold as a slave.[11] Menippus of Gadara also starts his life in a bad way as a slave who supported himself by begging. Cercidas of Megalopolis is compelled to come to grips with the moral bankruptcy of the world and the inhumaneness of war, when his homeland is destroyed by the Spartans. Maximus of Tyre also commences his journey through life as a slave. Dio Chrysostom, initially a distinguished and affluent rhetorician, finds himself exiled from Rome by Emperor Domitian in A.D. 82, and is compelled to wander for fifteen years through the remote provinces of the empire as a mendicant and destitute philosopher. Demetrius is an expatriate, who settles in Rome during the reign of Titus as a man without a country and without roots. Peregrinus Proteus, the last among the great Cynics, is banished from Parium, his homeland, for having strangled his father, and restlessly moves from place to place, admired *and* scorned, and welcomed *and* rejected wherever he goes, until his spectacular self-immolation in 165 B.C.[12] This list of Cynic 'tragedies' could be considerably enlarged, not leaving aside, of course, Diogenes' own 'tragedy'—his unhappy affair with the Sinopean currency and his banishment from his homeland.

It has been suggested by various scholars that it is principally in the unfortunate circumstances that accompanied the lives of the Cynics that we should expect to find the origin of their Cynicism. As if wishing to counterbalance their own personal misfortunes, then, the Cynics emerge as unhappy people who directed their anger at the world around them. Commenting on the reasons why Diogenes became a Cynic, K. O. Müller, for instance, notes that he was,

> either on his own account or that of his family, an outcast from his native city of Sinope; his asceticism was, in all probability, a refuge from his forfeited respectability and civic usefulness, and the socialism, which he openly preached, seemed to have been inspired by the recklessness of a man who had no character to lose.[13]

Applying this 'explanation' to all the Cynics, D. Henne writes that, "rejected by everybody and by fortune, all these wretched people, should they not have preferred to the laws of society the laws of nature, according to which all people, poor and rich, are equal?"[14] What else could have the Cynics done, having been mercilessly badgered by fortune and ill luck, and having been cast aside by others from a respectable place in society, but to turn against the world, as if intent on returning evil for evil, rejection for rejection, condemnation for condemnation? Only in death, it seems, some of them hoped to find freedom from misfortune and ostracism, which explains their inclination toward suicide, and when death was not chosen as an escape, then a life of indifference and a style of living divested of what others found necessary were seen by them as the best solution. Seneca's words about Diogenes are revealing in this regard:

> Diogenes acted in such a way that he could not be robbed of anything, for he freed himself from everything that is fortuitous. It appears to me as if he had said: "Concern yourself with your own business, Oh Fate, for there is nothing in Diogenes that belongs to you anymore." (*De tranquillitate animi* viii)

Undoubtedly, there is some value in this approach to the issue of the making of a Cynic. The adherents of Cynicism appear to have been precisely the sort of people who begin life on the wrong side of things and whose lives are especially beset by misfortunes, which explains in part their dissatisfaction with their human surroundings, their contempt for social conventions and political arrangements, and their systematic program to undermine the structure of the human world that could have been originally responsible for their misfortunes. It may account, too, for their style of life, so well exemplified by Diogenes. Like the typical Parisian *chiffonier,* a ragpicker, described by D. Rieger, Diogenes emerges as "a classless man, whose intemperance is proverbial and whose habits are depraved, and who is neither concerned with politics nor with the ordinary events of everyday life."[15] The poverty and isolation, initially imposed upon him by society, were transformed by him into a self-chosen mode of life, in which whatever value there may have been in his society was simply bracketed away. Like the famous fox of Aesop's fable, who was unable to reach the grapes and who walked away saying to himself, "These grapes must be sour," Diogenes, too, deprived by society of luxuries and comfort, and, above all, of the privilege of belonging to the community, turns his back to society, saying, "These things are useless." Something similar can be said with respect to other Cynics, for they often shared his initial ill fortune and his spirit of revolt.

Nevertheless, the approach entailed by these considerations, as well as by those related to the allegedly innate character of the Cynics, interesting and tempting as they may be, do not provide a solid explanation. There have been countless people, including philosophers, whose lives also began on the wrong side of things and who were also cruelly accosted by ill fortune and social ostracism, but who remained completely removed from the spirit of negativism and rebelliousness associated with Diogenes and his descendants, and who were able to become assimilated into their social and political contexts. The problem of appealing to psychological and sociological explanations in order to account for the emergence of a philosophical stance is that it sheds light only on certain cases and on certain situations, and always from a restricted point of view, but leaves untouched hosts of others that remain unexplained, and ignores the influence of intellectual currents on the formation of a philosopher. The process of the making of a Cynic, especially in relation to Diogenes, is, as G. Rudberg perceptively noted, both a cultural *and* a philosophical process.[16]

Likewise, it is unwise to opt exclusively for the approach that endeavors to explain the emergence of Cynicism in general and of Diogenes' stance in particular as a manifestation of the social struggle among socio-economic classes in ancient times. From this point of view, Diogenes has been seen as the precursor of the revolutionary spirit that more than two thousand years later would be responsible for the rise and revolt of the proletariat in the Western world. As a sort of philosophical Spartacus, the Thracian gladiator who in 73 B.C. led an army of slaves against the Roman military might, Diogenes, too, it has been suggested, raised the banner of revolt on behalf of the multitudes of dispossessed and disenfranchised—the slaves, the foreigners, the metics, the bastards, the poor— who constituted most of the population of classical nations. Not with the swords and shields of Spartacus' army, but with castigating words and shocking antics, the Army of the Dog, as Lucian calls Diogenes' sect, fought against the injustice and the cruelty under which the working masses lay buried under the crushing weight of the governing oligarchies. In the midst of the bourgeois decadence of Greek political and social institutions, Diogenes rose as the precursor of the revolution that would take place many centuries later.[17] From this point of view, Diogenes' ideology and preoccupations have been interpreted as an anticipation of those of modern communism. C. W. Goettling, for instance, has gone as far as to refer to him as "*ein bloss antiker Communist*" (a genuine ancient communist), for in him, we come upon the same impulse of modern communists to alleviate the unhappy condition of the proletariat, who must struggle against social, political, and economic oppression and deprivation.[18]

Unquestionably, an element of truth can be found in the above considerations. Diogenes, an unfortunate Sinopean exile, finds himself thrown into the turmoil of Athenian life, where the restrictions and limitations imposed by law and convention were designed to maintain outsiders and the poor outside the circles of influence. He reacts against such a world and affirms his alienation from that world by becoming a shameless dog, assuming the role of a social revolutionary with whom, according to Goettling, the proletariat—the poor, the workers, the slaves, the foreigners—can somehow identify.

Here again, as with the approaches mentioned earlier, we encounter only an element of meaningful interpretation, but not, by any means, an adequate explanation for the phenomenon of Cynicism and specifically for the processes responsible for the formation of Diogenes as a Cynic. Innate character and inborn predispositions, unfortunate circumstances and the blows inflicted by nature and society, and the bourgeois decadence or, more properly, the moral and intellectual bankruptcy that has characterized and still characterizes *all* nations and societies —all these may have been biographical, historical, and sociological factors that must have influenced Diogenes along the road toward Cynicism, and their impact on him and on other Cynics must be recognized. Still, by themselves, they are insufficient to explain the advent of Cynicism or the conversion to the Cynic mode of life on the part of any one among the Cynics. Cynicism, particularly in the case of Diogenes, must have had deeper intellectual roots. His revolt is more extreme than what we could expect from someone badgered by ill fortune and by society, or from someone who, like the ideal communist, constructs in his mind a program to reform the social fabric.

What needs to be explored, therefore, is the world of intellectual influences that could have been the catalytic agent responsible for crystallizing in Diogenes' mind the idea of Cynicism and for impelling him to transform it into a daily practice. What magic potion, then, did he imbibe in order to turn himself into a dog, and what powerful drug did he take daily in order to maintain alive within himself the necessary courage to hold fast to Cynic beliefs and practices?

The answer to these questions lies in the philosophical influences to which Diogenes was exposed, influences that can be classified into two groups: the immediate philosophical impact of Antisthenes and other Socratic philosophers, and certain Cynic-like ideologies with which we can assume that Diogenes must have been acquainted even before his arrival in Athens. It is not difficult to document the first group of influences, and, as we will see presently, it is possible to draw with some precision a 'succession' line that links Diogenes to Antisthenes and other Socratics, and ultimately to Socrates.[19] The second group, however, involves us in conjectures and assumptions of only *some* historical value, a circumstance, however, that should not compel us to ignore them altogether.

It is unquestionable that Diogenes' Cynicism is *not* a unique phenomenon in history. Both before, as well as during his own time, there must have been other Cynics, both in Greece and elsewhere. If, as Oscar Wilde said, "Cynicism is merely the art of seeing things as they are instead of as they should be,"[20] and if philosophy is, as Diogenes is reported to have said, "the art of calling things by their right name," Cynicism, as exemplified by Diogenes and his classical descendants, has to be viewed as a natural, although surely rare, human response to certain situations that on reflection demand a radical correction. All that we need for the making of a Cynic is the right mixture of the appropriate ingredients—a life that has been shaken by unfortunate natural or social circumstances, a temperament inclined toward inflexibility and extremism, a strong and proud will that is willing to face any situation, a mind endowed with an exceptional degree of lucidity or intellectual eyesight to be able to recognize the mistake of human existence for which we have been responsible, and the appropriate philosophical influences. As soon as these ingredients are present, a Cynic emerges into the scene, an occurrence that is bound to take place from time to time, although on very rare occasions, for the presence of mind and the strength of will that are required in the process are extraordinary anomalies in nature. For this reason, there should not be anything surprising in occasionally encountering Cynics in all cultures and at various times.

That only a few genuine Cynics emerge from time to time in the course of history, is understandable, for clarity of mind and a Herculean will are themselves uncommon human endowments. D'Alembert once noted that every century needs the presence of a Diogenes, but that the problem is to find human beings who have the *courage* to be like Diogenes, and, we may add, the required lucidity to see the world as he did.[21] In modern times, the example of Henry Thoreau (1817-1862) can be adduced in this regard. His rupture with his political and social context, his spirit of rebelliousness, his uncompromising unwillingness to make accommodations with a system that he found to be beyond repair, his contempt toward the American government and all other governments, his uncanny ability to pierce beneath the appearance of things, and his style of life—all these are reminiscent of Diogenes. When we read in Thoreau's *On Civil Disobedience* that "that government is best which governs not at all,"[22] and when we remember how well he understood the true meaning of the war waged by the Americans against the Mexicans, we hear a distinct echo of the Cynic anarchism that may be detected in Diogenes and other classical Cynics.[23] However, reminiscent of Diogenes as Thoreau and other Cynic-like figures in history may be, it remains true that what distinguishes Diogenes from all the rest is *not* his Cynic ideas and sentiments, but the extremes, both theoretical and practical, to which he was willing to take his Cynicism. In this sense, Diogenes remains unique and unequaled, which accounts well for his having been traditionally viewed as *the* stereotype of Cynicism.

Before Diogenes' time, we can identify Cynic-like ideas and practices, both among the Greeks and elsewhere, and numerous scholarly efforts have been made to discover antecedents of classical Cynicism in ancient cultures.[24] In India and in China, for instance, we come upon individuals and communities that appear to have anticipated much of what we associate with Diogenes and his Cynic sect. The Ch'an tradition in China and the Prasangika Madhyamika tradition in India, both of which antedate Diogenes, displayed beliefs and practices that remind us of him. In them, as with Diogenes, equanimity and asceticism were viewed as a shortcut to enlightenment and happiness. We also find in them a rejection of scriptures and sacred traditions as guides for human conduct, and the conviction that the only thing that matters is the present moment. They, too, like Diogenes, taught by example rather than by discourse, and imparted their teachings by means of seemingly irrational and often violent actions that were specifically designed to compel others to reflect on their own lives and to correct their behavior.[25] Likewise, in them, we come upon an emphasis on discipline, indifference, and simplicity, and even a welcoming attitude toward insults and vituperation.

Even more striking anticipations of Diogenes' Cynicism can be discerned among the adherents of a Shivaite sect of great antiquity, the Pasupatas, who, as A. Syrkin has pointed out,[26] were known in antiquity for their unusual austerities, their offending and anti-social behavior, their contempt for all social norms and conventions, and their commitment to poverty and simplicity. The Pasupatas, too, belonged to that strange group of people who since times immemorial have found themselves attracted to dogs and to a dog-like life. The Pasupatas had become apparently so divorced from their human context that, instead of speaking like human beings, they would bark among themselves and at other people, seeking to imitate the behavior of dogs in whatever they did. Like their remote and half-legendary ancestors, the Dog Heads described in Ctesias' *Indica*,[27] the Pasupatas displayed in their dog-like behavior the exhibitionism and primitivism that the sources associate with Diogenes. The name of the 'founder' of the Pasupatas—Lakulisa—to whom a text known as the *Pasupata Sutra* is ascribed, may be etymologically related to the name of Hercules, who, as has been noted, was viewed by the Cynics as *their* paradigm of virtue.[28]

The presence of the Indian Gymnosophists should also be mentioned. Possibly long before the campaigns of Alexander, the Greeks had become acquainted with these strange people—strange at least in the eyes of the Greeks—who, both in outward appearance and in behavior, bear some similarity with the most extreme among the Cynics, including Diogenes. Their designation as Gymnosophists is derived from the Greek word γυμνός (*gymnos*) that can be translated as 'naked' or 'lightly dressed', for their custom was to dispense with clothing. Like animals, then, they would go either naked or barely clothed, living on the fringes of society, rejecting the arrangements and amenities that civilized life provides. Neither laws, nor social norms, nor political associations ever entered their consciousness, living as if the whole world were their country and as if all things belonged to all and nothing to anyone in particular. They would reluctantly communicate their wisdom through gestures or short statements, and would avoid as much as possible any contact with ordinary people. Encounters between Greek travelers and the Gymnosophists begin to be documented during Alexander's campaigns, but earlier contacts cannot be discounted. Plutarch, perhaps on the testimony of a lost work by Onesicritus, recounts (*Alexander* lxv) how Onesicritus, originally a disciple of Diogenes and later the chief pilot of Alexander's fleet, was asked by the emperor to interview and question a group of Gymnosophists about their wisdom, which in his eyes must have been remarkable, for how, Alexander must have wondered, could destitute and naked men living in the wilderness be as happy as they were, while he, surrounded by wealth and richly attired, was always in a state of turmoil? Onesicritus tells the Gymnosophists about the greatness of three Greek philosophers—Pythagoras, Socrates, and Diogenes—to which a certain Gymnosophist named Dandamis replies, revealing thereby the essence of *their* wisdom, that such philosophers, great as they could have been, erred in a fundamental way in their search for wisdom, namely, "in having too much respect for the laws and customs of their country."[29] Obviously, the Gymnosophists themselves had no respect for the laws and customs of their own country, and in their beliefs and practices did in fact anticipate and duplicate much of what we associate with Diogenes and the Cynics.

The key question is, however, whether any among the many Cynic-like traditions of the ancient world, including those associated with the Gymnosophists and with Anacharsis, the legendary Scythian sage,[30] may have directly influenced Diogenes either in Sinope or after his departure for Athens. We could also ask whether or not Oriental influences, in particular those in which we can discern a prelude of Greek Cynicism, could have had any impact on Antisthenes and the quasi-cynics who echoed his ideas in the early fourth century B.C., men such as Simon the Shoemaker and Zoïlus of Amphipolis.[31] If such an influence is detectable, then Greek Cynicism turns out to be an offspring of an ancient ideology, the roots of which are traceable to remote cultures in the Orient.

In reality, however, the historical facts elude us and we are confined to interesting speculations of meager substance. It may be true, as A. Gladisch maintained,[32] that every major Greek contribution in philosophy has antecedents that transcend the Hellenic soil and an ancestry that takes us to cultures of greater antiquity than that of the Greeks. This may well be the case with respect to Cynicism. Nevertheless, at least in *this* respect, little of value can be affirmed, for nothing attributable either to Antisthenes or to Diogenes reveals a debt to philosophers who do not belong to Greek philosophical traditions. Still, if we bear in mind the geographical position of Sinope at the end of the caravan route that began in Persia and connected Persia with India, we must entertain the possibility that in his youth, Diogenes could have become acquainted with knowledge about the Indian Gymnosophists, as Sayre suggests,[33] or could have been in the presence of some wandering Gymnosophist near the shores of the Euxine.

R. P. Martin offers the tempting suggestion that it may have been from the north of Sinope, that is, from Scythia and from the northern shores of the Euxine, that the legends and stories about Anacharsis may have reached Diogenes.

Martin goes even further concerning the possible influence of Anacharsis:

> Sinope was a staging point for traffic across the Euxine toward Scythian lands; it was actually destroyed by the Scythians in the seventh century B.C.E. Could not a young man growing up in his town have heard travelers—even locals of Scythian descent—tell of the barbarian [Anacharsis] and his Hellenization? We know that the Cynics valued heroic models; who was Diogenes' hero? Could it be a Scythian who acted like a sage, and brought back, to his detriment,[34] the rites of the Great Mother from Cyzicus[35] (two hundred miles to the west of Sinope)? Was it an accident, or by design, that Diogenes of Sinope ended up, living an outdoor life, in the Metroön,[36] cult place of the same Great Mother, in the Athenian agora?[37]

This suggestion, no less than others that attempt to find non-Hellenic influences on the rise of Cynicism, may be only an interesting conjecture, although its plausibility cannot be altogether discounted, especially in view of the growing realization among historians and classical scholars that the Greek world was not a closed enclave in antiquity. Travel and communication between the Greeks and other nations in the sixth and fifth centuries B.C. appear to have been far more common than what nineteenth-century scholars were willing to concede, and, thus, the seeding of foreign ideas and modes of life among the Greeks, including the philosophers, must have been extensive.[38] Without wishing to question the uniqueness of the philosophical contributions of the Greeks or to diminish the merits of the conceptual revolution for which, especially in the context of the Presocratics, they were responsible, the presence of older sophisticated cultures, both around and *in* the Greek world, has to be considered.

In our endeavor to account for the making of a Cynic in the instance of Diogenes, we do not find ourselves as enmeshed in tempting and fanciful speculations when we consider the influence of Greek philosophical currents on him, for in this regard the sources provide some information. The streams of this influence appear to have reached Diogenes mostly through the agency of Antisthenes and other Socratics, but its sources are traceable to the Presocratics. Among them, beginning with Thales of Miletus, we encounter two themes that would reappear with great vigor in Diogenes: the acceptance of the supremacy of reason as the ultimate judge of nature and human experience, and a concomitant dissatisfaction with all traditional modes of thought and behavior. The conceptual revolution initiated by Thales' statement that all things are ultimately water, and by his search for the underlying and non-perceptible element ($ἀρχή$) that constitutes the universe, began, so to speak, a new chapter in the history of the human species, a chapter in which independence of thought declared war on blind faith and irrational opinions. Whether polytheism and superstition, or the fantasies and legends of the epic poets, or the obfuscated frame of mind of the masses, or the unrefined testimony of the senses—all these and other ordinary aspects of human experience were at one time or another brought before the tribunal of reason to be condemned as useless and detrimental by the Presocratics, whose preoccupation was basically the empowerment of human thought, unencumbered by the fetters of tradition and habit, as the only basis on which an understanding of the world and the right structuring of human life could be established.[39]

Eventually, through a tortuous path of speculation and controversy, and after almost two centuries of political and social turmoil, the legacy of Thales and the other Milesian philosophers would arrive in Athens in the middle of the fifth century B.C., and, through the intellectual activities of the Sophists and Socrates, would compel the human spirit to undertake a fundamental reassessment of its possessions. This reassessment was then directed almost exclusively toward questions and issues related to human concerns and activities, for the preoccupation with the universe and nature at large, which was at the heart of the early Presocratics' philosophical excursions, had lost its grip on the minds of philosophers in the second half of the fifth century. "Man," said Protagoras,[40] "is the measure of all things" (Frag. 1), which meant, among other things, that only human existence was worthy of consideration. The disdain toward natural science that is detectable in Diogenes and other Cynics had roots that are traceable to the time of the Sophists and Socrates. Human life, not the universe, Diogenes could have said in agreement with them, should be the only critical issue for philosophy, for everything else is inconsequential.

This subjective turn in philosophy was brought about by various circumstances, among which we could mention the sociological and political upheaval caused by the Peloponnesian War and the Greeks' discovery of cultures vastly different from their own, a discovery that forced them to question the value of their own traditions and customs. Eventually, the Sophists would enthrone epistemological skepticism, metaphysical indifference, and ethical nihilism as the epitomes of philosophical sophistication, while Socrates, dissatisfied with the impasse created by Sophistical philosophy and by the apparent futility of earlier cosmological and metaphysical speculations, devoted himself exclusively to the search for a new ground of moral certainty within himself, on which a virtuous and happy life could be attainable.

Fundamental both to the Sophists and to Socrates, however different they may have been from one another and however different their conclusions could have been, was their conviction that reason—the rational analysis of the world and of human experience, summed up by the word λόγος—is the last court of appeal in all matters. Neither conventions, nor traditions, nor religious beliefs, nor socially sanctioned norms had any value for the Sophists, nor, we may add, for Socrates.

With them, there arose the necessity of making a sharp distinction between νόμος (*nomos*)—the transitory and mutable domain of human customs—and λόγος (*logos*)—the rationality that distinguishes or should distinguish human beings from all other earthly creatures. This distinction, which had already been made clearly by some of the Presocratics, as with Heraclitus, compelled the Sophists to question the sanctity and infallibility both of the positive laws enacted by governments, whether in tyrannies or in democracies, and of the conventions by which people guide themselves. Social norms and values—the νόμισμα (*nomisma*) that, as we saw earlier, the Delphic oracle is said to have commanded Diogenes to deface— were, from the point of view of the Sophists, only expedient inventions fabricated by the ruling classes to maintain the masses under control, and modes of life that the inertia inherent in human thoughtlessness converts into unchanging natural principles, as we learn from the fragments of Critias,[41] for whom even the belief in gods falls into this category. Human laws, therefore, had little value in the eyes of the Sophists, and blind obedience to such laws revealed, according to them, the state of slumber and mindlessness that characterizes, as Heraclitus and the Cynics insisted, most people.[42] The point for them was, then, to be awakened from that slumber and to regain possession of one's own individual mind as the sole source of one's values—a socially dangerous idea, undoubtedly, and a political prelude to anarchism, as the Platonic Socrates suggests in the *Crito*[43], but ultimately the only solution available to anyone who has contemplated even for a moment, as Diogenes might have put it, the insanity of the human world. Thus, the Sophists were philosophical rebels and revolutionaries, who recognized the vacuity of their world and who proposed solutions, perhaps outlandish and extreme, leading to a stance of hedonistic individualism, or, as with Thrasymachus, to a rejection of all moral values,[44] or simply a withdrawal from the social and political world, which was precisely the influence that eventually affected Pyrrho of Elis and the Skeptics, and, through Antisthenes, also Diogenes.[45]

Nevertheless, the presence of Socrates as the ally of the Sophists in some respects and as their most formidable opponent in others, and as the direct mentor of Antisthenes, overshadows by far any other presence that could have influenced the development of Cynicism in general and the transformation of Diogenes into a Cynic in particular. We are told that Plato once referred to Diogenes as a "Socrates-gone-mad" (Σωκράτης μαινόμενος), as we read in Diogenes Laertius (VI, 54) and in Aelian (*Hist. Var.* XIV, xxxiii). This designation of Diogenes as a "Socrates-gone-mad," despite its perhaps questionable genuineness, is revealing. It does not matter whether or not Plato made such a comment, for it is clear that both from the point of view of ordinary people *and* in the eyes of the adherents of Plato's Socratic philosophy, Diogenes must have given the impression of being mad. In the previous chapter, we saw how, when someone called him a madman,

Diogenes replied, "I am not mad; it is only that my head is different from yours" (Stobaeus, III, iii, 51). He might have retorted to Plato in the same way, had he heard him call him a "Socrates-gone-mad." He might have added that it was Plato who was mad for having transformed Socrates into so vastly different a philosopher from what he actually was, and for having imputed to him so many strange metaphysical ideas and, in particular, so many perverse political views. How many lies, indeed, he could have said, has Plato told about Socrates![46] Madness is often a condition that we attribute to those whose ideas and style of life are so different from ours that it is impossible for us to establish a common ground between us and them. The 'head' of the madman, to use Diogenes' phrase, and ours are altogether different. Thus, when ordinary people called Diogenes mad, they were just acknowledging the abyss the separated him from them, an abyss that converted him, in their eyes, into an unexplainable aberration. Likewise, when *he* called *them* mad, *he* was recognizing in *them* what Machado called "*la terrible cordura del idiota*"—the terrible sanity of the idiot.[47] In calling Diogenes a "Socrates-gone-mad," what Plato is said to have done was merely to pass judgment on Diogenes' interpretation of Socrates and on his compulsive and exaggerated urge to actualize in his daily life what he understood to be Socrates' teachings. Obviously, Plato's interpretation of Socrates was profoundly different from that of Diogenes.

For us, however, the problem is especially difficult because whenever we speak of Socrates as a man and as a philosopher, our basis of historical knowledge is weak and questionable. In the presence of Socrates, we face a biographical and intellectual enigma that admits of no definitive deciphering. Perhaps even more than in the instance of Diogenes, it is difficult to make substantive statements about who Socrates was and what his teachings were, for here, too, we are at the mercy of sources that paint for us significantly divergent and even contradictory portraits. How, then, could we presume to know whether it was Plato, or Aeschines,[48] or Aristippus,[49] or Antisthenes, or Polycrates,[50] or any other associate or acquaintance of Socrates, who truly grasped or failed to grasp the enormous significance of the Socratic presence, especially in view of the fact, one of the few facts that can be affirmed about him, that no writings can be attributed to him? The extensive testimony of Xenophon and the dialogues of Plato present to us different representations of him, and even within each one of these sources, there are irreconcilable areas of disagreement, so that one is tempted to assume that the various Socratic writers of the early fourth century B.C. were engaged in making use of the name and memory of Socrates to give expression to their own ideas.[51] Thus, it turns out to be an impossibility to reach a determination concerning the degree of 'madness' ascribed by Plato to Diogenes' interpretation of the Socratic presence. Unable to have a clear picture of who and what Socrates was, we must suspend judgment on the matter. Perhaps Plato, in using the name and style of Socrates to construct the grand political scheme of his *Republic*, was no less mad than the eccentric and exhibitionist Diogenes. Perhaps, too, if Diogenes ever had the opportunity to read the concluding section of Plato's *Crito*, where Socrates is portrayed as a subservient and faithful servant of the Athenian laws, and as a man who was willing to die rather than to break the laws, he would have thrown away this dialogue, saying, not only what he is said to have remarked about Plato's lectures ("a waste of time"), but that Plato's madness had led him to compose such an embarrassing travesty of Socrates.[52]

Still, it must be granted that there are common elements in the various representations of Socrates that emerge from the sources, principally in Xenophon's Socratic writings and in Plato's early dialogues, that can provide for us an avenue to understand how an account of his ideas and mode of life could have influenced Diogenes. We could mention, for instance, Socrates' repeated affirmation that his life was lived as a fulfillment of a divine mission, for it was God who sent him to the Athenians as a pestering gadfly to arouse them from intellectual and moral somnolence.[53] In him, we witness a commitment to a simple and disciplined life, divested of luxuries and extravagances, and a resolution to live in poverty and vigilant austerity. In him, too, we detect a condemning attitude toward the blind pursuit of pleasure and power that characterizes the behavior of most people. There was also in him a skeptical uneasiness in the presence of religious superstition and blind faith, and a disdainful stance toward the mythological legends created by the epic poets and perpetuated by the rhapsodists, in which ordinary people found the basis for their religious beliefs and practices. We discern in him an attitude of unyielding arrogance in his dealings with people in power, whether tyrants like Critias or jurors like the ones who sentenced him to die.[54] Unquestionably, despite his confession of ignorance and his ironic humility, we perceive in him a tremendous sense of pride, almost as if he viewed himself as a monarch, that manifested itself in his constant reminder that the opinions and modes of life of the masses—the οἱ πολοί, as he calls them in the *Crito*—are not worth anything and should be disregarded. Then, too, was his conviction that only a life devoted to rational self-examination is worth living, and that evil enters the soul when reason is set aside, and when impulses and desires become the guides of human behavior. Evil, too, which ultimately is ignorance in the form of spiritual obfuscation, invades the soul when language is misused: "You may be sure," he says to Cebes in the *Phaedo* (115e), "that inaccurate language is not only in itself a mistake, but is something that implants evil in the human soul." This fundamental conviction explains why, with Socrates, philosophy must begin with an elenchical analysis of language in order to achieve the initial goal of what Diogenes himself would define as a precondition for clarity of mind, namely, "calling things by the right name."

In Socrates, there was also an exemplary indifference about the accidents and circumstances of nature and fate—where and how we were born, how beautiful or ugly we may appear to be, how long we are allowed to remain in this physical world, and other such things for which we are not responsible. Equanimity, abnegation, endurance, patience, independence of judgment, the willingness and ability to speak only the truth, and many other virtues were present in him. As he taught others to follow his example, he did it, not by means of learned treatises or lengthy speeches that, as he ironically observes in the *Protagoras* (334c), he himself had difficulty retaining in his memory, but by means of his example, because, like Diogenes, he lived precisely as he thought. In him, theory and practice were one and the same reality. Ideas that are unrelated to the immediacy of human experience, and those philosophical and scientific endeavors that force us to turn our eyes toward domains of existence that transcend our present reality, were for Socrates both useless and detrimental, which explains the contempt toward speculative philosophy and science that Xenophon attributes to him and that he himself mentions in Plato's *Apology* (19c-d).

Possessing an unparalleled degree of lucidity, and always, as Guthrie puts it, with "an unerring eye for humbug,"[55] and, we may add, with an uncanny ability to see beneath and around things, Socrates succeeded in detecting and identifying the deceptions and confusions in which social existence involves us from the moment we were born, and the countless falsehoods and illusions that, like the blurry and unstable shadows of which he speaks in Plato's *Republic* (7.514a ff.), distract the mind from the right path. Socrates knew, possibly more than any other human being, how to distinguish reality from appearance, certainty from opinion, and truth from falsehood. He understood with unforgiving clarity the nonsensical character of the games in which politics and social conventions entangle human beings, and through which they become the easy prey of perfidious manipulation on the part of the ruling classes. His medicine—the elenchus[56]—was invariably painful, and his art of spiritual midwifery caused anger and hatred in those on whom it was administered. As he remarks in the *Theaetetus* (151c), "people have often felt like that toward me, and have been positively ready to bite me for taking away some foolish notion that they have conceived,"[57] and during his trial he reminded the jurors that it was his elenchus that gave rise to his bad reputation.

In each one of these convictions and characteristics, especially in Socrates' unwavering belief in the redeeming efficacy of reason as the healer of personal, social, and political ills, we can identify a prelude of Diogenes' Cynicism. In the construction of a catalogue of significant Cynic concepts, which we will undertake in a later chapter, it will become clear that each one of those concepts can be discerned in Socrates' philosophy. It is obvious, however, that Diogenes' Cynicism emerged as a radicalization of the Socratic stance, that is, as a carrying to the ultimate consequences what Socrates believed and exemplified in his life. In that sense, then, but only in that sense, is there some justification in accepting Plato's reported designation of Diogenes as a "Socrates-gone-mad": he actualized point by point, word by word, and without ambiguity or accommodations what he learned about Socrates.

From those who, like Antisthenes, had the benefit of being in the presence of Socrates, Diogenes must have heard recounted, over and over again, stories and anecdotes about him, and, let us not forget, an account of his execution. He must have heard how the man, whom Plato called the wisest and most just,[58] and whom the other Socratics loved so dearly and of whom they spoke so highly, was unjustly sentenced to death by a legally constituted Athenian jury—the jury of the King-Archon.[59] How, Diogenes might have wondered, could it have been possible for a sensible person not to revolt against a political system that made Socrates' execution possible? How could have a clear-minded person not turned, like an angry hound, against that undeserving world? Would it not have been a manifestation of madness or of utter dishonesty to remain indifferent in such a morally desolate world?

As we saw in chapter 1, the biographical and doxographical traditions are emphatic in associating Diogenes with Antisthenes, as is exemplified in Diogenes Laertius' testimony (VI, 21). That Diogenes became a direct disciple of Antisthenes, is a circumstance about which all the sources stand in agreement or, at least, about which none of the sources expresses serious doubts. Modern scholarship, as noted in chapter 2, has thrown a veil of doubt over this matter, and for this reason, whether or not such a direct association can be regarded as a historical fact remains a matter of controversy. It may be correct to assume that Diogenes arrived in Athens *after* Antisthenes' death around the year 366 B.C. and even *after* Plato's death in 347 B.C.,[60] which would then compel us to regard the numerous reports about Diogenes' encounters with Antisthenes, Plato, and other Socratics as fabrications possibly rooted in the Stoics' desire to validate the legacy of the philosophy of Zeno of Citium, the founder of their school, as traceable to Socrates, through the invention of the 'succession' Socrates-Antisthenes-Diogenes-Crates-Zeno.[61] Still, neither the numismatic evidence nor a review of the literary testimonies *compels* us to dismiss this 'succession' as a fabrication. Despite the hypercritical stance assumed by several modern scholars, it remains possible, if not probable, that Diogenes' arrival in Athens anteceded the death of Antisthenes, and that, as other exiles and foreigners, he would have naturally gravitated toward the Cynosarges, where he could have met Antisthenes. But even if we insist on rejecting this possibility, the truth of the matter is that Antisthenes' writings and those of Xenophon, which, as A. H. Chroust has correctly maintained,[62] were themselves influenced by Antisthenes, were available in Athens in the second half of the fourth century B.C. Thus, if not directly from Antisthenes, then from his writings and from those of Xenophon, Diogenes must have been able to derive a great deal of information about Socrates, and could have come to regard him as a man worthy of emulation.

In order to understand and appreciate Antisthenes' impact on the formation of Diogenes as a Cynic philosopher, it is necessary to examine several aspects of Antisthenes' life, personality, and thought, most of which, however, are known to us through the agency of secondary sources, because most of his writings are not extant. The details about his life emerge from various sources, principally Diogenes Laertius (VI, 1-19), and his ideas and personality are outlined for us in Xenophon's *Symposium*. While the references to him in Plato's dialogues are insignificant (actually only one explicit reference in *Phaedo* 59b), there are extended commentaries about him in Aristotle's writings, especially with regard to his logical and political ideas (e.g., *Topics* 104b21, *Metaphysics* 1043b24-28, *Politics* 1284a15). The year of his birth cannot be fixed with certainty, although some time between 455 and 450 B.C. seems to be a reasonable assumption. Plutarch (*Lycurgus* xxx) speaks of him as having made a comment about the battle of Leuctra in 371 B.C., and Diodorus Siculus (XV, lxxvi, 4) says that he was still alive in the year 366 B.C.

His place of birth was Athens. We know little about his background and early life, except for an important detail, namely, that whereas his father was an Athenian citizen, his mother was a Thracian slave, which, as pointed out in chapter 2, rendered him a bastard and a non-citizen in the context of Athenian law. We also know that at some point in his life he became associated with the Sophists, specifically Gorgias of Leontini, Hippias of Elis, and Prodicus of Ceos, from whom he must have derived valuable lessons in rhetoric, as can be inferred from the surviving fragments of his early works. His constant preoccupation with the meanings of words and his excursions into the realm of logic, too, must have originated during his years as a Sophistical apprentice, and possibly also his uneasiness with the social and political world, because the Sophists had much to say in the way of criticism about the Athenian polity.

It would have been difficult to be under the tutelage of the Sophists without assimilating at least some of their skepticism and agnosticism. Whether concerning religion, or the value of tradition, or the possibility of knowledge, or the value of speculative and scientific endeavors, the Sophists generally assumed a negative stance, reaching sometimes the most extreme conclusions, as exemplified in these words from Gorgias: "Nothing exists. If anything existed, it could not be known. If anything could be known, it would be impossible to communicate that knowledge" (Frag. 3). We can discern in Sophistical thought, as expressed in the radical agnosticism and skepticism so clearly manifested in this fragment, the seeds that would eventually germinate in the mature Antisthenes as manifestations of Cynicism, and that would be then transplanted, augmented and intensified, in

Diogenes, although adapted to the requirements of *his* own version of Cynicism.

At a later point in his life, some time between the years 426 and 421 B.C., Antisthenes 'discovered' Socrates and left the company of the Sophists to devote himself exclusively to him. Saint Jerome provides for us a glimpse of that moment of discovery:

> It is a fact that Antisthenes, who had been teaching rhetoric in so excellent a manner, after he heard Socrates, said to his disciples: "Get yourselves going and find a teacher, for I have made a discovery." At once, he sold all his possessions and distributed the money among the people, keeping only a cloak for himself. (*Adv. Jovin.* II, xiv)

The theme of discovery is important in the history of Cynicism, and is found on a multitude of occasions: just as Antisthenes 'discovered' Socrates, so did Diogenes 'discover' Antisthenes, and Crates Diogenes, and Hipparchia and Zeno Crates, and so on. In each instance, the discovery is sufficient to transform the discoverer's life and to impel him to follow a different path, often symbolized by giving up all possessions, as with Crates, who is said to have thrown all his money into the sea as soon as he heard Diogenes speak (D.L. VI, 87). Like a leaping spark that ignites the soul and becomes self-sustaining, the Cynic is converted into Cynicism by the presence of another Cynic or, in the case of Antisthenes, of a Cynic-like person like Socrates. From that moment on, his life (or *her* life, if we remember Hipparchia) is changed. Wealth, possessions, rank or the lack of rank, erudition and learning, the need to belong to a political structure such as a country, amenities and pleasures, fears and anxieties, and all such things are thrown overboard, and even the physical appearance and the attire undergo a transformation. Expensive clothing is replaced by a rugged and torn cloak, hair is worn long and unkept, shoes and sandals disappear, and a leathern wallet and a wooden stick become the only treasured belongings, as if the converted Cynic had gained admission into a sect.[63] There is a sense of liberation, a being-set-free, as Epictetus notes with regard to Diogenes' discovery of Antisthenes:

> Diogenes used to say, "From the time that Antisthenes set me free, I have ceased being a slave." How did Antisthenes set him free? Listen to what Diogenes says: "He taught me what is mine and what is not mine. Property is not mine; kinsmen, members of my household, friends, reputation, familiar places, social intercourse with people—all these things are not my own. 'What, then, *is* yours? The power to deal with external circumstances and impressions'. He showed me that I possess *that* without any hindrance or constraint. No one can hamper me, and no one can force me to deal with them otherwise than as I choose." (*Discourses* III, xxiv, 67-70)

Diogenes' liberation from 'slavery' through the magnetic mesmerism of Antisthenes can be understood at least partially if we bear in mind on the one hand the circumstances of the former and, on the other, the ideology and style of life of the latter. As an exile from Sinope and as a man whose reputation as a currency defacer may have preceded him, Diogenes enters the Athenian world as an outcast and is thus somehow 'enslaved' by the external circumstances of his life. The pronouncement of the Delphic oracle that enjoined him to proceed with the defacement of the social and moral currency, whether a genuine oracle or an invention about Diogenes, places him in a peculiar position, that is, as a man who is set to undermine the foundations of the polity that provides for him at least a place of refuge. He finds his way to the Cynosarges, the Athenian park and gymnasium, where, as we saw in chapter 2, foreigners and outcasts like him would congregate in freedom.

It is there, as the traditions insist, that he met Antisthenes, a man of illegitimate birth and a man who had traveled extensively along the tortuous roads of the mind, only to come to a negative and condemning stance toward the world at large. Their meeting is described by Diogenes Laertius:

> On reaching Athens, he [Diogenes] came under the influence of Antisthenes. Being rejected by him, because he never welcomed disciples, Diogenes wore him out by sheer persistence. Once, when Antisthenes stretched out his staff against him, Diogenes offered his head with the words, "Strike, for you will find no wood hard enough to keep me away from you, so long as I think that you have something to say." From that time on he was his disciple, and, exile as he was, set out upon a simple life. (VI, 21)

As we might expect, Sayre and other scholars have dismissed this meeting as fiction and fantasy, not only, as we have seen, on account of the chronology of Diogenes' arrival in Athens, but, as Sayre argues, because "it is inconsistent with the characters of both Antisthenes and Diogenes as they are represented elsewhere."[64] Nevertheless, it is difficult to see what such an inconsistency could be, for, on the contrary, what the account of the meeting reveals is fully in accord with what the sources tell us about both philosophers. Antisthenes is known to have been a less than welcoming person and someone who did not enjoy the company of disciples or associates. When asked why he had so few followers, he replied that it was his custom to strike them with his staff (D.L. VI, 4), which explains why, aside from Diogenes, no other disciples are associated by the sources with him. Diogenes' impetuosity and stubbornness, moreover, are repeatedly emphasized by the sources. Once his purpose was set, no one or anything could dissuade him from pursuing it. Thus, he 'discovers' in Antisthenes what he wants and needs, and not even blows on the head can keep him away from him.

Concerning the chronology of his arrival in Athens, we must reiterate the fact that no definitive assertions can be made in that regard. It might even be possible, as Long suggests,[65] that early in his life Diogenes could have traveled to Athens, where he would have met Antisthenes, and then could have returned to Sinope, where he became engaged in the defacing of the currency. This, however, is an interesting supposition, but, still, merely a supposition, although it falls well within the realm of possibility.

The important point for us is to gain some understanding of the reasons for Diogenes' attachment to Antisthenes, an attachment that must have been decisive in his turning in the direction of Cynicism. The Cynic predispositions that, as noted earlier, may have dwelled in him, as well as the circumstances related to his exile and whatever non-Greek Cynic-like influences may have affected him earlier in his life, may not be sufficient to explain his conversion into the ferocious dog that he eventually became. Antisthenes, then, provides for us the decisive clue for our grasping the process of the making of a Cynic. The man who called himself 'the absolute Dog' (Ἀπλοκύων) and who taught in the Cynosarges, the Park of the White Dog, and who inherited from Socrates, as he himself says in Xenophon's *Symposium* (iv, 34-44), his convictions and style of life, was the catalytic ingredient necessary for Diogenes' transformation.

Various ideological elements and a certain style of life associated with Antisthenes can be identified in this regard. There are, for instance, Antisthenes' logical ideas, which he inherited from the Sophists. Among these, we could mention his conviction that contradiction is altogether an impossibility (expressed in his language as οὐκ ἐστιν ἀντιλέγειν),[66] and the related belief that definition other than ostensive definition is a useless linguistic game.[67] From these two contentions, we can draw the outlines of Antisthenes' theory of language, a theory that insists that language has only one function, namely, to identify without elaboration the objects that constitute the physical world. Hence, discursive language, as found in philosophical and scientific treatises, and even in ordinary speech, is pointless and misguided, which explains why Antisthenes and the Cynics after him turned their back on the world of speculative philosophy and scientific pursuits. Even reading and writing were viewed by Antisthenes and Diogenes as detrimental diversions. Intelligent people, said Antisthenes, should not even bother learning how to read, lest they become perverted by bad influences (D.L. VI, 103).[68] When, as Diogenes Laertius reports (VI, 40), Diogenes challenged Plato's definition of Man as a featherless biped by plucking a chicken and presenting it to Plato's audience, he was putting into practice an important component of Antisthenes' logic: nothing can be either defined or explained, except by pointing to the object. Diogenes' bent toward teaching through example and toward using his body to give expression to ideas can be, therefore, traced to Antisthenes' disregard of discursive language. Likewise, Diogenes' distrust of language (he might have preferred barking to speaking) is traceable to Antisthenes' taciturn behavior and laconic style of speaking. For Diogenes, if it can be *shown,* then it should not be *spoken,* and if it cannot be *shown,* then it is not worth thinking about. Eventually, this distrust would grow to extremes, as when we find the followers of Pyrrho of Elis, whom we mentioned earlier, abandoning language altogether and using only their hands to express themselves. Among the late Cynics, too, there is the instance of Secundus the Silent, a Cynic and Pythagorean philosopher of the time of Hadrian, who, after a certain point, remained in absolute silence for the rest of his life, refusing to speak even to the emperor and willingly choosing to die rather than to break his silence.[69]

Antisthenes' style of life, specifically *after* his encounter with Socrates, displays characteristics that anticipate what we witness in Diogenes. Unmarried and living generally on the fringes of society, Antisthenes remained unattached to most of the things that people then and now deem necessary for a good life. To him, his poverty was a source of pride, his only possessions being those that he could carry wherever he went (Xenophon, *Symposium* iv, 44) and, of course, the wisdom that Socrates "with bounteous hand," as he remarks (ibid.), bequeathed to him. Diogenes Laertius reports (D.L. VI, 8) that once, when Socrates noticed the torn part of Antisthenes' cloak, he remarked to him, "I spy your love of fame through your cloak." This story has been viewed as an anachronism foisted on Antisthenes at a much later time, when, as Sayre remarks,[70] poverty had become a required element of Cynic life. It should also be noted that, despite his protestation of poverty and indifference to material things, Antisthenes is portrayed by Xenophon (*Symposium* ix, 60) as "dressed in a becoming manner." We could dismiss, however, Sayre's comment about the anachronism allegedly involved in the story about Socrates' comment, and interpret the matter in a different way. *Before* his meeting Socrates, Antisthenes could have been a man of some means, as is implied by the fact that he took lessons from the Sophists, who charged dearly for their teaching. Even owning property and having a decent income, as is suggested by Xenophon (*Symposium* iii, 8), can be ascribed to Antisthenes. *After* his encounter with Socrates, however, we may presume that he commenced his journey toward Cynicism, and that his commitment to poverty and to indifference began to grow in him, and that other manifestations of an incipient Cynicism started to emerge in him. We know of other instances of Cynics, who were once affluent and prominent in their communities, but, who, when they heard the call to Cynicism in their conscience, abandoned, sometimes all at once as with Crates, sometimes slowly but steadily, the materialistic fetters that tied them to the world. This latter occurrence, we propose, is relevant in Antisthenes' case. Twenty-five years in the company of Socrates must have eventually impelled him toward his ultimate destination.[71]

The trial and execution of Socrates in 399 B.C. may have been the final push, so to speak, and may have sealed Antisthenes' rupture with the world, for in convicting and killing Socrates, what the Athenian polity did was to reject all the convictions and ideals for which Antisthenes himself stood, and to attempt the destruction of his principles and mode of life.[72] Even Plato came close to effecting his own rupture with that world, as we read in one of his letters (*Epist.* 7.325b): "Finally I saw clearly in regard to all states now existing that without exception their system of government is bad. Their constitutions are almost beyond redemption except through some miraculous plan accompanied by good luck" (*Epist.* 7.325b). The key phrase in this passage is "almost beyond redemption," because Plato, despite the moral bankruptcy of the world that condemned Socrates, maintained some degree of optimistic idealism that allowed him to envision the regeneration of society at large and guided him to construct the grand educational and political scheme of his *Republic* and his *Laws*. It would be futile, however, to search for *that* kind of optimism in Antisthenes or in Diogenes, or, in fact, among other classical Cynics. They may have been optimistic about changing the character and behavior of individuals, but with respect to reforming society at large, we would be unable to find one single Cynic who could have entertained such a hope, which accounts for their aloofness from the political world. The Cynics saw the social and political world, not as *almost* beyond redemption, but as *totally* beyond redemption, and this appears to be one of the first lessons that Diogenes learned from the disillusioned Antisthenes.

These lessons, as Chappuis perceptively noted, were assimilated by Diogenes as exaggerated versions of what Antisthenes himself had learned from Socrates, just as those learned and practiced by Diogenes were hyperbolic renditions of what Antisthenes had taught and exemplified.[73] The independence of judgement that Socrates displayed before the jurors during his trial became transformed in Antisthenes into an attitude of disdain and indifference toward the State, and this, in its turn, was converted by Diogenes into a harsh stance of rebelliousness and contempt. The skepticism of Socrates toward popular religious beliefs, especially those embodied in the writings of the poets, about which we learn in Plato's *Euthyphro*, was inherited by Antisthenes in the form of a critical and agnostic attitude toward all forms of religious ideas and practices. This same attitude surfaced in Diogenes as a sarcastic and unforgiving condemnation of such things. Antisthenes' preoccupation with language and the use of the 'correct' words to identify things surfaced in Diogenes as a distrust of all forms of language and as the practice of signifying things and people by pointing and gesturing. The poverty and simplicity of Socrates emerged in Antisthenes as a renunciation of most of what the material world can provide, but this renunciation was carried by Diogenes one step further—he lived in a tub and begged for his daily sustenance. Socrates' ascetic uneasiness toward pleasure and comfort appeared in Antisthenes as a condemnation—"I would prefer a state of madness than a life of pleasure" (D.L. VI, 3; Sextus Empiricus, *Adv. math.* XI, 73). Diogenes, for his part, would take this idea again one step further—he sought pain and suffering as a means to strengthen his character. Socrates was a married man and the father of three children, and marriage and parenthood, as Schopenhauer noted, are unmistakable signs that one has made peace with the world and that one is willing to perpetuate the social order.[74] Antisthenes remained unmarried and childless, although was not unwilling to seek pleasure in the company of women, as we read in Diogenes Laertius (VI, 3) and in Xenophon's *Symposium* (iv, 38).[75] With Diogenes, however, neither marriage nor procreation ever entered his plan of action, and *nothing, absolutely nothing* is said by any of the sources that could lead us to believe that he established any close relationships with anybody. The gentle irony with which Socrates pursued his search for wisdom and virtue eventually changed itself in Diogenes into limitless sarcasm and harsh vituperation.[76] His rupture with the world was, therefore, complete and irreversible.

As we reflect on the process through which Diogenes became a Cynic, the influence of Antisthenes appears to have been decisive, whether or not we are willing to envision them as having ever met. Behind the presence of Antisthenes, however, we can easily discern the presence of Socrates, who had the ability to alter radically people's lives—at least some people. It is said (D.L. III, 5) that when Plato met Socrates for the first time, he experienced so profound a change in himself that he proceeded to burn his rhetorical and poetical writings, as if wishing to begin a new life. Antisthenes probably experienced the same overwhelming force of Socrates' presence (so eloquently described in Plato's *Meno*), and he, too, abandoned the path of Sophistical philosophy and the distractions of rhetorical and poetical activities. The Socratic "magic and witchcraft" of which Meno speaks (*Meno* 80a) also touched Diogenes, albeit at a distance, and touched him so intensely that he lost his mind, so to speak, and became a veritable Socrates-gone-mad. We may not be altogether justified in agreeing with Erasmus, who insisted on placing Socrates and Diogenes on the same exalted plane of philosophical worth, but we would err in not recognizing in Diogenes a distinct reflection of the Socratic presence.

Notes

1. A. Schopenhauer, *The World as Will and Representation.* Translated by E.F.J. Payne (Indian Hills, Colo.: The Falcon's Wing Press, 1958), Vol. 2, p. 574.

2. Ibid., Vol. 2, p. 576.

3. Schopenhauer recognized the gap that separated his pessimism from that of the Cynics and rejected as useless their solution to the problem of existence, which, in his view, amounted to renouncing the world, "seeking to disarm every misfortune by preparedness for all and contempt for everything." This "cynical renunciation," he adds, "prefers to reject once for all every means of help and every alleviation. It makes us dogs, like Diogenes in his tub" (ibid., Vol. 2, p. 577).

4. Schopenhauer, *Complete Essays of Schopenhauer.* Translated by T. B. Saunders (New York: Willey Book Company, 1942), Book V, p. 23.

5. For an examination of Schopenhauer's conception of the Will, see L. E. Navia, "The Problem of the Freedom of the Will in the Philosophy of Schopenhauer" (Ph.D. diss. New York University, 1972).

6. For a discussion of Cercidas' Cynicism, see L. E. Navia, *Classical Cynicism: A Critical Study* (Westport, Conn.: Greenwood Press, 1996), pp. 159-166.

7. For a study of Schopenhauer's character determinism, see L. E. Navia, "Schopenhauer's Concept of Character." *The Journal of Critical Analysis* 5 (1974), pp. 85-91.

8. According to Philostratus, who had advised Titus to take Demetrius wherever he went, Titus' response was: "Give me your dog to accompany me, and I will even let him bite me, in case he feels that I am committing injustice" (*Life of Apollonius of Tyana* VI, xxxi). For comments on Demetrius as a watchdog, see Navia, *Classical Cynicism: A Critical Study*, pp. 175ff.

9. See Chapter 1, note 16.

10. An excellent example to a scholar who despite his erudition failed to understand and appreciate classical Cynicism is F. Sayre. His books on the subject are useful for the documentation that they provide, but not for the understanding of Cynicism that they purport to provide. See chapter 1, note 58.

11. According to Diogenes Laertius (IV, 46), this is how Bion introduced himself to Antigonus Gonatas, the Macedonian king (c. 320-239 B.C.): "My father was a freedman, who wiped his nose on his sleeve, a native of Borysthenes, with no face to show, but only the markings on his face, a remainder of his master's cruelty. My mother was the type of woman whom only my father would have chosen for a wife, a whore from a brothel."

12. For a discussion of various biographical details of the lives of Diogenes' Cynic descendants, see Navia, *Classical Cynicism: A Critical Study*, pp. 119-192.

13. K. O. Müller, *A History of the Literature of Ancient Greece*. Translated by G. C. Lewis and J. W. Donaldson (London: Longman, Green, and Co., 1884), Vol. 2, pp. 177-178.

14. D. Henne, "Cynique (École)," in *Dictionnaire des Sciences Philosophiques*. Edited by A. Franck (Paris: Librairie Hachette, 1885), p. 335.

15. Adapted from D. Rieger, *Diogenes als Lumpensammler. Materialen zu einer Gestalt der französischen Literatur des 19. Jahrhunderts* (Munich: Wilhelm Fink Verlag, 1982), p. 20.

16. G. Rudberg, "Zur Diogenes-Tradition." *Symbolæ Osloenses* 14 (1935), pp. 22.

17. The 'socialism' inherent in Diogenes' Cynic revolt has been emphasized by various writers, for instance, I. M. Nakhov, "Der Mensch in der Philosophie der Kyniker," in *Der Mensch als Mass der Dinge. Sudien zum griechischen Menschenbild in der Zeit der Blüte und Krise der Polis*. Edited by R. Müller (Berlin: Akademie-Verlag, 1976), pp. 361-398. The socialistic basis of classical Cynicism has also been underlined by H. Schulz-Falkenthal, who recognized in Diogenes' "*Umwertung aller Werte*" (παραχάραττειν τὸ νόμισμα) a call for a radical questioning of all social values and norms, *and* a commitment to elevate the worth and dignity of the working class. See in this regard his "Zum Arbeitethos der Kyniker." *Wissenschaftliche Zeitschrift der Martin Luther Universität* 29 (1980), pp. 91-101.

18. C. W. Goettling, "Diogenes der Cyniker oder die Philosophie des griechischen Proletariats." *Gesammelte Abhandlungen aus dem classischen Alterthume* (Halle, 1851), p. 275.

19. I use the word 'succession' in the sense in which Diogenes Laertius uses the word διαδοχαί, the meaning of which can be understood in terms of a school of ideas. When the ideas of a philosopher are 'transmitted' to another, we are in the presence of a philosophical succession.

20. O. Wilde, *Sebastian Melmoth*. Quoted in *The Cynics: The Cynic Movement in Antiquity and Its Legacy*. Edited by R. Bracht Branham and M. O. Goulet-Cazé (Berkeley: University of California Press, 1996), p. vii.

21. Quoted in *The Cynics: The Cynic Movement in Antiquity and Its Legacy*. Edited by R. Bracht Branham and M. O. Goulet-Cazé (Berkeley: University of California Press, 1996), p. vii.

22. H. D. Thoreau, *On Civil Disobedience* in *The Fundamental Questions: A Selection of Readings in Philosophy*. Edited by E. Kelly and L. E. Navia (Dubuque, Iowa: Kendall/Hunt, 1997), p. 231.

23. Whether or not there is some justification in ascribing anarchism to Diogenes, is an issue that will be discussed in chapter 4.

24. See, for instance, J. Romm, "Dog Heads and Noble Savages: Cynicism Before the Cynics" in *The Cynics: The Cynic Movement in Antiquity and Its Legacy*. Edited by R. Bracht Branham and M. O. Goulet-Cazé (Berkeley: University of California Press, 1996), pp. 121-135.

25. T. McEvilley, "Early Greek Philosophy and Madhyamika." *Philosophy East and West* 31 (1981), p. 159.

26. A. Syrkin, "The Salutary Descent." *Numen* 35 (1988), pp. 1-23, 213-237.

27. Ctesias of Cnidos (late fifth century B.C.) was a physician in the court of the Persian king Artaxerxes. His ethnographic treatise *Indica* contains valuable information on the Indian Dog Heads. A discussion of Ctesias' account of the Dog Heads is found in Romm, "Dog Heads and Noble Savages," pp. 133ff.

28. D. Ingalls, "Cynics and Pasupatas: The Seeking of Dishonor." *Harvard Theological Review* 55 (1962), pp. 281-298.

29. For comments on Onesicritus' conversation with the Gymnosophists, see Navia, *Classical Cynicism: A Critical Study*, p. 149. Obviously, if Diogenes knew about the Gymnosophists, it is certain that the Gymnosophists, at least those interviewed by Onesicritus, knew nothing about Diogenes, for, otherwise, how could they have objected to *his* respect for the laws of his country?

30. Reliable information about Anacharsis is unavailable. Mentioned by Herodotus and by other sources, he remains a shadowy figure of the early sixth century B.C. Diogenes Laertius (I, 101-105) devoted one of this biographies to him, in which we are told that his mother was Greek and that his father a Scythian nobleman. Many of his maxims and deeds do contain elements that are reminiscent of what the Cynics said and did, for which reason it has been suggested that he could have influenced the tradition that eventually gave rise to Diogenes. See in this regard R. P. Martin, "The Scythian Accent: Anacharsis and the Cynics," in *The Cynics: The Cynic Movement in Antiquity and Its Legacy*. Edited by R. Bracht Branham and M. O. Goulet-Cazé (Berkeley: University of California Press, 1996), pp. 136-155.

31. Simon the Shoemaker is said to have been a friend of Socrates. Historical information about him is meager, although his name is mentioned in various sources, as in the so-called *Epistles of Socrates*. Some archaeological evidence supports that fact that he was a shoemaker during Socrates' time. See in this regard, D. B. Thompson, "The House of Simon the Shoemaker." *Archaeology* 13 (1960), pp. 235-240), and H. A. Thompson, "Excavations in the Athenian Agora." *Hesperia* 23 (1954), pp. 30ff. For comments on the philosophical significance of Simon as a Cynic, see R. F. Hock, "Simon the Shoemaker as an Ideal Cynic." *Greek, Roman and Byzantine Studies* 17 (1976), pp. 41-53. Zoïlus of Amphipolis (c. 400-320 B.C.) was a grammarian whose vitriolic attacks on Homer earned for him the title of "the scourge of Homer" (Homeromastix). His writings also included pieces condemning Plato, Isocrates, and others among his contemporaries. His style and inclination have been viewed by some as a justification for classifying him among the early Cynics. According to Aelian (*Hist. Var.* XI, x), Zoïlus became known as the "Rhetorical Dog" (κύων ῥητορικός). It is unquestionable that even if we do not classify him as a Cynic, the tenor of his writings influenced the Cynics, and that the tradition of Homeromastigy—the tradition of whipping or scourging Homer—was maintained alive among them. For a study of this tradition, specifically as revealed by the Geneva Cynic papyrus (Pap. Genev. inv. 271), see J. T. Katridis, "A Cynic Homeromastix." *Serta Turyaniana: Studies in Greek Literature and Paleography in Honor of Alexander Turyn*. Edited by J. L. Heller (Urbana:

University of Illinois Press, 1974), pp. 361-373.

32. For instance in his *Einleitung in das Verständniss der Weltgeschichte* (Posen, 1841), where Gladisch establishes a parallelism between the Cynics and the Indian Gymnosophists, from whom, he maintains, the Cynic style of life was derived.

33. F. Sayre, *The Greek Cynics* (Baltimore: J. H. Furst, 1948), pp. 39ff.

34. According to Herodotus (IV, 76), Anacharsis was killed for having introduced in Scythia the cult of the Great Mother.

35. Cyzicus was a Milesian colony on the island of Arctonnesus, near the coast of northern Phrygia.

36. See Appendix, note 15.

37. Martin, "The Scythian Accent," p. 155.

38. In regard to the appreciation of Oriental influences on the development of Greek philosophy, Gladisch appears to have been the exception. In various works, he endeavored to show that in practically every single major Greek philosophical contribution, we can discern the presence of Oriental or non-Greek thought. The more traditional approach to the issue, announced clearly by Hegel in his *Lectures on the History of Philosophy*, insisted on the idea that the origin of Greek philosophy had no precedents and was an exclusively Hellenic accomplishment.

39. For a discussion of the role of the idea of λόγος among the Presocratics, see L. E. Navia, "The Meaning and Origin of Philosophy," in Kelly and Navia, *The Fundamental Questions*, pp. 1-33.

40. Protagoras of Abdera was an older contemporary of Socrates and one of the most influential among the Sophists.

41. Critias (c. 460-403 B.C.) was a relative of Plato and at some point an associate of Socrates. A Sophist of some literary talent, he was the leader of the Thirty, who in 404 B.C. assumed the control of Athens. In one of his works, of which a long fragment has been preserved, Critias offers a rationalistic explanation of the origins of religious beliefs, arguing that the tales about the gods were invented by the ruling classes for the purpose of manipulating the masses.

42. Some statements associated with Heraclitus have been occasionally ascribed to Diogenes. Heraclitus' conviction that most people live as if in a deep state of sleep is reminiscent of what the Cynics said concerning the cloud of mist or fog (τῦφος) that envelops human existence. Likewise, Heraclitus' contempt for the masses appears in statements ascribed to Diogenes, who could have said what Heraclitus is reported to have said: "What intelligence or understanding do people have? They believe in the stories of the poets and accept only the populace as their teacher, not knowing that the majority are bad and the good are few" (Frag. 104). Heraclitus' advise to the people of Ephesus, namely, that they should hang themselves for being morally worthless (Frag. 121), reminds us of Diogenes. The influence of Heraclitus' philosophy on the development of Cynicism has been recognized by various scholars. See, for instance, J. F. Kindstrand, "The Cynics and Heraclitus." *Eranos* 82 (1984), pp. 149-178.

43. In the *Crito* (50d-54c), the Platonic Socrates argues that obedience to the laws is the necessary condition for the existence of civilized communities and that, consequently, those who disregard or break the laws of the State are ultimately calling for its destruction.

44. Thrasymachus of Chalcedon (late fifth century B.C.) was a Sophist, who is known to us through the testimony of Plato's *Republic*, where he is depicted as defending the view that justice is a game played in the interest of those who control society (*Republic* 336b ff.). If Plato's testimony about him is accurate, there is ample justification in regarding him as an ethical nihilist, that is, a man for whom moral values amount to nothing.

45. For a discussion of the common roots of Cynicism and Skepticism, see M. Luz, "Cynics as Allies of Scepticism," in *Scepticism: Inter-Disciplinary Approaches. Proceedings of the Second International Symposium on Philosophy and Inter-Disciplinary Research. September 27-31, 1988* (Athens: The Ministry of Culture, 1990), pp. 101-114.

46. Diogenes Laertius (III, 35) tells us that once, when Socrates heard someone reading from Plato's *Lysis*, he exclaimed, "By Hercules, what a collection of lies this young man has written about me!"

47. A. Machado, "Un loco," in *Obras. Poesia y Prosa* (Buenos Aires: Editorial Losada, 1964), p. 140.

48. Aeschines of Athens was an associate of Socrates and the author of Socratic dialogues, only fragments of which are extant.

49. Aristippus of Cyrene was an associate of Socrates and the founder of the Cyrenaic school of philosophy.

50. Polycrates of Athens, a younger contemporary of Socrates, was a rhetorician. He composed a piece of anti-Socratic literature entitled Κατηγορία Σωκράτους (*The Indictment of Socrates*) that can be partly reconstructed from the *Declamations* of Libanius. Diogenes Laertius (II, 38) suggests that Polycrates' work was written as the speech that Meletus, one of the prosecutors of Socrates, was expected to read in court. For an examination of Polycrates' work, especially in relation to Xenophon and Libanius, see J. Mesk, "Die Anklagerede des Polykrates gegen Sokrates." *Wiener Studien* 32 (1911), pp. 56-84.

51. For a documented examination of the sources of information concerning Socrates, see L. E. Navia, *The Socratic Presence: A Study of the Sources* (New York: Garland Publishing, 1993). For the vast and exceedingly varied bibliography that has been produced about the sources, consult L. E. Navia, *Socrates: An Annotated Bibliography* (New York: Garland Publishing, 1988), especially the chapter on the Socratic problem (pp. 105-120).

52. The views imputed to Socrates in Plato's *Crito* have given rise to much controversy among scholars, some of whom have called attention of their inconsistency with Socrates' stance of independence and defiance in Plato's *Apology*, while others claim to be unable to detect any such inconsistency. For an annotated bibliography on the *Crito* and on Socrates' political ideas, see Navia, *Socrates: An Annotated Bibliography*, pp. 339-358. The idea that Plato's rendition of Socrates in the *Crito* and, in fact, throughout his dialogues is a travesty of Socrates' personality and thought is defended by K. Popper in his *The Open*

Society and Its Enemies (New York: Harper Torchbooks, 1963). Popper compares the Platonic "perversion" of Socrates to Fichte's "deformation of Kantian philosophy." The latter, Popper writes, "happened only one hundred years ago and can be easily checked by anybody who takes the trouble to read Kant's and Fichte's letters, and Kant's public announcements; and it shows that my theory of Plato's perversion of the teaching of Socrates is by no means so fantastic" (Vol. 2, p. 313).

53. In Plato's *Apology* (30e), Socrates describes himself as a gadfly sent by God to awaken the Athenians from a state of spiritual slumber.

54. Socrates' 'arrogance' (μεγαληγορία), according to Xenophon (*Apology* 1), was noticed by those who were present at his trial, and it was, he says, for the purpose of giving an adequate explanation of it that he wrote his *Apology*. The disdain with which Socrates dealt with the threats of the prosecutors and with the supreme power of the jurors, also attested to in Plato's *Apology*, was an apparent manifestation of a proud and unyielding mind.

55. W.K.C. Guthrie, *Socrates* (London: Cambridge University Press, 1977), p. 163.

56. Socrates' elenchus (ἔλεγχος), which in Plato's seventh letter (*Epist.* 7.344b) is defined as "a disputation by use of question and answer," was a structured way to search for the truth by analyzing the language of those with whom he conversed. For a discussion of the Socratic elenchus, see G. Vlastos, "The Socratic Elenchus," in *Oxford Studies in Ancient Philosophy*. Edited by J. Annas (Oxford: The Clarendon Press, 1983), Vol. 1, pp. 27-59.

57. Among the most celebrated statements of Socrates is his reference to himself as a midwife (μαῖα). In the *Theaetetus* (149a-151e), he reminds us that his mother was a midwife and that he, like her, is also engaged in midwifery, but with a difference: for, whereas his mother aided women in the process of childbirth, he, for his part, helps people give birth to thoughts.

58. In the *Phaedo* (118a), Plato describes Socrates as "our comrade, who was, we may fairly say, of all those whom we knew in our time, the bravest and also the wisest and most upright man." Xenophon's *Apology* (32) concludes with this remarkable words of encomium: "As for myself, as I reflect on Socrates' wisdom and nobility of character, I am unable either to forget him or, in remembering him, to refrain from praising him."

59. The court of the King-Archon was the court before which Socrates was tried and sentenced to death in 399 B.C. Presided by one of the archons or chief Athenian magistrates, it was composed of 501 jurors selected yearly to hear cases involving irreligiosity or impiety (ἀσέβεια). As in the case of all other Athenian juries, its decisions were final and unappealable.

60. A. A. Long, "The Socratic Tradition: Diogenes, Crates, and Hellenistic Ethics," in *The Cynics: The Cynic Movement in Antiquity and Its Legacy*. Edited by R. Bracht Branham and M. O. Goulet-Cazé (Berkeley: University of California Press, 1996), p. 45.

61. Ibid., p. 28, where Long notes that "the early Stoics can be assumed to have readily propagated such stories, determined as they were to connect their founder with Socrates. Hence they publicized the philosophical succession Socrates, Antisthenes, Diogenes, Crates, Zeno. In the Stoic canon of saints and quasi saints, Socrates and Diogenes form a ubiquitous duo."

62. A. H. Chroust, "The Antisthenian Elements in the Two Apologies of Xenophon," in *Socrates: Man and Myth; The Two Socratic Apologies of Xenophon* (Notre Dame, Ind.: University of Notre Dame Press, 1957), pp. 101-163.

63. There is a recurrent representation of Antisthenes, both in the sources and in modern literature, that, although somewhat idealized, reflects well his spirit after Socrates' death: "Wearing only a cloak, barefoot, a beggar's wallet on his shoulder, his beard and hair in disarray, holding a walking stick, he sought, through his example, and offering no other attractive feature than such a miserable appearance, to lead human beings to the simplicity of nature" ("Antisthène," in *Dictionnaire des Sciences Philosophiques*. Edited by A. Franck, Paris: Librairie Hachette, 1885, p. 76).

64. Sayre, *Diogenes of Sinope: A Study of Greek Cynicism* (Baltimore: J. H. Furst, 1938), p. 60. It is not unfair to affirm that Sayre's treatment of Antisthenes, no less than his treatment of Diogenes and other Cynics, provides an example of a scholarly petitio principii, the fallacy of assuming in the premises of an argument the conclusion that is to be proven. Sayre begins by assuming (1) that the Cynics were worthless charlatans, (2) that practically all the information provided by the sources is fiction and fabrication, and (3) that Antisthenes was himself a respectable Socratic philosopher. Accordingly, he concludes that whatever Cynicism could have been, Antisthenes had nothing to do with it. How strange for a scholar to have wasted his energies in so empty and worthless a philosophical movement!

65. Long, "The Socratic Tradition," p. 45.

66. Antisthenes' contributions in logic and the theory of language have been subjected to much scrutiny in modern times, and the most divergent assessments have emerged. G.M.A. Grube, for example, minimizes the significance of Antisthenes' ideas on logic and describes him as "an earnest, blunt, vigorous and sharp-witted man," whose logical works are only "obviously moral diatribes" ("Antisthenes Was No Logician." *Transactions and Proceedings of the American Philological Association* 81, 1959, p. 24). For a more positive study of Antisthenes' denial of the meaningfulness of predication, see H. D. Rankin, "Οὐκ ἔστιν ἀντιλέγειν," in *The Sophists and Their Legacy*. Edited by G. B. Kerferd (Wiesbaden: Steiner, 1981), pp. 25-37, and "That It Is Impossible to Say 'Not' and Related Topics in Antisthenes." *International Logic Review* 10 (1979), pp. 51-98.

67. For an examination of Antisthenes' views on definition and language, see C. M. Gillespie, "The Logic of Antisthenes." *Archiv für Geschichte der Philosophie* 26 (1913), pp. 479-500; 27 (1914), pp. 17-38, and A. Brancacci, Οἰκεῖος λόγος. *La filosofia del linguaggio di Antistene* (Naples: Bibliopolis, 1990).

68. There is no need to reject prima facie the report that Antisthenes recommended that neither reading nor writing should be learned, as F. Decleva Caizzi does (*Antisthenis fragmenta*, Milan: Istituto Editoriale Cisalpino, 1966, p. 111), on the basis that he was a learned man and a prolific writer. It is not inconceivable that such a recommen-

dation may belong to a period in his life when, possibly after Socrates' death, he realized that reading and writing are futile endeavors that promote neither virtue nor happiness.

69. Solid historical information about Secundus is lacking. For a discussion of the available information about him and a translation of the anonymous work *The Greek Life of Secundus*, see B. E. Perry, *Secundus the Silent Philosopher* (Ithaca, N.Y.: Cornell University Press, 1964).

70. Sayre, *Diogenes of Sinope: A Study of Greek Cynicism*, p. 58.

71. There is no certainty concerning the year when Antisthenes met Socrates, although various references in the sources allow us to advance a reasonable supposition. First, there is possibly a tacit allusion to Antisthenes in Plato's *Sophist* 251b, where we hear about "certain elders who have taken to learning philosophy late in life." What "late in life" means is unclear, except for the fact that it establishes a contrast with Plato's own first encounter with Socrates — when Plato was a young man. Secondly, the *literary* date of Xenophon's *Symposium* seems to be around the year 421 B.C., and it is clear from the content of this work that the friendship between Socrates and Antisthenes was already firmly established. Thirdly, in Libanius' *Apology of Socrates* (v, 23), Antisthenes is described as "an older man" at the time of Socrates' death. Combining these three references and a few others, we can say that Antisthenes may have become an associate of Socrates around the year 425 B.C., just about the time when Gorgias left the city.

72. It is known that after the execution of Socrates some of the Socratics, including Plato, left Athens, possibly out of fear of accusations similar to those lodged against Socrates. Antisthenes, however, seems to have remained, as if willing to face any eventuality. Diogenes Laertius (VI, 10) reports that he was responsible for the punishment inflicted by the State upon the accusers of Socrates, Meletus having been executed, while Anytus was exiled. From a historical perspective, nothing is known about such punishments, and it appears that the story is a typical Cynic χρεία that still does not lack in value: Antisthenes, recognized in antiquity as the most authentic follower of Socrates and as his closest associate, is made responsible for attempting to redress the wrong wrought upon his master.

73. C. Chappuis, *Antisthène* (Paris: Auguste Durand, Libraire, 1854), p. 20.

74. Schopenhauer, *The World as Will and Representation*, Vol. 2, p. 616.

75. Much has been written about Antisthenes' view of pleasure and on his apparent wavering between asceticism and hedonism. For a balanced treatment of this matter, see A. Brancacci, "Érotique et théorie du plaisir chez Antisthène," in *Le Cynisme ancien et ses prolongements. Actes du Colloque International du CNRS*. Edited by M. O. Goulet-Cazé and R. Goulet (Paris: Presses Universitaires de France, 1993), pp. 35-55. For a discussion of the passage in Xenophon's *Symposium* in which Antisthenes speaks about his involvement with women, see P. Roy, "Antisthenes' Affairs with Athenian Women: Xenophon, *Symposium* iv, 38." *Liverpool Classical Monthly* 10 (1985), pp. 132-133.

76. For a study of the transformation of Socrates' irony into Cynic contempt, see L. Ucciani, *De l'ironie socratique à la dérision cynique. Éléments pour une critique par les formes exclues* (Paris: Les Belles Lettres, 1993).

Chapter 4

The Building Blocks of Cynicism

In his discussion of Cynicism, Hegel notes that "there is nothing particular to say about the Cynics, for they possessed but little philosophy, and did not bring what they had into a scientific system."[1] He concludes that the Cynics were,

> generally speaking, nothing more than swinish beggars, who found their satisfaction in the insolence that they showed others. They are worthy of no further consideration in philosophy, and they deserve fully the name of dogs, which was early given to them; for the dog is a shameless animal.[2]

Although this last statement is meant to apply especially to the late Cynics of Roman times, it is unquestionable that Hegel had little regard for the philosophical basis of Cynicism in general and of Diogenes' thought in particular. Even about Antisthenes he had nothing positive to say: "Antisthenes' principles," he writes, "are simple, because the content of his teaching remains general; it is hence superfluous to say anything further about it."[3]

Hegel's estimate of the philosophical basis and value of Cynicism has had considerable influence on subsequent modern scholars and popular writers, from many of whom we hear repeatedly the same negative assessment. G. H. Lewes, for instance, speaks about Cynicism as "an imposing blasphemy"[4] and as "a very preposterous doctrine,"[5] and adds that

> that which prevents our feeling the respect for the Cynics which the ancients seem to have felt, and which, indeed, some portions of the Cynical doctrine would otherwise induce us to feel, is the studious and uncalled-for outrages on common decency and humanity which Diogenes, especially, perpetrated.[6]

Such a view of Cynicism has been echoed vehemently by others, for whom, it seems, even one serious thought about Diogenes would be a wasted thought, except perhaps for the purpose of debunking what has been called "the Diogenes legend."[7] What benefit, they argue, could there be in examining the ideas and actions of someone who was and remains an embarrassing philosophical scandal?

In recent times, however, especially since the publication of D. R. Dudley's *A History of Cynicism from Diogenes to the 6th Century A.D.* in 1937, the need for a fresh reappraisal of the contributions of the Cynics, especially those of Diogenes, has been increasingly felt, and various important studies on the subject have surfaced and continue to surface. R. Höistad's *Cynic Hero and Cynic King: Studies in the Cynic Conception of Man*, for instance, has forced us to view classical Cynicism in a new light and to return to what Lewes called "the respect for the Cynics that the ancients seem to have felt." This process has been strengthened by new and refreshing studies on Antisthenes and in particular on his relationship with the Socratic philosophy. Increasingly, too, the importance of Antisthenes as possibly the most authentic witness of the Socratic presence has been recognized, and his place as the originator of the Cynic movement, seldom questioned in ancient times, has been reasserted by recent scholarly work. Thus, the canonical tradition that links Diogenes to Antisthenes, and Antisthenes to Socrates, appears to have undergone a process of positive reassessment. Likewise, the unquestionable ideological connection between Cynicism and Stoicism has been reappraised, and this has led to the conclusion that the ideas and mode of life of the early Cynics, particularly Diogenes, must be examined with great care, because it is in them that we find, not only the presence of genuine Socratic elements, but also the seeds that would later fructify in the philosophy of the Stoics. We can readily agree in this regard with a statement of A. A. Long, who observes that "of all the routes by which Socrates' philosophy was transmitted to the Hellenistic world, that followed by the Cynics was the most startling and, in certain respects, the most influential."[8]

The recent efforts to reappraise the worth of classical Cynicism have yielded fruitful results, especially in what concerns the contributions of Diogenes. The man who was called a "Socrates-gone-mad" may not have been mad after all. His 'madness' may turn out to be something quite different from what his contemporaries saw in him and from what some modern scholars insist on detecting in him. Once the basis of his philosophy is understood and once the building blocks of his Cynicism are put together, his 'madness' becomes philosophically understandable, although probably impossible to duplicate. If we have the patience to sift through the evidence, and the necessary perspicuity to see *through and behind* the anecdotes and reports, with all their jokes and occasional vulgarity, with all their exhibitionism and histrionics, with all their half-valid ascriptions and exaggerations, what we may find is not a crackpot philosopher or a psychopath, or a "good-for-nothing" man whose only interest was to call attention to himself through his outrageous antics, or a charlatan who had little, if anything, to offer in the realm of ideas. Then, we may not be as easily tempted to dismiss him as an inconsequential man during his own time and as an irrelevant philosopher in modern times. We could then discover that his ideas, veiled as they may have been under a mantle of histrionic and theatrical manifestations, were firmly implanted in his consciousness, and that his mission, outlandish and preposterous as it may have appeared (and still appears) in the eyes of the advocates of the Establishment and the status quo, was well designed and very carefully executed. His sense of urgency and his compulsive diatribal style would then be explainable, not only by reference to what he himself was, but also by reference to what the human world around him was. How could a sensible man, Diogenes might have often pondered, think and behave differently in a world in which, as Plato puts it in the *Republic* (6.496d), a man of clear mind—a philosopher—is like "a man who has fallen among wild beasts, and who is unwilling to share in their misdeeds, and is unable to hold out singly against their savagery?"

We might not be mistaken in affirming that what distinguishes Diogenes from many other philosophers and people in general, past and present, is this, namely, that he recognized the spiritual poverty and the moral depravity of his world, and was able and willing to denounce it in word and in deed, without even one passing thought about the consequences that such a mode of life could bring to him. Other philosophers have sometimes recognized what Diogenes once did, but have had neither the ability nor, more often, the will to denounce it. To *them*, not to Diogenes, we could apply the words of Ovid in *Metamorphoses* VII, 20: "*Video meliora, proboque; deteriora sequor*" (I see what is good and I approve of it; and yet, I do what is bad).[9] There are many who may be aware of the absurdity inherent in much of what people do, but who, unlike Diogenes, are unwilling or incapable to oppose it. The essence of Diogenes' 'madness' is the singularity of his reaction to the world, a reaction that was relevant not only to his own time and culture, but to any other time and culture. The elements of human nature that he denounced have remained unchanged, and the intellectual confusion and moral depravity of his contemporaries have not diminished with the passing of time. The statement of D'Alembert quoted in the previous chapter remains as true today as it did in the eighteenth century or in the fourth century B.C.: "Every century needs the presence of a Diogenes," if nothing else to serve as an awakening call of conscience in the midst of the intellectual slumber and moral moroseness that characterize human existence. We may add that every century also needs the courage to endure the presence of a Diogenes in order to force itself into an examination of conscience and a reevaluation of the moral 'currency', for the presence of a genuine Cynic in our midst can serve as a useful corrective to our confusions and inertia. It is for this reason that on repeated occasions the ghost of Diogenes has been conjured back from his grave or, if we remember Cercidas' epigram,[10] from his celestial abode, for when nothing else seems to work, the presence of a barking and biting dog can at least keep us awake and aware of the right track. Foucault's 'return' to Diogenes manifests clearly the need of those who have themselves attained some degree of intellectual lucidity, and who hunger for existential honesty, to resurrect the man who insisted on calling things by the right name and who practiced so unabatedly the art of 'saying it all', which goes by the name of παρρησία (*parrhesia*) and is a fundamental concept of Cynicism.[11]

In an earlier chapter we endeavored to lay bare and elucidate the *practice* of Cynicism as exemplified by Diogenes, and the comment was made that this practice must be understood as the manifestation of a set of convictions that were sufficiently strong to determine and structure the conduct of his life. We would be in error if we were to assume that Diogenes' practice of Cynicism did not spring from a theoretical ground, just as we would be wrong if we insisted on dealing with this theoretical ground in isolation from its practical manifestations, because with Diogenes, theory and practice were intimately intertwined and almost indistinguishable. The exaggerated emphasis on behavioral manifestations, in terms of which most reports about Diogenes are couched, may easily lead us to ignore the theory behind such manifestations, or, as with certain scholars, even to deny its very existence and to conceive of his Cynicism merely as a way of life or a religion.[12] The problem is that in Diogenes, we generally *witness* a certain action, or *hear* a comment about this or that specific circumstance, or *see* a certain physical movement, but seldom, if ever, do we come upon a discourse about his ideas and convictions in his own words or even in the words of those who wrote about him. Perhaps if the writings attributed to him were extant, we might be able to have a window to look into the recesses of his mind, but in the absence of such writings, we are confined to the secondary sources that, as we have seen, take generally the path of anecdotal reports that describe his *practice* of Cynicism, not the underlying theoretical basis that could have supported it. Still, it would be unimaginable that a man who was so greatly influenced by Antisthenes and by the Socratic tradition, and whose life exhibited so remarkable a degree of consistency and directedness, would have simply spoken and acted without a set of firmly held convictions. The eccentricity of Diogenes' conduct, as V. Brochard noted, can lead us to ignore the greatness of his convictions, especially his moral principles.[13] We would then be no different from the crowds of gaping onlookers who surrounded him, peeping at his antics and listening to his strange comments, without the slightest idea as to their meaning and origin.

The question, therefore, that confronts us now is what those convictions could have been and what the underlying theoretical basis of Diogenes' Cynicism was. Obviously, this question is not easy to answer, for the sources lend us only the most limited assistance. For a discursive account of Diogenes' ideas, we must appeal to Roman sources, such as certain writings of Epictetus, Dio Chrysostom, and Emperor Julian, but in them, it is not a simple matter to separate the genuine elements that could have belonged to Diogenes' philosophy from those that are of Stoic heritage, because one of the two branches of early Cynicism that grew out of Diogenes' philosophy and practice—the most sophisticated and fruitful, we might say—blended itself so intimately with Stoicism that it lost its Cynic distinctiveness. When Epictetus, for instance, endeavored to reconstruct the principles of Diogenes' thought and to vindicate its value as a meaningful philosophical option, it is hard to say whether he was giving expression more to his own Stoic leanings than to what may have been the actual core of Diogenes' Cynic stance. Moreover, the section of Diogenes Laertius' biography (VI, 73) that deals with Diogenes' opinions (δόξαι) is unfortunately brief and sketchy, and, belonging as it does to an unknown source borrowed by the biographer, cannot give us a clear and reliable representation of Diogenes' thought. Here, too, the presence of Stoic conceptions may be indiscriminately mixed with elements of Diogenes' philosophy.

From the *other* branch of Cynicism that sprang from Diogenes, moreover, little assistance seems to be forthcoming. This branch, represented by the innumerable Cynics of the Hellenistic and Roman world, remained surely more faithful to the external aspects of Diogenes' Cynicism than his Stoic descendants, and maintained truly alive the spirit of revolt against the 'currency' of late classical times, but lacked the theoretical structure that we suspect was present in Diogenes. The late Cynics furnish us with wonderful examples of what constitutes a Cynic with regard to his mode of life, his attire, his condemning and barking at institutions and values, and other similar aspects of Cynicism, but give us no meaningful clues concerning their beliefs and convictions, for which reason Julian was probably justified in attempting to resurrect what he viewed as the genuine spirit of Diogenes, while thundering against the Cynics of his time and accusing them of being thoughtless people. We encounter a similar situation in the instance of Lucian of Samosata, the great satirist, who spared no efforts in ridiculing Cynicism as an empty husk containing nothing and meaning nothing, except a series of bombastic manifestations of dissatisfaction with the world, as he makes it abundantly clear in his treatment of the life and suicide of Peregrinus Proteus. Lucian, himself a sort of Cynic, did not fail to realize that the Cynics of his time had lost most of what was valuable in the earlier Cynics—Antisthenes, Diogenes, Crates—that is, the conceptual basis of their Cynicism. The Cynics of late Roman times, in Lucian's view, had kept the appearance of Cynicism, but had forgotten its essence.

Epictetus, for his part, also condemning the Cynics of his time, reminds us of the gap that separated them from Diogenes. As a certain young man, who was considering becoming a Cynic, approached Epictetus in search for guidance, the philosopher offered him these reflections:

> Think carefully about this matter, for it is not by any means what you

think it is. "I will wear a rough cloak, and I will sleep on a hard bed. I will carry with me only a wallet and a walking stick, and I will begin to go from place to place, begging for my sustenance and reviling all those who cross my path. And if I see anyone getting rid of superfluous hair or cutting his hair in a fancy way, or walking about in scarlet clothes, I will come down hard on him." If you think that this is what Cynicism is, keep yourself as far from it as you can. Don't even think about coming near it, for it has nothing to do with you. But if you are able to understand it correctly, begin by considering the magnitude of the enterprise that you are about to undertake. (*Discourses* III, xxii, 9-12)

The important idea in this passage is clearly that genuine Cynicism cannot be viewed merely as a practice. A leathern wallet, a wooden staff, bare feet, disheveled hair, a harsh voice, a barking and snarling attitude, living in a tub, gesturing obscenities at mindless and wicked people—these are only the external manifestations of Cynicism, not its essence or its guiding force. For those who are contemplating becoming Cynics, if indeed one can become a Cynic by an act of will, Epictetus' advise makes sense: first gain an *understanding* of what Cynicism is before you put on the Cynic uniform. For us, moreover, his advise would not be altogether different: we must first pierce through the appearances and manifestations in order to arrive at the conceptual basis of Cynicism.

It must be emphasized that in the search of such a conceptual basis, especially in regard to Diogenes' Cynicism, we should not expect to find a *system* of philosophy, or not even a cogent and well-arranged collection of philosophical statements. Already beginning with Socrates and Antisthenes, but far more in the context of Diogenes, philosophical ideas became subservient to immediate moral concerns,[14] and speculation for its own sake and the need to establish philosophical concepts within the framework of a system began to be set aside. Hence, the building blocks of Diogenes' Cynicism cannot be neatly arranged in a systematic or hierarchical scheme, for which reason his philosophy gives the impression of being a truncated collection of insights and undeveloped notions about the world and about human existence. Diogenes' Cynicism is primarily a philosophy of revolt[15] and a reaction against what he perceived to be the dismal spectacle of human existence, and consequently it should not surprise us to find that his ideas lack the completeness and development that we may encounter in other philosophers. Undoubtedly, the negativism of his life and the overwhelming force of his mission as a defacer of values prevented him from putting the building blocks of his thought into a well developed philosophical edifice, but this circumstance, as the fundamental characteristic of his mission, is perhaps what paradoxically constitutes the real merit of his accomplishment. He challenged, rejected, ridiculed, dismissed, condemned, and literally defaced the 'currency' of his time and set for us an example how we, too, should be prepared to do likewise in a true Cynic spirit. Much more he did not accomplish, but in accomplishing what he did, he did more than most other people of his time and of all subsequent times.

Still, despite the truncated and incomplete character of Diogenes' philosophy, it is possible to identify its building blocks and to arrange them in some sort of order that, on the basis of *our* reflections on the matter, makes some sense. These blocks can be arranged in two categories, first a series of *propositions* and secondly a collection of Cynic *concepts*. These propositions and concepts emerge in the testimonies about Diogenes only in passing and almost incidentally, a circumstance that is explainable by reference to the fact that he was reluctant to use discursive language to give expression to his thought: he preferred to *show* and *exemplify* it through actions and gestures rather than to give a linguistic account of it. Moreover, for their development, we must wait either for the Stoics or for the later Cynics, but by then, the spirit of revolt and the Cynic enthusiasm that permeated their genesis in Diogenes' mind would be somewhat diminished: both the Stoics and the later Cynics were often willing to make peace with the world and use its 'currency'. Furthermore, while some of the building blocks of Diogenes' Cynicism appear to have been created by him, others are as ancient as philosophy itself and can be found among the Presocratics and the Sophists, and particularly in Socrates and Antisthenes. Still others emerge in Diogenes in a blurry outline and are found with some degree of precision only in his successors, both among the Stoics and the later Cynics.

The *first* proposition of Diogenes' thought can be stated thus: the one and only object of philosophy is human existence, and any other object can only be a source of distraction and an inconsequential way to satisfy the unhealthy sense of curiosity that afflicts human beings. To Protagoras' assertion that Man is the measure of all things, that is, the only point of reference that invests the world with meaning, Diogenes would have given his unqualified assent. The universe at large, with its countless worlds and stars, the realm of nature, with its innumerable species and phenomena, and the very structure of Being that so powerfully engaged the imagination of the Presocratics—all these things and the human concerns about them are to be ignored and bracketed away. For Diogenes, no less than for Socrates, the world begins and ends with the presence of every human being. Science, metaphysics, and all sorts of intellectual activities that transcend human existence had, accordingly, no significance for him.

The *second* proposition is this: in our endeavor to make sense of human existence, we must direct our attention exclusively to this physical world in which we live. Other worlds and other dimensions may or may not exist. We may have existed as disembodied spirits and as other people before our birth, and may yet remain in existence after death, as is maintained in religious creeds, but however that may be, the truth is that no one can claim to *know* anything about such things. In matters of religion, therefore, we must suspend judgment and be willing to confess our ignorance. We may still entertain what Socrates calls in the *Phaedo* (114d) pious hopes about another world, but must not convert such hopes into articles of faith, for that would be intellectual dishonesty. Concerning God or the gods, and concerning the stories about divine intervention in human affairs that abound in religious traditions, we really know nothing, and neither do we know anything about the efficacy of religious rituals and practices, nor about the legitimacy of those who claim to speak on behalf of God or the gods, for which reason Diogenes displayed so disdainful an attitude towards all matters related to religious beliefs and practices.[16] Oracles and divination, as we saw in chapter 1, were viewed by Diogenes as ways in which simple-minded people hide their ignorance under a mantle of false knowledge. Once again, Diogenes would have given his unqualified assent to a statement attributed to Protagoras: "As for the gods, I have no way of knowing whether they exist or not; nor, if they exist, what their nature could be. For the obstacles to that sort of knowledge are many, including the obscurity of the subject and the brevity of human life" (Frag. 4).

Protagoras' phrase "the brevity of human life" can lead us now to an important aspect of Diogenes' thought. That every human life is short and ephemeral, and that, before we realize it, it has passed from us like water through our fingers, does not need to be emphasized, except for the strange fact that most people live as if they were going to live forever in this world, planning ahead quite convinced of the certainty of the future, as if they could continue in existence for endless ages. Reality, however, intrudes upon our activities, constantly reminding us that neither is the future an assured possession, nor is the past a retrievable commodity. Only the here-and-now actually exists for us—the present moment—and the collection of moments that constitutes each human life soon comes to an end, often when least expected. Therefore, Diogenes might have reasoned, given the brevity and uncertainty of life, would it not make more sense to live each moment as if it were the only moment and each day as if it were the last day? Here then we come upon the *third* proposition of Diogenes' Cynicism: live each moment as if it were the only moment of life. This explains his preoccupation with the immediacy of human existence and his disinterest in all other human concerns such as the historical past, the future, the actions and behavior of people who are distant and unrelated to us, the world of gossip that goes by the name of 'the news', and so on. Indeed, Diogenes lived as if the entire world were limited to what he could see and hear in his surroundings, as each morning he would emerge from his tub.

Aside from its brevity and uncertainty, human life has yet another inherent characteristic that Diogenes and other Cynics after him must have recognized with great clarity. From birth to death, even though we struggle so frantically to be happy, both personally and collectively happiness manifests itself as something elusive and deceiving, and life turns out to be a constant oscillation between misery and boredom, happiness being only the brief transitory passage from one extreme to another. To avoid boredom, people invent distractions and pastimes, and all forms of entertainment, and to shun misery, they seek pleasures and excitement, and devise complicated and ingenious ways to attempt to circumvent the conditions under which nature meant for human beings to live. Somehow, however, neither individually nor collectively happiness is attained, and nothing, not even the dreams and illusions perpetuated by religion, or the grandiose schemes created in the name of nationalism, appears to render it more accessible. But why should this be so? Why the senseless going back and forth in all directions in the search for that which, like an enticing ghost, eludes us each time we come close to it? "Instead of useless toils," Diogenes noted (D.L. VI, 71), "people should choose those that nature recommends and that lead to a happy life. Yet, so great is people's madness that they choose to be miserable," and they do so precisely by identifying happiness with what happiness is not and by searching for it where it cannot be found. In their vain quest for happiness they only succeed in rendering it more inaccessible not only for themselves, but for everybody else.

Herein lies the *fourth* proposition of Diogenes' thought: happiness cannot be achieved as long as we fail to understand its nature, for this failure makes us look for it where it does not reside. Hence, the aim of philosophy must be conceived of as the correct understanding of happiness, and its purpose as the rendering of human life happy, any other aim or purpose being either inconsequential or detrimental. Julian captured well this point when he insisted that "the happy life is regarded as the goal and final aim in the philosophy of the Cynics" (*Or.* VI).[17] In attempting to make sense of Diogenes' choice of life as a destitute mendicant, Seneca, too, understood the point when he remarked: "We must consider [according to Diogenes] how much less painful it is not to have something than to lose it, and we should understand that the poor have less to suffer the less they have to lose" (*De tranquillitate animi* viii).

In enthroning happiness as the only aim of philosophy, Diogenes was obviously not unique, for practically all major philosophers, from Aristotle to the Utilitarians, have placed this idea at the very center of their ethical philosophies. Differences, however, surface as soon as we begin to consider (1) what the nature of happiness is and (2) what the means for its attainment are, and it is here that Diogenes' thought gains in distinctiveness and uniqueness, especially in the context of those philosophers who are unrelated to Cynicism. For with him, happiness has a specific meaning and the path that leads to it is precisely delineated,[18] and here then we encounter the *fifth* proposition of Diogenes' thought: happiness, understood in its Greek sense of εὐδαιμονία (that is, well-being) cannot be defined in terms of possessions, pleasures, comfort, power, fame, erudition, a long life, and other similar things that, in the opinion of ordinary people, are its essential components. The opinions of the multitude, as Julian reports (*Or.* VI), were, in Diogenes' view, only worthy of rejection, especially in what concerns the understanding of happiness. According to Ibn-Hindu (Diogenes 30), he is reported to have said that anybody who wants to be happy must begin by following a path that runs contrary to that of the majority of people, an idea that he exemplified by entering the theaters at the end of the performances, just as the spectators were leaving, or by walking backwards through the streets of Athens.

But, then, if happiness is not what people think it is, what could it be? What could be the path that is contrary to that of the multitude? Diogenes' answer, particularly through the example of his life, furnishes us with the *sixth* proposition of his thought: happiness is living in accordance with nature (κατὰ φύσιν). But, again, what could this mean, for the answer is bound to remain unclear unless we gain some understanding of the meaning of 'nature'? Could it be that in saying this, Diogenes was advocating a return to primitivism and to a theriomorphic transformation of human beings into animals, preferably into undomesticated dogs? Could it entail a total renunciation of all the accomplishments and advantages of civilized life, and a casting away of the artificiality with which historical and cultural 'progress' has invested human existence? Diogenes claimed to have learned how to live well by watching the behavior of a mouse in the marketplace. Once, as we have seen, he threw away his cup after seeing a boy drinking water out of his hands, saying that he was not aware until then that "nature had already provided him with a cup" (Saint Jerome, *Adv. Jovin.* II, xiv). Again, those, who report that his death was caused by his eating a raw octopus, maintain that he ate it raw because he did not believe in the use of fire. Other examples of this return to 'naturalism' abound in the sources. In chapter 2 we had the opportunity of mentioning some of them, and a review of them could lead us to the hasty conclusion that he was indeed a primitive man who defined happiness in terms of a return to the most primitive modes of life. What else indeed could we say about someone who attended to his physical needs in public, who lived in the streets or in a tub, who ate raw meat, who in his writings had no compunction about cannibalism and incest, and who proudly called himself a dog? For dogs, at least wild and street dogs, live fully in accordance with nature. For them, neither conventions, nor complicated norms, nor etiquette, nor manners, nor 'the proper way of doing things', nor the distinction between what is right and what is wrong, have any meaning. They belong to no country and pledge allegiance to no flag, and are not burdened by titles or possessions. Neither are they consumed in thoughts or perplexities about the nature of virtue or about the immortality of the soul, nor do they have the ability to pass judgment as to what is natural and what is not. They simply live and die precisely as nature intended them to live and die.

It has been alleged that Diogenes' advocacy of a life lived according to nature involves a call for the return to bestiality, with all the connotations and consequences that this entails—antisocial behavior, anarchism, brutality, aloofness, and similar 'bestial' forms of behavior.[19] Nevertheless, a balanced review of the evidence points in another direction, even if we are willing to lend credence to the most uncomplimentary reports about the man in the tub. For side by side with Diogenes' call for a return to nature and with his condemnation of conventions and social norms, we must keep in mind another proposition of his thought that is as clear as the rest. This, the *seventh* proposition, can be stated in these terms: reason, that is, clarity of mind, is that which must determine what is and what is not in accordance with human nature. Neither desire nor emotion, nor the ingrained human tendency to revert to animalism, nor, in fact, anything else, can be the judicial court that renders the final decision as to what is natural and what is unnatural for human beings. Accordingly, Diogenes' call for a return to nature is not by any means a call for a return to bestiality or naked primitivism, because beasts, while living according to nature, do not have the *capacity* to reason and understand, a capacity potentially present in human beings, although seldom put into use. We would not be mistaken in asserting that when Diogenes transformed himself into a dog, a transformation originally initiated in him by the way in which he was seen by ordinary people, he could not have meant literally that he viewed the life of a dog or of any other animal as preferable to the life of a human being who succeeds in guiding his affairs through the use of reason.

It is the use of reason that allows us to gain some understanding of the meaning of nature. This concept—φύσις (*physis*) in Diogenes' language—had a long linguistic and intellectual history before him. Among the Presocratics, we find it persistently present as early as the time of the Milesian philosophers, for whom it had a meaning significantly different from that with which it has been invested in modern languages. When *we* speak of nature, images of the jungle, the undergrowth, wild animals, savage tribes, naked natives, and other such things are often conjured in our minds, for that is what in popular parlance 'nature' signifies. But that is not what the concept must have aroused in the minds of the ancient Greeks. As Aristotle points out in his discussion of the Presocratics, φύσις meant something akin to the idea of the processes and transformations that constitute the *physical* world, that is, the recurrent ways in which, according to their nature, things, living and inanimate, arise, remain in existence, and pass away. These processes and transformations were perceived by the Presocratics as repetitious and predictable, and as controlled by certain physical or natural laws, which are themselves manifestations of the structure that permeates the universe and that the Greeks called λόγος (*logos*). Thus, 'nature' among them stood for the ways in which, in accordance with the 'logical' laws that govern the world, things come into being and cease to exist. Expressing this idea in different language, we could say that 'nature' signifies the natural and expected ways in which all the components of the universe exist or, in the instance of human beings, *should* exist. In modern languages, we retain this meaning, as when we speak of the 'nature' of a chemical reaction or of the 'nature' of the behavior of a certain species. Thus, 'nature' could be made to signify the natural characteristics, both actual and potential, that are inherent in every existing thing.

A human life lived in accordance with nature (κατὰ φύσιν) is *not*, therefore, a life that imitates the life of a beast or of any other nonhuman creature, for *that* would render it altogether contrary to *its* nature. It is right for a dog to live as a dog and for a snail to carry its 'home' on its back, for in so doing, they are living in accordance with what is natural for them. A human being, however, is not by nature either a dog, a snail, or any other animal, and it would be therefore unnatural for him to attempt to live as animals do. Yet, Diogenes called himself a dog and, like a snail, carried his 'home', that is, his tub, from place to place. Furthermore, he once said that he learned how to live well by watching a mouse in the marketplace. What could he have meant, when he said that it was from animals that we should learn to live according to nature? The answer, we think, is discernible in a statement attributed to him by Diogenes Laertius: "He was in the habit of saying that he followed the example of the trainers of choruses. For they, too, set the note a bit too high to insure that the singers hit the right note" (VI, 35).

The two key phrases in this passage are "set the note a bit too high" and "hit the right note," for they furnish us with the password that opens for us the gates that lead to Diogenes' thought. Living in a world in which, from his point of view, most people lived in ways that are contrary to what nature intended human beings to be, and surrounded by specimens of humanity who were, as Marcus Aurelius would call them (*Meditations* II, 16), "malignant growths in the universe," what else could have Diogenes done except to "set the note a bit too high," when his remarkable lucidity made him aware of such unnatural aberrations? Hoping to compel them to "hit the right note," he called himself a dog and carried his 'home' on his back, and on repeated occasions did behave like an animal, as is confirmed by the blatant shamefulness with which he flaunted social norms. Still, there were also numerous occasions when he chastised his contemporaries for behaving like animals and when he hurled back the designation of himself as a dog to those who wanted to insult him by calling him a dog. Muhtasar Siwan al-hikma reports (Diogenes 27) that once, when Alexander went to visit him, he found him sleeping, whereupon the young emperor kicked him to awake him. Diogenes' remark is revealing: "Conquering cities may not be held against kings, but kicking like a donkey should be." The same source (Diogenes 14) tells us that Diogenes' advise to his associates was, "Abandon the ways of the beasts," and from other sources we learn that when he wished to call attention to the depravity of people, he would compare them to animals.

Thus, the truth appears to be that in calling himself a dog and in extolling the virtues of animal life, what Diogenes was doing was "setting the note a bit too high," as if he wished to say to people, "Look at me, you fools and scoundrels, I am a man who appears to have abandoned his human nature and his capacity to reason, and who on purpose seems to have become a wild dog. What do you think of me now? You, on the other hand, who claim to be human, are worse than animals, for you, too, have abandoned your human nature, but in ways far greater and more real than I, and have allowed your minds to become atrophied and enfeebled by the smoke produced by your endeavors to be something that by nature you are not. I have observed you for many years, day after day, sometimes from my tub and sometimes reluctantly walking backwards among you, and have been a witness to your depravities, deceptions, idiocies, and lack of mind. I have seen how each one of you endeavors to take advantage of others, and how you are enslaved by your unnatural desires and appetites. I have seen how your monarchs and governments use and abuse the people, and how this thing that you call the State works only for the advantage of the wealthy and the powerful. I have contemplated the sad spectacle of your amassing possessions and coveting fame, as if these things added even one bit to your human worth. Nature gave you a pair of feet that you can well protect with one pair of sandals, and yet some of you appear not to be happy unless you own three thousand pairs of shoes. How sad indeed! In vain I have searched among you for a human being, a true human being, but have only found rascals and scoundrels. I have gone to your public baths and theaters, where I have found many living creatures, but not one single human being. I have called for you to come to listen to me, but when you have come, I have been surrounded by strange aberrations of nature. For all this, I no longer speak to you, but merely bark at you, and I no longer approach any of you without striking him with my stick. I am not the mouth for ears such as yours.[20] Perhaps, I have thought, by shocking you with my shamelessness and by soiling with mud the rugs of the affluent and the pretentious, and by converting myself into an intolerable clown who calls himself a dog and who is always willing to 'say it all', you may in the end come to see what you have become, namely, lamentable refutations of what nature meant you to be. For this, too, I have lived among you as a perambulating negation of practically everything that you are, always amazed at the curious fact that you have not decided to do away with me.[21] Behaving like the trainers of choruses, I have set the note as high as possible, hoping that eventually some of you may hit the right note, for I have been sustained by the conviction that no matter how stupid and dense you are, each one of you still has the chance to reflect on your condition and return to your true nature, and reach the goal that you have been seeking, but along a mistaken path. I have sought to show you a shortcut to happiness, and the spark of reason that may still flicker in the recesses of your confused consciousness can guide you to it."

    This imaginary yet somehow quite genuine diatribe from Diogenes can lead us now to the *eighth* proposition of his thought, which can be expressed in these terms: the possibility of a return to nature, understood, of course, as a return to true humanity, exists for every human being, no matter how distant he or she may be from living in accordance with nature. If, as noted in chapter 3, human life is, in Schopenhauer's language, "some kind of a mistake," this mistake was never intended by nature, but is the result of human choices. There is, however, a shortcut that can be pursued to correct it.[22] It does not involve intellectual speculation or even much learning or education, but two seemingly simple and interrelated components, one belonging to the mind and the other to the will. The former, referred to by later Cynics as ἀτυφία (*atyphia*), that is, clarity of mind or lucidity, is the ability to 'see things as they are' and to recognize the inherent value of things and activities as means to attain happiness. Diogenes' craft, he once said according to Muhtasar Siwan al-hikma (Diogenes 46), had to do with "examining the condition that is proper [natural] to me at first, at the end, and in between," and this craft, he might have added, can be learned by practically anyone.

The latter component involves the *method*, that is, the way, through which ἀτυφία can be developed in the mind. How can we learn to see things as they are, except by divesting ourselves of the inveterate modes of thinking and acting that have removed us from our true nature, and by defacing and throwing away the 'currency' that has been in circulation in the social and political world for such a long time? Diogenes' answer, couched in terms that are traceable to Antisthenes and even to Socrates, is clear, and we find in it his *ninth* proposition: through discipline, expressed in his language as ἄσκησις (*askesis*, from which we derive our word 'ascetic'), we cleanse the mind of confusion and obfuscation, and the body of detrimental substances and unnatural habits, and succeed in strengthening the will. The asceticism that lies at the core of Diogenes' thought does not entail a blank renunciation of pleasure, and neither does it call for the mortification of the body, as among Christian monks and certain sects such as the Indian Gymnosophists, for *that*, he would have argued, is as removed from what is natural for us as a life devoted to the pursuit of pleasure. Through discipline we learn to endure pain and suffering, and to develop in ourselves the indifference that is necessary to cope with all eventualities, those brought about by fate and chance, and those burdened upon us by the actions of others. Through discipline we succeed in taming the passions and desires that befog the mind and render people unable to use their reason. Through discipline we develop in us the habit of dispensing with the innumerable things that ordinary people deem required for happiness, and through discipline we strengthen the will and cleanse the mind. If we wish to "set the note a bit too high," hoping thereby eventually to be able to "hit the right note," we might even imitate the example of the legendary Hercules, who is said to have looked for suffering and vicissitudes, not in the mode of a vulgar masochist who finds pain preferable to pleasure, but because of his conviction that pain and suffering augment in us our strength, that is, our virtue (ἀρετή). Thus, when we find Diogenes rolling over hot sand in the summer and walking barefoot in the winter, or when we hear that his diet consisted of lupines, lentils, and water, and that he avoided, as if they were poisonous, the delicacies with which the wealthy feed themselves, we must realize that we are in the presence of an athlete who must exercise and who must subject himself to the severest training in order to attain his goal, a goal that, as he said, is more difficult than that of the Olympic athletes who compete against people, for what he must compete against is the host of unnatural monsters that enslave human beings—gluttony, lust, envy, anger, laziness, and other similar vices.

In considering what Diogenes understood as the goal of his life, the *tenth* proposition of his thought surfaces: if a happy, natural and virtuous life is what we must pursue, given the social context in which we are condemned to live, it is imperative that we aim at developing in us an imperturbable and total state of self-sufficiency (αὐτάρκεια).[23] In Diogenes' concept of self-sufficiency or independence, we come upon a notion that sums up the essence of classical Cynicism. The precise meaning of this concept can be extracted both from many of the statements attributed to Diogenes and from the descriptions of his mode of life. It entails a complete renunciation of the need to need the world, and a bracketing away of the senseless impositions and requirements that society places upon its members. Accordingly, it sets the Cynic apart from all things and virtually removes him from the obligation to be a part of the social world. Neither civic responsibilities, nor the duty to obey the laws, nor the obligation to respect and follow the conventions and norms of others, nor the need to belong to the community, nor, in fact, any of the customary bonds that tie ordinary people to their social context, have any relevance or value for the Cynic. Living among people, he is not one of them, and being in the world, he is not part of the world, for he claims to have become self-sufficient —he needs only himself—and independent—he abides only by those laws and precepts that *he himself* has certified as authentic 'currency'.

In the *Politics*, Aristotle emphasizes the political or social nature of human beings, saying, for instance, that "man is more of a political animal than bees or any other gregarious animals" (1253a). To be truly human, he argues, requires community life and the integration of the person within the socio-political fabric that constitutes the State. Nature, Aristotle maintains, does nothing in vain, and the mere fact that it has endowed human beings with the gift of speech—a gift denied, he believes, to other creatures—proves that we were meant to live as social or political beings. He then proceeds, as if Diogenes' ideal of self-sufficiency was the target of his remarks, to show that self-sufficiency is both unattainable and undesirable:

> The proof that the State is a creation of nature and prior to the individual is that the individual, when isolated, is not self-sufficient; and therefore he is like a part in relation to the whole. But he who is unable to live in society, or who has no need because he is sufficient for

> himself, must either be a beast or a god: he is no part of a state. (*Politics* 1253a)

Accordingly, from Aristotle's point of view, those who, like Diogenes, called for a life lived according to nature, and who somehow insisted on undermining the foundations of the State, were guilty of intellectual blindness, for they failed to understand that the most natural condition for human beings is a life within the structure provided by the State, a structure that is even more basic and natural than that of the family. Neither beasts nor gods need such a structure, for that is not in their nature, and when a person turns his back to the State, he must think of himself either as a beast or as a god.

As noted earlier, the manifestations of Diogenes' self-sufficiency abound in the sources. An Arabic source provides us with an anecdote that, despite its possibly apocryphal character, is valuable. Alexander once summoned Diogenes to come to his presence, but the philosopher sent back to him this ironic message: "You are too powerful to need me and I am too self-sufficient to need you." Various other accounts of the interaction between Alexander and Diogenes, some of which appear to be based on a modicum of historical fact, furnish us with the same message: Diogenes does not need Alexander, and neither does he need that for which Alexander stood, namely, the State.[24] In Diogenes Laertius, there are several reports about such an interaction. For instance, we are told (D.L. VI, 38) that when Alexander visited Diogenes in Corinth and asked him for whatever he wished from him, Diogenes' answer was, "Stand out of my light." Obviously, he needed nothing from the emperor, except his moving out of the sunlight that was warming him. The man who had so much had nothing that could have been of use to Diogenes, who needed only those things that, as he says, could be gotten for nothing—sunlight, water, air, and a place to lie down. Other things, Diogenes contended, have the tendency of entrapping the mind and the will until they enslave us and take away the most precious possession that we can have, freedom (ἐλευθερία), which, as he would insist, Hercules called the most valuable thing in the world (D.L. VI, 71). This world, Diogenes would say, is like a marketplace on the road, and the sensible traveler is he who passes by it, buying only those few things that will sustain him in his journey. Hence, if we are to attain self-sufficiency and preserve our freedom, we must abandon the socially created need for things and relationships, have and own as few things as possible, and be detached from human bonds, especially those that tie us to the State. True power and true kingship do not reside in those who, like Alexander, succeed in conquering the world, or in amassing fortunes, or in collecting titles and honors, but in those who are self-sufficient and free.[25]

Diogenes' ideal of self-sufficiency is the source of various other important concepts that would have a lasting influence in the Western world, especially through the agency of the Stoics. Among these, there is the concept of cosmopolitanism, which is at the basis of the *eleventh* proposition of Diogenes' thought and which can be stated in these terms: the world belongs equally to all its inhabitants, human and otherwise, and we, as human beings, belong to the entire world. According to Diogenes Laertius (VI, 63), when asked what his country was, Diogenes replied, "I am a citizen of the world." In this passage, we come upon the first known occurrence of the word 'cosmopolitan' (κοσμοπολίτης), which literally means a citizen (πολίτης) of the universe (κόσμος), and which could have been a term coined by him.[26] In other passages from the sources, the same idea is expressed. Thus, for instance, in a report from Ibn-Abi 'Awn, we are told that when asked where his home was, his answer was that his home was any place where he could find some rest, and in a quotation from one of Crates' tragedies (D.L. VI, 98), we find a statement that appears to be an expansion of Diogenes' designation of himself as a citizen of the world:

> Neither a tower nor a roof does my homeland have,
> For its citadel is indeed as wide as the whole world.

Few other concepts associated with Diogenes have given rise to more controversy and have been subjected to more scrutiny than his idea of cosmopolitanism. As a "phantom that has haunted the pages of scholarship,"[27] it has been interpreted in the most diverse ways and has been viewed as expressing a variety of different ideas. The time of Diogenes was a time when the very notion of the Greek city-state, the πόλις (*polis*), was being challenged in the name of nationalism, as exemplified in the political ideas of Demosthenes and Isocrates, both of whom recognized a fundamental weakness in the fragmentation of the Greek nation into a multitude of city-states, and in the name of internationalism, as exemplified, according to some, in the political ideas that have been associated with Alexander. It is often maintained that what the ultimate goal of Alexander's campaigns entailed was the creation of a universal State that would embrace all nations and races under one rule. To subject the entire human species to a process of homogenization (ὁμόνοια) was the fundamental ideal, we are told, that motivated him, as he marched with his Greek and Macedonian phalanxes through Egypt and Persia, and deep into India, the expected result of his enterprise being the emergence of the Universal Man, who would have neither city nor country as his home, but only the world.[28]

Whether or not we are justified in ascribing any such ideas to the historical Alexander, is a question that transcends the parameters of this study of Diogenes. Alexander *may* have been responsible for what W. W. Tarn calls "one of the great revolutions in human thought,"[29] namely, the vision of a universal nation, where neither national allegiances nor frontiers exist. It is possible that such a vision *may* have been born in his mind as a result of Cynic influences, either from Diogenes or from Onesicritus, the Cynic who accompanied him in his campaigns,[30] or even from the Gymnosophists with whom he became acquainted in India, although such suppositions are difficult to document and support. Nevertheless, Alexander's style of life and character, as these became progressively manifested throughout his short life, point to a man so vastly removed from Cynicism that it is difficult to imagine any lasting influence on him on the part of any among the Cynics.[31] Furthermore, it is indisputable that immediately after his death in 323 B.C., whatever seeds of internationalism there may have been in him disappeared completely among his successors, who, forgetful of the symbolism of the wedding in Babylon of hundreds of Greek and Macedonian officers with Babylonian maidens, divided the empire and instituted once more national and ethnic divisions, just as they had existed before and as they would continue to exist in subsequent ages.[32] If Alexander ever dreamed of a united and homogenized humanity, we can rest assured that those who divided his possessions did not shelter such dreams.

Now then, the question is whether in calling himself "a citizen of the world" Diogenes himself had such dreams. The answer, although as tentative as anything that can be said about Diogenes, is that his cosmopolitanism had a radically different orientation. Tarn insisted on this point, and we think correctly, when he argued that in calling himself 'cosmopolite', Diogenes meant, "not that he was a citizen of some imaginary world-state—a thing he never thought about— but that he was not a citizen of any Greek city,"[33] nor, we may add, of any human city or nation. He, who had been banished from Sinope, conceived of himself as an exile and a foreigner everywhere and at all times. His true home was literally the entire world and his citizenship was universal. Diogenes Laertius tells us (VI, 72) that Diogenes would insist that the only true commonwealth is that which is as wide as the universe (ὀρθὴ πολιτεία ἡ ἐν κόσμῳ), not in the sense that he belonged to a universal community of which every person was a member, but simply that he did not belong to any specific community at all. Perhaps, as a modern scholar has suggested, he viewed the human species as divided into two unequal communities, a large community of fools and a small community of wise men and women, and conceived of himself as part of the latter.[34] More likely, however, is that he regarded himself as a member of no human community, not even that provided by the family, because he advocated the idea that men and women should live with one another without the bonds of marriage (cf. D.L. VI, 72). Diogenes' rejection of the idea of ownership or property fits well within this frame of reference. Nothing in the world belongs to any specific person, except inasmuch as certain things are necessary for survival. There is nothing, therefore, improper or reprehensible, for instance, in stealing from a temple (D.L. VI, 73) or in taking food from the rich to feed the poor and the hungry (D.L. VI, 28), for the universe is the property of all its inhabitants. The true Cynics, that is those human beings who have attained wisdom, he maintained, own everything, for that is their kingly right. He expressed this idea in terms of this syllogism: "All things belong to the gods. The wise are friends of the gods, and friends own everything in common. Therefore, all things belong to the wise" (D.L. VI, 37).

Clearly, his cosmopolitanism was so negative and radical that he could not have thought otherwise, as the testimony of Philodemus of Gadara makes it abundantly clear,[35] for which reason those who have discerned in Diogenes a bent toward anarchism, that is, toward a rejection of even the most primitive forms of human association, may not be altogether misguided.[36] Unfortunately, however, the surviving fragments of his *Republic* are brief and their character is of dubious authenticity, and thus we cannot draw definitive conclusions about the details of his proposed utopia. It is possible that the ideal commonwealth envisioned by Crates, about which we do have some information, may reflect what Diogenes himself envisioned for his own utopia. In one of Crates' fragments, we come upon this description of his utopia, the Island of Πήρα ('Pera', in honor of one of the few possessions of every Cynic—his leathern wallet, which was called πήρα):

> Pera, so name we an island, girt around by the sea of Illusion,
> Glorious, fertile, and fair land unpolluted by evil.
> Here no trafficking knave makes fast his ships in the harbor,
> Here no tempter ensnares the unwary with venal allurements.
> Onions and leeks and figs and crusts of bread are its produce.
> Never in turmoil of battle do warriors strive to possess it,
> Here there is respite and peace from the struggle for riches and honor.

The phrase 'the sea of Illusion' is expressed in Greek by the phrase οἴνοπι τύφῳ that can be rendered as 'a wine-colored sea of fog'. It includes what is possibly the most important idea of classical Cynicism, τῦφος (*typhos*), which will be elucidated in the following chapter. Let it suffice at this point to say that Crates' utopia is an island surrounded but not affected by the immense world of intellectual confusion and spiritual obfuscation in which humanity has always been immersed. There, and only there, human beings live at peace and free from the madness that generally characterizes human existence, and there the Cynic finds his dreams realized.

Still, even Crates' utopia remains for us only a blurry vision of unclear outlines, a chimerical 'no-place place' (which is what 'utopia' literally means), although it does play the opening notes of a long symphonic poem that would be composed after him, first by the Stoics and then by all the idealists of later times, who, like Rousseau, would dream of a place divested of the constraints and perversities created by civilization. Diogenes' utopia, however, is even blurrier than that of Crates, not only because of our lack of source materials about it, but because of the negative and extreme character of his philosophical stance. Far more than Crates, he devoted himself more to defacing and destroying what he found around him than to building and developing what might replace what is in existence. Thus, whatever such a cosmopolitan utopia might have been in his mind, both his behavior vis-à-vis the political institutions of his time, and his comments about the laws and the governing structures of the State with which he was acquainted, lead us to the conclusion that he regarded all such arrangements as worthy of defacement. Neither patriotism nor loyalty to the laws, nor the need and desire to belong to a community, nor any attachment to ethnic or racial roots, nor a belief in property rights, nor support for family covenants, nor, in fact, any inclination toward the various aspects of human existence that render human beings "political animals," to use Aristotle's phrase, can be detected in Diogenes' thought. Just as, according to Diogenes Laertius (VI, 50), he did not hesitate to praise those who kill tyrants and break the laws, he would not have been unhappy at the prospect of the dissolution of *all* political arrangements. The State, he would have said in agreement with Max Stirner,[37] is the most formidable enemy of human happiness, for it creates dependency and brings about a multitude of misfortunes and ills to persons and communities, war, destruction, and slavery being only some among them. The greater the dominance of the State in human life, he would have said, the further we move away from a life lived in accordance with nature. The greater the power of the State is, the more diminished human freedom becomes.

There is no need to emphasize the obvious fact that this idealistic and chimerical cosmopolitanism of Diogenes exemplifies well the somewhat truncated and undeveloped character of his thought, for it unveils for us a program of human reform that is strictly utopic, and is neither practical nor achievable.[38] We suspect, moreover, that this assessment would remain valid, even if we had the benefit of possessing the complete text of his *Republic* or of his other works, for our information about them, scant as it may be, points decisively in the same direction. His cosmopolitanism is ultimately a *negative reaction* to the dismal spectacle that he saw around him: nations at war with one another, cities destroying cities, monarchs and oligarchs satisfying their whims at the expense of the masses, ordinary people allowing themselves to be duped by political and nationalistic ideologies and slogans, laws created and enforced only for the benefit of those in power, philosophers and theologians spinning out of their confused and confusing heads cobwebs of speculation and fantasy designed to dull and mystify the masses, people in general living in accordance with the demands of their desires and passions—in a word, the madhouse atmosphere that he discerned everywhere. Had he been able to accompany Alexander in his campaigns, as the young emperor ravished city after city, crucifying and putting to the sword so many thousands of people, setting the example for the countless rulers, dictators, and politicians of subsequent times, while being greeted and acclaimed wherever he went as the great and exalted savior of nations, Diogenes would have reflected on the time in Corinth, when he hardly even moved from the ground where he was lying as Alexander approached him

(Plutarch, *Alexander* xiv). Alexander, the man who embodied the idea and the structure of the State, Diogenes might have said to himself, deserved then nothing but contempt, and the course of his life and especially his miserable end in Babylon proved this beyond any doubt. He, too, had to be bracketed away, for his 'currency' was counterfeit and had to be defaced. The 'currency' of the multitudes that blindly followed him and made possible his senseless and pointless enterprise also deserved the same fate.

Here, then, we come upon the final building block of Diogenes' Cynicism, the *twelfth* proposition of his thought, that, as a cornerstone, supports the incomplete edifice of his philosophical stance and contains all the elements of classical Cynicism, both theoretical and practical. We encountered this proposition as we endeavored to give an account of Diogenes' life, specifically in relation to the point of departure from which he launched his onslaught on society. This point of departure, as we saw, was the oracular pronouncement that reportedly commanded him to deface or adulterate the currency. "Παραχάραττειν τὸ νόμισμα" were the words of the Pythia, and that was exactly what he did until his death. *That* was his only mission and *that* is his legacy. Lucian tells us that in Hades *that* is precisely what he has continued to do without abatement, in such a way and to so extreme a degree that those who share with him some corner of the Underworld cannot wait for the moment when they can move away from him. What else, indeed, can *they* do, condemned as they are to share eternity with someone who endlessly reminds them that their lives on earth were a waste and that their currency—the fortunes they amassed—was counterfeit and useless, and that their other 'currency'—their values and habits—was also false and valueless?

The essence of Diogenes' thought, is succinctly expressed by the phrase 'Deface the currency', of course, not in the sense that every single piece of 'currency' deserves defacing, for even Diogenes understood that, in the light of reason, there are certain rare pieces that appear to be both sanctioned by convention *and* dictated by nature. Because of this, then, we discover that his shamelessness, that is, his ability and willingness to deface norms and conventions, was *not* absolute and total, and that he often appealed to his contemporaries' feelings of shame, both conventional *and* natural, when he reprimanded them. Still, such pieces of the social currency in which convention and nature are manifested must have been exceptional from his point of view: like rare coins kept in antiquarians' drawers, they are few and generally kept out of circulation. Therefore, Diogenes' campaign to deface the values and customs of his world took on the garb of an all-out war against the world. Those who, like Hegel, have emphasized the lack of positive elements in Diogenes' thought may not be entirely mistaken. In his inspection of the world as the great overseer and scout of God on earth, to use Epictetus' phrase (*Discourses* III, xxii, 24),[39] and "scenting the world, looking it full in its face," in the expression of Robert Browning,[40] Diogenes found little in his world worth preserving. The grand building erected by civilization, he would have said, is beyond repair and must be demolished, if there is to be any hope of amelioration for the human condition. The demolishing tactic that he advocated and practiced, his rhetoric of Cynicism, is as clear as daylight and emerges with distinctness in every one of his words and actions. The plans for the construction of the new building, however, remain undefined and only their outlines—the twelve propositions that we have identified in this chapter—are discernible in his legacy throughout the centuries that have elapsed since his death.

Notes

1. G.W.F. Hegel, *Lectures on the History of Philosophy*. Translated by E. S. Haldane (London: Routledge and Kegan Paul, 1963), Vol. 1, p. 479.

2. Ibid., Vol. 1, p. 487.

3. Ibid., Vol. 1, p. 481.

4. G. H. Lewes, *The Biographical History of Philosophy From Its Origins in Greece Down to the Present Day* (New York: D. Appleton and Company, 1883), Vol. 1, p. 177.

5. Ibid., Vol. 1, p. 181.

6. Ibid., Vol. 1, p. 182.

7. F. Sayre, *Diogenes of Sinope: A Study of Greek Cynicism* (Baltimore: J. H. Furst, 1938), pp. 99ff.

8. A. A. Long, "The Socratic Tradition: Diogenes, Crates, and Hellenistic Ethics," in *The Cynic Movement in Antiquity and Its Legacy*. Edited by R. Branham and M. O. Goulet-Cazé (Berkeley: University of California Press, 1996), p. 28.

9. Cf. *Romans* 7:18-19, where Saint Paul uses language that is reminiscent of that of Ovid.

10. In one of Cercidas' fragments (Frag. 54) Diogenes is referred to as "the Celestial Dog."

11. Michel Foucault, who died in 1984, devoted his last course at the Collège de France in Paris to an examination of the philosophy of Diogenes, focusing on his practice of παρρησία. For Foucault, the *parrhesiast*—the person who is able and willing to 'say it all'—is a genuine philosopher and an authentic human being. For an examination of the significance of παρρησία in Foucault's understanding of the role of philosophy in the modern world, see T. R. Flynn, "Foucault as Parrhesiast: His Last Course at the Collège de France" in *The Final Foucault*. Edited by J. Bernauer and D. Ramussen (Cambridge, Mass.: MIT Press, 1991), pp. 102-118.

12. J. Ferguson, *Moral Values in the Ancient World* (London: Methuen & Co., 1958), p. 145. According to Ferguson, Cynicism was "not really a philosophy; it was a way of life, almost a religion."

13. V. Brochard, "Diogène le Cynique," in *La Grande Encyclopédie. Inventaire Raisonné des Sciences, des Lettres et des Arts* (Paris: H. Lamirault et Cie, n.d.), Vol. 14, p. 601.

14. L. Robin, *La pensée grecque et les origines de l'esprit scientifique* (Paris: La Renaissance du Livre, 1923), p. 199.

15. A. O. Lovejoy and G. Boas, *Primitivism and Related Ideas in Antiquity* (New York: Octagon Books, 1965), p. 118-119.

16. For a study of the early Cynics' attitude toward religious beliefs and practices, see M. O. Goulet-Cazé, "Les premiers Cyniques et la religion" in *Le Cynisme ancien et ses prolongements. Actes du Colloque Internationale du CNRS.* Edited by M. O. Goulet-Cazé and R. Goulet (Paris: Presses Universitaires de France, 1993), pp. 117-159. The author notes that Diogenes and the other early Cynics "mounted a radical attack on religion, making on their part absolutely no concessions to traditional beliefs and practices" (p. 141). For a different approach to the issue, see H. Rahn, "Die Frömmigkeit der Kyniker." *Paideuma* 7 (1959-1961), pp. 280-292, where the author recognizes in what he calls "true Cynics" (Diogenes included among them) positive elements of religiosity, despite their rejection of polytheistic beliefs.

17. Long ("The Socratic Tradition," pp. 29-30) lists seven propositions as the basis of classical Cynicism: (1) Happiness is living in agreement with nature; (2) happiness is something available to any person willing to engage in sufficient physical and mental training; (3) the essence of happiness is self-mastery, which manifests itself in the ability to live happily even under adverse circumstances; (4) self-mastery is equivalent to, or entails, a virtuous character; (5) the happy person is the only person who is wise, kingly, and free; (6) things conventionally deemed necessary for happiness, such as wealth, fame, and political power, have no value in nature; and (7) prime impediments to happiness are false judgments of value, together with the emotional disturbances and vicious character that arise from these false judgments. Long's propositions, while reflecting the essence of the message of Cynicism, appear in need of being extended, as I have done in this chapter.

18. For comments on the role of the concept of happiness in classical Cynicism, see G. Messina, "L'uomo e la felicità nel pensiero ellenistico." *Civiltà Cattolica* 107 (1956), pp. 598-609.

19. See, for instance, W. Riley, *Men and Morals: The Story of Ethics* (Frederick Ungar Publishing Co., 1960), where we are told that Diogenes "confused a return to nature with a return to bestiality" (p. 132). In A. O. Loveyoy and G. Boas, *Primitivism and Related Ideas in Antiquity* (New York: Octagon Books, Inc., 1965), we come similar comments, for the authors contend that "the Cynic ethics may be said to reduce, in its practical outcome, almost wholly to primitivism" (p. 118). Long ("The Socratic Tradition") has gone a long way in refuting so superficial an interpretation of Cynicism.

20. Cf. F. W. Nietzsche, *Thus spake Zarathustra*, #4. After Zarathustra had finished speaking to a crowd, he stood silently looking at the people and then said to himself: "There they stand.... There they laugh. They understand me not, for I am not the mouth for these ears." The comparison of Zarathustra with Diogenes is tempting. In the presence of the multitude, Zarathustra remarked in an obviously Cynic mood: "Must one first batter their ears, that they may learn to hear with their eyes? Must one clatter like kettledrums and penitential preachers? Or do they only believe the stammerer?"

21. In Plato's *Apology*, Socrates notes that it is surprising that the Athenians did not dispose of him earlier, but were willing to endure his presence for so many years.

22. V. E. Emeljanow, "A Note on the Cynic Short-Cut to Happiness." *Mnemosyne* 18 (1965), pp. 182-184.

23. For comments on Diogenes' concept of self-sufficiency, see A.N.M. Rich, "The Cynic Conception of αὐτάρκεια." *Mnemosyne* 9 (1956), pp. 23-29.

24. The juxtaposition of Diogenes and Alexander appears in numerous passages in the sources, the most significant among which are those found in Plutarch, Dio Chrysostom, Lucian, and Diogenes Laertius, and in Arabic gnomologies. What historical truth there is in them, is ultimately anybody's guess, although the number of such reports and their consistency seem to point to some element of historicity. After all, there is nothing impossible in imagining that Alexander, the newly 'elected' commander of the Greek and Macedonian armies, may have wished to visit the best tourist attraction in Corinth, Diogenes the Dog. What took place between Alexander and the philosopher, is not known, except for the fact that they stood as two irreconcilable poles in ideology and style of life. Their encounter has been an inspiration for numerous artists, both ancient and modern, who have directed their talents to depicting graphically the opposition between two very different types of humanity. It has also been an inspiration for writers such as Shakespeare, in whose writings, albeit with different names, the same opposition is dramatically presented. See in this regard D. K. Hedrick, "'It is no novelty for a prince to be a prince': An Enantiomorphous Hamlet." *Shakespeare Quarterly* 35 (1984), pp. 62-76, and S. Doloff, "'Let me talk with this philosopher': The Alexander/Diogenes Paradigm in *King Lear*." *The Huntington Library Quarterly* 54 (1991), pp. 253-255. The cultural sources of the legends that link Alexander and Diogenes have been explored by many scholars, among whom there have been some who have discerned roots in Buddhist traditions of great antiquity. See in this regard A. M Pizzagalli, "Influssi buddhistica nella leggenda di Alessandro." *Rendiconti dell'Istituto Lombardo* 76 (1942-1943), pp. 154-160.

25. The notion of the Cynic as 'king' is explored in R. Höistad, *Cynic Hero and Cynic King: Studies in the Cynic Conception of Man* (Uppsala: C.W.K. Gleerup, 1948).

26. This statement of Diogenes is reminiscent of a statement attributed to Anaxagoras (D.L. II, 7): when asked if he was concerned about the affairs of his country (Clazomenae), Anaxagoras replied, pointing to the sky, "I am greatly concerned with the affairs of my country (τῆς πατρίδος)." The sky, of course, symbolized for him the universe at large.

27. E. Badian, "Alexander and the Unity of Mankind." *Historia* 7 (1958), p. 425.

28. W. W. Tarn, "Alexander the Great and the Unity of Mankind," in *Makers of the Western Tradition: Portraits from History.* Edited by J. Kelly Sowards (New York: St. Martin's Press, 1979), Vol. 1, pp. 73-80. Tarn's attribution of internationalism to Alexander has been disputed by various scholars such as H. C. Baldry and E. Badian. Baldry speaks of Tarn's interpretation of Alexander as untenable. For his comments in this regard, see his *The Unity of Mankind in Greek Thought* (Cambridge: Cambridge University Press, 1965), pp, 101ff.

29. Tarn, "Alexander the Great," p. 73.

30. According to Tarn, the influence of the Cynics on Alexander's political ideas must have been negligible, because "the Cynics had no thought of any union or fellowship between Greek and barbarian" ("Alexander the Great," p. 75).

31. Examples of Alexander's reckless behavior and weakness of mind, traits opposed to Cynic ideals, abound in the sources. In Plutarch (*Alexander* lxxii), for instance, we come upon the following scene that shows that Alexander learned nothing from Diogenes:

> When he came to Ecbatana in Media, and had dispatched his most urgent affairs, he began to divert himself again with spectacles and public entertainments, to carry on which he had a supply of three thousand actors and artists, newly arrived from Greece. But they were soon interrupted by Hephaestion's falling sick of a fever, who, being a young man and a soldier, could not confine himself to so exact a diet as was necessary; for while his physician, Glaucus, was gone to the theater, he ate a fowl for his dinner, and drank a large quantity of wine, upon which he became very ill, and shortly after died. At this misfortune, Alexander was so transported beyond all reason that, to express his sorrow, he immediately ordered the manes and tails of all his horses and mules to be cut, and threw down the battlements of the neighboring cities. He crucified the unfortunate physician, and forbade playing on the flute or any other musical instruments in the camp.

32. The famous nuptial festival celebrated at Susa can be viewed as a token sign of the integration of nations into one universal community. According to Plutarch (*Alexander* lxx), Alexander married Statira, Darius' daughter, while hundreds of Greek and Macedonian officers married Persian women.

33. Tarn, "Alexander the Great," p. 75.

34. Baldry, *The Unity of Mankind*, p. 110. In Baldry's opinion, Diogenes' cosmopolitanism "does not unite the human race, but draws a single great dividing line across it, separating the few wise men from the many fools, whom Diogenes described as 'one finger removed from lunacy'."

35. For a discussion of Diogenes' *Republic* and Philodemus' testimony about his political ideas, see T. Dorandi, "La *Politeia* de Diogène de Sinope et quelques remarques sur sa pensée politique," in *Le Cynisme ancien et ses prolongements. Actes du Colloque International du CNRS*. Edited by M. O. Goulet-Cazé and R. Goulet (Paris: Presses Univer-

sitaires de France, 1993), pp. 57-68.

36. For comments on Diogenes' political ideas, especially in relation to his seemingly anarchistic inclinations, see M. Gigante, "Sul pensiero politico di Diogene di Sinope." *La Parola del Passato* 16 (1961), pp. 454-455. Gigante, while referring to Diogenes as "*cittadino del mondo, banditore del cosmopolitanismo*," maintains that there is no justi-fication in calling him an anarchist: "*Il Cinico non è un anarchico, ma vuol superare la formula democratica della città-stato*" (The Cynic is not an anarchist, but is someone who strives to go beyond the democratic arrangements of the city-state).

37. Max Stirner (1806-1856) is one of the most radical and consistent anarchists in the history of philosophy. His *The Ego and His Own: The Case of the Individual Against Authority* may be regarded as *the* manifesto of anarchism.

38. G. B. Donzelli, "Un'ideologia 'contestaria' del secolo IV a.C." *Studi Italiani di Filologia Classica* 42 (1970), pp. 225-251.

39. The word used by Epictetus is most appropriate: κατάσκοπος, for it describes the Cynic as a *spy* or a *scout* in the employment of God. He lives among human beings and takes note of their words and deeds, and prepares a report card about them to inform God about their affairs. He is, therefore, to use Schopenhauer's phrase, a sort of 'eye' that inspects all things and records the madness of the world.

40. Robert Browning's "How It Strikes a Contemporary" expresses an image that is reminiscent of Diogenes. This poem, originally published in 1855, describes an elderly poet in Valladolid, who, wearing an old cloak and accompanied by a bald and blindish dog, attentively inspects people's actions and behavior, as if silently engaged in the preparation of a report to be submitted to "our Lord the King." As a spy of God and as "a recording chief-inquisitor," the poet goes among people, scenting their ways and secretly evaluating their conduct. For a discussion of Browning's poem, particularly in the context of its Cynic message, see M. W. Schneider, "Browning's Spy." *Victorian Poetry* 17 (1979), pp. 384-388. Schneider recognizes numerous parallels that link the poet in Browning poem and Diogenes: the poet, he notes, "living the ascetic life of a Cynic, like Diogenes observing men, has a profound, even mystical, insight into human life, being not only a *sophos* but a seer" (p. 387).

Chapter 5

The Legacy of Diogenes

After the death of Diogenes in 323 B.C., classical Cynicism underwent a series of transformations and split into two main streams of development. In one of them, we find it transformed into Stoicism, and, in the other, we come upon a long list of Cynics, who, beginning with Crates of Thebes and ending with Sallustius[1] during the last decades of the Roman Empire, maintained alive some of the principles and practices that had animated and characterized Diogenes' life. Through the agency of Zeno of Citium, a disciple of Crates, Stoicism became a firmly established school of philosophy, the roots of which are traceable not only to Diogenes, but also to Socrates. The Stoics inherited from Diogenes and indirectly from Socrates the conviction that reason alone must be the determining factor in human conduct and that only a life lived in accordance with nature is worth living. According to the Stoics, virtue is the only necessary and sufficient condition for happiness, and external circumstances such as one's place of origin and station in life are inconsequential contingencies in the presence of which we must behave with absolute indifference. These and other distinctively Stoic ideas can be found in one form or another in the sayings attributed to Diogenes and can be clearly associated with the example of his life, for which reason the Stoics insisted that their philosophical stance was an offshoot of that of Diogenes.

Zeno, the founder of Stoicism, is said to have commenced his philosophical journey in a curious way. According to Diogenes Laertius (VII, 2-3), he, too, like Socrates and Diogenes before him, received an oracular pronouncement that changed his life. "Take on the complexion of the dead" was the oracle, which he understood, not in the sense that he should resemble the dead, but that he ought to devote himself to the study of ancient authors. After being shipwrecked on a voyage from Phoenicia to Athens, and having lost thereby a cargo of precious goods, he found his way to Athens, where he did as the oracle had commanded, that is, he began to read books of authors who were dead. At a bookseller's shop, we are told, he read Xenophon's account of Socrates in the *Memorabilia*, and so impressed was he with Socrates' character and style of life that he asked the bookseller where if anyone like Socrates could still be found. At that precise moment, Crates was passing by and the bookseller, pointing to Crates, said to Zeno, "There, follow that man." And he did so, transforming himself first into a Cynic like Crates and like Crates' teacher, Diogenes, and then into a Stoic, authenticating in this way the ideological validity of the canonical 'succession' Socrates-Diogenes-Crates-Zeno. The tradition that sprang from Zeno, the philosophy of the Stoa,[2] would remain one of the major intellectual currents of the ancient world for several centuries, and would give rise to important concepts that shaped the development of classical thought.

Whether or not, as in the instances of Socrates and Diogenes, the story of the oracle that was given to Zeno is historically reliable, and whether or not the reports about the shipwreck that brought him to Athens and about his direct association with Crates are biographically accurate, are not decisive questions. As with Socrates and Diogenes, we often come upon anecdotes and reports about Zeno and other Stoics that serve more the purpose of illustrating an ideological point than the exigencies of historical reporting. What is undeniable, however, is that Diogenes' thought was in one way or another the principal source responsible for the emergence and development of Stoicism. For this reason, there is ample justification in affirming that Diogenes' interpretation and adaptation of the Socratic presence, exaggerated and hyperbolic as it may have been, constitutes one of the most critical moments in the history of ideas, for it was the point of departure from which Stoicism began its journey.[3]

This journey would take the Stoics along a path, already outlined by Diogenes, on which several decisive ideas would be 'discovered'. Among these, possibly the most influential is the notion of natural law. Diogenes' juxtaposition of custom (νόμος) and nature (φύσις), his insistence that reason (λόγος) must always take precedence over emotion or instinct (ὁρμή), and his refusal to accept the socially sanctioned fragmentation of humanity into nations, races, and classes, were ideas that, albeit incomplete and truncated in his mind, would provide the ground on which the Stoics' notion of natural law would grow in late classical times, and would eventually reappear in the Middle Ages and in modern times, ultimately transforming itself into the theory of innate and inalienable human rights. There is nothing *natural* in the structuring of society into social classes, Diogenes believed, and nothing *natural* either in the artificially created gap between the rich and the poor, or between free persons and slaves, or between citizens and foreigners. By nature, we are all born into the same world, a world that belongs to all, and by nature, too, we all have the ability to claim and reclaim what is ours, that is, our natural rights, which have not been granted to us by the State, or by the statutes embodied in systems of laws, or by the whimsical decisions of monarchs and governments. The State, the laws, and those who rule human communities are all to be measured by the absolute standard of natural law, which, as Cicero taught us, echoing a distinct Stoic doctrine with roots in Cynicism, is discoverable by the use of reason. The laws and the customs of society deserve to be obeyed and respected only when, in the light of reason, they are found to be morally acceptable.

Somehow, then, the man in the tub, who walked backwards and shocked his contemporaries by so many words and acts of defiance, gave birth to a conception of rationality that would underlie in time the efforts of so many theorists and revolutionaries of later times who have struggled to free human beings from the bondage created by atavistic fetters, by irrational desires, and by the brute force possessed by the oligarchies. Whether behind a street barricade in Paris, or in the mountains of Bolivia, or in the Walden woods, or creating hope for humanity in the solitude of a writer's studio, all those souls who have endeavored to unsettle the status quo of the socio-political world, have carried with them the lighted lamp of the man in the tub, searching generally in vain for a speck of true humanity in their midst, but reminding us that if human life is a mistake, it is only because we have allowed it to be so.

This is undoubtedly the legacy of Diogenes, the intellectual components of which were secured by the Stoics and bequeathed by them to the Western world, although not without significant variations and occasional embarrassing accommodations. For Stoicism became in time, in fact not long after Zeno's death, mummified into a *system* of doctrines that often assumed a compromising position vis-à-vis the State and speculative philosophy. The emphasis on practice that, as we saw in chapter 2, permeated Diogenes' stance was replaced in certain manifestations of Stoicism by a preoccupation with theory, and the urgency with which Diogenes approached *human* issues was subsumed in Stoicism under mountains of speculative and cosmological concerns. This explains the increasing chasm that separated some of the late Stoics from those who regarded themselves, to use Lucian's phrase in *The Runaways* (16), as soldiers of the Army of the Dog, that is, the Cynics of Hellenistic and Roman times, who believed that *they*, more than other philosophers, were the bearers of the torch of Diogenes' spirit.

Nevertheless, Cynicism and Stoicism, despite their differences, remained allied philosophical responses toward the disintegrating world of late classical times. In both, no less than in the skepticism of Pyrrho and his successors, we encounter what a scholar has aptly called "*la réaction humaine des philosophes*"[4] in the presence of what he identifies as "*la caparace vétuste d'une société moribunde*" (the decrepit trappings of a dying society).[5] In both, too, this reaction, initially a negative and iconoclastic outburst of rebelliousness, as is perfectly clear in Diogenes and Zeno, paved the way for what has been called "a common feeling of humanity,"[6] that is, the conviction that despite the many differences that fragment the human community into alienated groups and individuals, humanity is ultimately *one* body, *one* organism. The Cynic term φιλανθρωπία (*philanthropia*), related to but not identical with what we call 'philanthropy', is said to have been coined by Crates, although it is possible that its origin may be traceable to Diogenes. Its history in classical times takes us along the tortuous paths of the development of Stoicism and along the even more winding byways of late Cynicism. It conveys the idea of love for human beings, but not in the sense of loving humanity at large in an abstract and sentimental way, and giving token donations to charitable causes, as is the custom of modern philanthropists. The classical term 'philanthropy' reflects the ideal relationship that, from the point of view of the Cynics and to some extent the Stoics, should exist between the philosopher and the masses. The former is an enlightened and lucid human being, who, by nature and luck, and especially by disciplined training (ἄσκησις), has succeeded in seeing through the appearance of things and the deceptions of the world, and has attained a stage of intellectual and spiritual development known among the Cynics as ἀτυφια (*atyphia*), generally understood as clarity of mind or lucidity. The latter, that is, most human beings, are the many, who remain, in Plato's language, chained by heavy fetters at the bottom of a dark cave (*Republic* 7.514ff.), contemplating unstable and indistinct shadows that they mistake for reality, and are immersed in what the Cynics called τῦφος (*typhos*), that is, obfuscation and confusion, or, literally, smoke and fog. They are afflicted by madness, Diogenes would have said, and have abandoned their true nature only to become slaves of the illusions and phantoms that structure their state of psychotic normalcy. They are truly sick and are, therefore, in need of assistance.

Should then the philosopher turn his back on them and walk away, seeking for himself the solace of his solitude in some distant mountain range or in the isolation of his tub? Or should he not rather plunge himself into their midst, with a lighted lamp and a stick, and begin his missionary task as a *physician* of the mind, a ἰατρός (a term that the sources use repeatedly in describing Diogenes and other Cynics)? As we reflect on Diogenes' practice of Cynicism, the answer is obvious: he may have slept in his tub, but, when awake, he spent every moment pursuing his contemporaries as a hunting dog pursues its prey. Aware of their sickness and madness, and convinced of the eventual efficacy of his Cynic medicine, he, like Socrates,[7] set the example for later Cynics and even for the Stoics of a philosopher who undertakes the task of reforming the human world, first by defacing its 'currency' and dissipating the fog that permeates it, and then, perhaps somewhat clumsily in his case, by instilling in the minds of his patients certain propositions, possibly platitudes for him, but surely novelties for them, that could initiate the process of their recovery. This, too, is an essential component of his legacy, namely, a commitment to ameliorate intellectually, spiritually, and physically the existential condition of human beings. This is, indeed, the meaning of his philanthropy.

Diogenes' legacy was bequeathed to posterity not only through the increasingly sophisticated philosophy of the Stoics, but also through the agency of the philosophers who since his death until the demise of the Roman Empire insisted on calling themselves Cynics and who were part of the enormous and multifaceted Army of the Dog that we encounter everywhere in late classical times, from the streets of Athens and Corinth to the gardens and street corners of Alexandria and Pergamum, from the poor neighborhoods of distant Gadara and Cyrene to the imperial court in Rome. Several late Cynics can be identified by name and often by their contributions,[8] although it is reasonable to assume, judging by the vigor with which Lucian and Julian attacked them, that their number was considerable. Lucian (*The Runaways* 16) complains that "every city is filled with such upstarts, particularly with those who enter the names of Diogenes, Antisthenes, and Crates as their patrons and enlist in the Army of the Dog." Their ranks included men and women, Greeks and Romans, Pagans and Christians, and individuals from practically all the regions and walks of life of the classical world, including some of the liberated and vociferous slaves described by Philo of Alexandria (*Quod omnis probus liber sit* xxi), who would live in temples and public places. Some of them achieved fame and were influential in maintaining alive Diogenes' legacy,[9] while others, the majority, remained anonymous.

It has often been noted that the presence of the Cynics in late Hellenistic times was important for the development of early Christian ideas and practices. Elements of Cynicism have been discerned in numerous passages of the Pauline letters, and even in the style of life associated with Jesus some have recognized unmistakable Cynic traits. It has been suggested that, divested of his Jewish messianic and theological attire, Jesus emerges as a typical Cynic philosopher of the first century A.D.[10] Raised in Nazareth, a town only a few miles from Gadara, he could have become acquainted with the Gadarean Cynics, who preached and practiced a mode of life not significantly different from his. The rise of monastic orders among the Christians, moreover, may have been influenced by certain Cynic traditions, especially those related to the Cynic community in Gadara, where poverty, asceticism, abnegation, equality, simplicity of life, and other similar virtues were practiced. The Christian mendicant monk, carrying a leathern satchel and a wooden stick, begging for his daily bread and detached from the surrounding world, preaching and moralizing wherever he went, and acting as an itinerant physician of the soul, is a vestige of what classical Cynicism practiced and is a bearer of at least some of the aspects of Diogenes' legacy.[11]

The development of Cynicism in late classical times was characterized not only by a great variety of ideas and modes of life, but also by what appears to have been a loss of the vigor and directedness of purpose that are associated with Diogenes. Epictetus, Lucian, and Julian, the three major admirers of the early Cynics—Antisthenes, Diogenes, and Crates—and the principal chastisers of the late Cynics, stand in agreement in their insistence that the latter were more inclined to perpetuate the external marks and traits of Cynicism than to preserve the principles and convictions to which Diogenes gave expression. Epictetus, for instance, as mentioned in the previous chapter, reminds a prospective Cynic that there is much more in Cynicism than a torn cloak, a staff, disheveled hair, bare feet, and a condemning attitude toward customs and conventions, and adds that if anyone imagines that such things are sufficient to become a Cynic, he should keep himself as far away from Cynicism as possible (*Discourses* III, xxii, 9-12).[12] Lucian, for his part, spared no castigating words to describe the Cynics of his time (second century A.D.) as charlatans and performers, who, like Peregrinus Proteus, had little in their minds and who presented to the world only the appearance of Cynicism. For them, according to Lucian, all that it took to become a Cynic was to wear the expected Cynic 'uniform', set up a stand on some street corner, and begin to shriek platitudes about virtue and hurl insults at passers-by (*The Passing of Peregrinus* 3).[13] Julian, living two centuries after Lucian, complained that at least with respect to the Cynics with whom he was acquainted, "the rivers are flowing backwards"(*Or.* VI), an often quoted line from Euripides' *Medea* (413) that conveys the sense that the world is ultimately upside down and that things are terribly wrong. For, in his view, the new Cynics were nothing but sham preachers who had nothing to offer in the way of serious philosophy, and who had distorted and trivialized the legacy of Diogenes.

It is difficult to determine the historical accuracy of the testimonies of Epictetus, Lucian, and Julian concerning the presence or absence of philosophical substance among the late Cynics. Their negative assessment must be viewed in the context of their inclination to idealize and canonize the older Cynics, especially Diogenes, and, in the instance of Lucian and Julian, against the background of the ideological agenda that lurks behind their literary undertakings. Their impartiality, therefore, cannot be taken for granted. It cannot be doubted that some of the Hellenistic and Roman followers of Diogenes managed to distance themselves from the teachings and example of the early Cynics, and that, like the Stoics, were sometimes willing to make peace with the world. It is also probably correct to affirm that, as happens in the development of practically every intellectual, religious, and political movement, late Cynicism lost the pristine quality of its origins and was on occasion preoccupied more with the appearance of Cynicism than with its substance. Nevertheless, in what concerns the legacy of Diogenes, it is also undeniable that among the late Cynics there were some who kept fully alive its flame and exemplified with great earnestness its principles. Self-sufficiency, shamelessness, cosmopolitanism, indifference, poverty, asceticism, and, above all, the ability and willingness to 'say it all'—these and other unmistakable manifestations of Diogenes' Cynicism abound in numerous late Cynics. They, too, like Diogenes, lived in the world, but were not part of the world. Like him, they contemplated the maddening spectacle of human existence and did precisely what Diogenes did, for they spat on it, unconcerned about how the world would retaliate. Just as Diogenes expressed contempt toward Alexander and other rulers of his time, the late Cynics, as shown by the behavior of Demetrius, wasted no opportunity to insult the Roman emperor and his imperial magistrates. Like Diogenes, too, they saw themselves as aliens in the strange world of human beings, and, like him, they undertook the task of defacing the 'currency' of that world.

Thus, even with diminished vigor and despite the predictable crowds of pseudo-Cynics who enrolled in the Army of the Dog—the ancestors of modern *cynical* people, about whom we will have much to say presently—the late Cynics were responsible for having impressed on the consciousness of the classical world the distinguishing marks of Diogenes' legacy, and it was through them that the thread that connects him to medieval and modern times remained unbroken. They exemplified the practice of Cynicism and did not fail to remind their contemporaries of the counterfeit character of *their* 'currency'. Their message, expressed both in words and in acts, was genuinely a reflection of that of Diogenes. This message, as we saw in the previous chapter, can be understood in terms of twelve propositions that were identified there as the building blocks of Cynicism. Among the late Cynics, however, we encounter an even less structured philosophical position than what we can associate with Diogenes, for which reason his legacy among them took the form of an adherence, not so much to principles, but to certain practices that can be appreciated by a review of some of the principal *concepts* of Cynicism. These, too, were exemplified by Diogenes and the older Cynics, but among the late Cynics, they became the essence of their stance, which explains why philosophers like Cicero and Epictetus complained so bitterly about the lack of philosophical principles among the Cynics of *their* time.

Among such concepts, mention should be made of self-sufficiency (αὐτάρκεια): the Cynic is self-sufficient and only needs himself, and is, therefore, able to dispense with the support provided by human society; contempt for the opinions of the many (ἀδοξία): the Cynic looks with contempt or at least with suspicion at the values and customs by which ordinary people guide themselves, including those that are embodied in laws and statutes, and especially at the need to be honored or appreciated by others, for the Cynic welcomes repudiation and insults[14]; shamelessness or impudence (ἀναίδεια): the Cynic is not ashamed to break even the most sacrosanct rules of decorum, either when such rules are found by him to be senseless or when he feels that by breaking them he can express his absolute freedom; indifference (ἀδιαφορία): the Cynic is unconcerned about all the circumstances and contingencies that come to him from the external world of nature or from his surrounding human world, and about all things over which he has no control; insensibility (ἀπάθεια), a central concept also in Stoicism: the Cynic's aim is, as Julian reports (*Or.* VI), to make himself insensible to pleasure and pain; ignorance (ἀμαθία): the Cynic restricts his intellectual activities to those concerns that are of immediate value for human existence, and glances away from philosophical speculations and investigations that relegate human issues to a secondary plane; disciplined training (ἄσκησις): the Cynic is committed to a program of self-training that leads to the strengthening of his character and lessens his dependency on social and physical needs, and that allows him to maintain all his desires and impulses under the strictest rational control; strength of character (καρτερία): the Cynic aspires at developing in himself a character and a physical constitution that, like those associated with Hercules, render him impervious to the vicissitudes and sufferings that accompany human life; poverty (πενία): the Cynic understands that virtue and happiness cannot be found in the search and acquisition of physical possessions, and thus divests himself of as many things as possible, retaining only the bare necessities that are required to maintain him alive and that assure for him the freedom (ἐλευθερία) that Hercules esteemed to be the most precious thing in the world (D.L. VI, 71); and philanthropy (φιλανθρωπία): the Cynic recognizes his moral obligation to make himself useful in the task of dispelling the illusions that rob people of their ability to be happy and live in accordance with nature, and regards his rendering assistance as a compassionate physician of the mind as his highest moral duty and as an indispensable requirement of his calling.

    Other concepts could be added to this list of Cynic notions, all of which played a role in the lives of the classical Cynics that followed Diogenes' path. There are, however, two additional concepts that merit more detailed consideration, because of their importance in our endeavor to gain some appreciation of how Diogenes' legacy has managed to survive until our own time. These two notions are τῦφος (*typhos*) and the related concept of ἀτυφία (*atyphia*), and παρρησία (*parrhesia*). In them, we encounter what may be conceived of as *the* common denominator that is discernible in *all* classical Cynics, although in varying degrees, from Antisthenes to Sallustius, and as the link that ties all subsequent Cynics, even those of modern times, to what we have called the legacy of Diogenes. As we reflect on the meanings of these two notions, too, we understand that their *presence* or their *absence* is ultimately what constitutes the gap that separates Cynicism in its classical sense from cynicism in its modern sense.

    The idea of τῦφος does not appear explicitly in any of the sayings or anecdotes associated with Diogenes, except possibly in a passage from Aelian (*Hist.* Var. IX, xxiv) quoted in chapter 2, in which we are told that once, when Diogenes was at Olympia, he noticed a crowd of young athletes from Rhodes wearing fancy robes. "Here," Diogenes said, "I see nothing but *smoke*." Soon after, he saw a group of Spartan athletes wearing rugged and soiled clothes, upon which he remarked, "Here again, I only see *smoke*." Still, even in the absence of any other explicit occurrence of the idea of τῦφος in the testimonies about Diogenes, its Cynic meaning remains persistently present in practically all that was said and written about him in ancient times.

The primary meaning of the Greek word τῦφος (*typhos*) can be rendered in English by words such as 'smoke', 'mist', and 'cloud', and various verbal forms related to τῦφος convey the same meaning. For instance, τύφω means 'to raise a smoke' or 'to make a cloud of smoke'. Beyond the primary meaning of the word, moreover, there are other meanings and connotations, all of which express in one way or another the idea of something dark and obscure, of something that is difficult to perceive or that obstructs our ability to see clearly. To be in τῦφος, therefore, means to be in darkness. The mythological legends about Typhon, the grisly monster who, according to Hesiod (*Theog.* 820ff.), was born of the union of Earth and Tartarus as their youngest son, and who with his one hundred heads, hands, and feet inflicted so much suffering wherever he went, capture well the primary sense of τῦφος: the *darkness*-producing monster was eventually plunged by the might of Zeus into Tartarus, and, in his descent to the *dark* infernal regions below the earth through the mouth of Mount Aetna, caused vast volcanic clouds to cover the sky. As the mythological personification of volcanic forces and great winds, Typhon stands in Western traditions as the symbolic source of physical and spiritual darkness. Modern words such as 'typhoon', '*typhon*' in French, '*taifung*' in Chinese, and others, are vestiges of the presence of Typhon in Greek mythology.

There is also a legend about Hercules that is of significance because of his connection with the Cynic movement. Hercules is said to have slain the great Nemean lion, who was an offspring of Typhon, and to have worn afterwards the skin of that creature as his only garment. The great Cynic hero, then, who in Cynic traditions traceable to Diogenes symbolized so much of what the Cynics viewed as paradigms of virtue—courage, self-sufficiency, asceticism, and strength—was responsible for the death of the Nemean lion, who himself had come into the world as the bearer of darkness. Dio Chrysostom (*Or.* LXI) understood well the relevance of Hercules' slaying of the Nemean lion in the context of Diogenes' legacy: like Hercules, Diogenes, too, had to struggle against the fiercest enemy of the human mind, namely, τῦφος, which in the language of the Cynics stands for the darkening madness that permeates human existence in all its manifestations, blinding the eye of the soul and obfuscating the mind. Like Hercules, Diogenes' task was to obliterate the offspring of the primeval Typhon.

The oldest clear occurrence of τῦφος in its Cynic sense is found in one of the fragments of Crates, already quoted in the previous chapter where his cosmopolitanism was discussed.[15] There, we saw that Crates' utopic island is named Πήρα ('Pera', in honor of the Cynics' leathern wallet, which was called πήρα). This island, which must be understood more as an ideal state of mind than as an actual ideal place, is described by Crates as a "glorious, fertile, and fair land unpolluted by evil," where neither the prompting of sensual passion nor the allurements of illusion have any place. Its happy inhabitants are immune to such things. Surrounding the island, Crates observes, there is a vast sea, the home of turbulent storms and tragic shipwrecks, of anguish and unhappiness, and of blind coveting and senseless desiring, an enormous universe of darkness, that he calls τῦφος.

From the peaceful shores and placid plains of Pera, its inhabitants contemplate the immensity of that "wine-colored sea of fog" that surrounds their home. There, they see, humanity drowns in wretchedness and pain, and there, they know, is where the mind is caught in currents of irrationality and madness, for what has human history been from the beginning but irrationality and madness? Fortunate are indeed the inhabitants of Pera, the Cynics, who have managed to escape from the treacherous waters of the sea of confusion and illusion that surrounds their island. But their good fortune does not render them either arrogant or disdainful, and neither does it move them to aloofness. Their contempt and disdain, as shown by Diogenes, are not directed at the many who drown in τῦφος, but at the conditions and customs that create and sustain it. Thus, they feel compelled to lend whatever assistance they can to those who have not reached their shores. Like the liberated prisoner of Plato's cave (*Republic* 7.516c-e), who, after seeing the sun, "recalls to mind his first habitation and what passes for wisdom there," and who, moved by pity, chooses to return to the darkness of the cave to spread the good news among those who remain in chains, the inhabitants of Pera act as emissaries of reason and physicians of the soul among their fellow-human beings. Their missionary love of people, their philanthropy, manifests itself in all their activities, especially in those in which they must awaken others by means of shocking acts and insulting phrases—the manifestations of Diogenes' Cynic rhetoric—that are like the painful medicine that a man suffering from typhoid fever must be given.[16]

These and other similar images are useful in clarifying for us the sense in which the Cynics understood the concept of τῦφος. Its philosophical meaning among them is perfectly clear. It stands for the lack of mental clarity that prevents people from attaining the only goal of their existence—happiness. It stands, too, for the webs of senseless customs, atavistic traditions, irrational beliefs, illusory expectations, and so many other things that enmesh the mind. When Diogenes looked at people and especially at their bizarre modes of behavior, *that* and only *that* is what he saw. As a well-trained physician, he recognized at once the symptoms of their illness: a delirium-like state of emotional agitation that impels them to act thoughtlessly, a mental obfuscation that prevents them from seeing things as they are, a spiritual blindness that converts them into puppets of political ideologies and religious mystifications, a disequilibrium of mental abilities that moves them away from their true nature and makes them arrogant—*that* is their τῦφος.

The second fundamental notion of Diogenes' legacy is παρρησία (*parrhesia*), a concept about which we have already commented in various contexts. Its Cynic meaning is not difficult to understand, particularly since so many among Diogenes' actions exemplified it. The term παρρησία is generally translated as 'freedom of speech', but its Greek meaning is more precise. It includes two words, πᾶς (*pas*) and ῥῆσις (*rhesis*), that stand, respectively, for 'all' and 'speech' or 'speaking'. Thus, παρρησία literally means 'the kind of speech in which we say it all'—no ambiguities, no euphemisms, no hidden meanings, no deceiving nuances of language, and, above all, no intention to cover up linguistically the way things are. As a Cynic once put it, in παρρησία we actually and literally 'vomit the truth', nothing more and nothing less. We could put it more gently and say that in παρρησία we *spit out* the truth, which is the obvious meaning of the anecdote in which we are told that once, when Diogenes was in the presence of a certain despicable man, he spat on his face and justified his action, saying that he could not find a more appropriate place to deposit his phlegm (D.L. VI, 32). It might be difficult to find a more compelling instance of the Cynics' freedom of speech.

Surely, as with other Cynic notions, παρρησία was not invented by the Cynics. It is found in various contexts long before Antisthenes and Diogenes with a meaning not altogether different from that with which the Cynics invested it. As an essential component of the democratic ideology of the Athenians of Pericles' time, for instance, παρρησία was understood *and* often practiced in Athens as the right of any citizen to speak his mind whenever and however he chose to do it. In the Athenian Assembly, citizens exercised that right, although sometimes with dire consequences for themselves, and on the comic stage it was taken for granted that the comic poets could make their actors speak with absolute freedom of speech.

Few clearer examples of παρρησία can be adduced than the comedies of Aristophanes, where nothing, absolutely nothing, is left unsaid, and where nothing is sacred. Nothing escapes his diatribal sarcasm, and nobody is safe from his thundering ridicule. Not even the gods, with the notable exception of Athena, are spared. Mingled with the expected vulgarities and occasional blasphemies, no less than with the considerable amount of τῦφος of Aristophanes' own mind, there is a great deal in his comedies that exemplifies unadulterated freedom of speech. Out of them, we could even construct a dictionary of new meanings, perhaps as anticipations of Diogenes' own 'definitions', truer and more realistic than those found in ordinary speech. What is a juror? A wasp that is anxious to sting his victims. What is a general? A donkey driver who leads men to death. What is war? A senseless game created by politicians for their own ends. What is peace? Pacification through extermination. What is a politician? An unscrupulous scoundrel who lives solely to take advantage of others. What is a theologian? Another scoundrel who mystifies people with things nobody understands. What is democracy? A form of oligarchy in which the dregs of society assume control. What is the government? A group of clever fools who have seized power to promote their own advantage and abuse the people, who are greater fools. What is a philosopher? A madman who lives suspended in a hanging basket, and who endlessly talks nonsense about this and that, and succeeds in disorienting those who listen to him. What is a Sophist? Another madman who employs language to manipulate people and become wealthy. What is a scientist? Still another madman characterized by arrogance, who spends his time thinking about the stars and the shape of the earth. What is love? Normally nothing but a camouflaged sexual urge. What is education? The process by which young persons are indoctrinated in the ways of the old and by which they grow effeminate and lazy.

The list of Aristophanic 'definitions' could be extended almost indefinitely, for it contains innumerable new meanings, as if the poet had been bent on remaking the language of his time, unmasking the deceptions in which, from his point of view, his contemporaries lived, and bursting the bubbles of their illusions. Undoubtedly, this element of unmasking deceptions is also at the root of Diogenes' attachment to παρρησία. He, too, like Aristophanes, mounted repeatedly the comic stage, not impersonated by professional actors, but assuming himself the role of a performer, wasting no opportunity to practice philosophy *precisely as he defined it*, that is, as the art of calling things by their right name (ὁ οἰκεῖος λόγος), which he must have learned from Antisthenes and indirectly from Socrates. Endowed with tremendous mental lucidity and with a remarkable store of will, he guided in all directions what he interpreted to be the light of reason, and, as if with a lighted lamp, walked among people unmasking deceptions and bursting the bubbles of illusion, hoping to compel others to recognize the truth—ἀλήθεια— inherent in things, not a transcendent or metaphysical truth, but the truth that things speak out for themselves.[17]

For this recognition, Diogenes insisted, it is necessary to have good eyesight and plenty of light to see, not a world beyond this world, as with Plato, but *this* world, the world of immediate human experience. Then, once things are recognized for what they are, we must be willing to call them exactly what they are —we must speak out their names. Inaccurate language, as Socrates says in the *Phaedo*, is not merely a source of deception, but is something that infects the soul with evil. It turns us into inauthentic persons and augments in us the τῦφος that is itself at the basis of our existential dislocation. Every lie, every attempt to cover up what is with what is not, every slip into deceitfulness, every compromise with what Jonathan Swift calls in *Gulliver's Travels* "the Thing-which-is-not,"[18] and even every hesitation to 'say it all', plunges us deeper into the sea of τῦφος. Herein, then, is the essence of Diogenes' notion of παρρησία.

As with Aristophanes, and perhaps even more, we can construct a long list of 'definitions' and synonyms that can be associated with Diogenes and that, through him, became the common stock of ordinary speech among later Cynics both in classical times and in modern times. Just a few examples can illustrate this point. Money becomes the mother of all vices; luxury and an easy life, the dream of a sloth; poverty, a blessing; toils and vicissitudes, another blessing; wealth, theft, and great wealth, greater theft; a woman, grief; a man, still more grief; marriage, entrapment; family relations, still more entrapment; sexual satisfaction, the delight of pigs; a mouse, a paradigm of good life; a dog, something we should all strive to become; a beautiful face and an ugly face, precisely the same thing; a long life and a short life, again, the very same thing; a Greek, a Persian, and an Egyptian, once more, exactly the same unhappy thing; wine, the drink of fools; a man who takes pride for being a gourmet, a mindless fool; a human being, generally an aberration of nature; a politician, a rascal and a thief; an orator, a demented demagogue; a priest, a dispenser of lies; the belief in the gods, the consolation of dumb heads; speculative philosophy, especially that of Plato, a waste of time; education, another waste of time; news about people and places, useless gossip and still another waste of time; the stars in the sky and the beauty of the universe, an absurdity with which we should not be concerned; destiny and fate, excuses for poor behavior; a soldier, a trained killer, and a general, a trainer of killers; a policeman, a thief who is licensed to steal; a tax collector, a professional thief; a common thief, a person who reclaims what is his own; the State, the enemy of human freedom; one's country, the place where one happens to be at any given time; allegiance to a city or to a country, a manifestation of lunacy; democracy, a government in the hands of many fools; oligarchy, a government controlled by a few fools; monarchy, a government by one fool; a king, a tarantula; a prince who mingles with the poor, a liar; a man who commits a crime and denies it, a coward; a prostitute, someone who does what others do, but admits it; a friend, a rare occurrence in nature; an honest person, an almost impossible phenomenon; obedience to the laws, a form of idiocy; abidance by rules of etiquette and decorum, sheer stupidity; spectacles and diversions, a temporary cure for boredom and peepshows for unintelligent people; athletes who become famous and rich, the proof of human thoughtlessness.

  It does not require much mental clarity to realize that such a list of Cynic synonyms includes a heavy dosage of exaggeration and distortion. Not every woman is grief, and neither is every king a tarantula. There may be many policemen or law officers who do not make it a practice to steal and to abuse their power. Ibn-Hindu (Diogenes 36) reports that once, when Diogenes saw a policeman (probably a Scythian archer[19]) beating a thief and dragging him along, he exclaimed, "Wonder of wonders! A thief who steals in public disciplining a thief who steals in secret!" Such an occurrence was probably as common then as it is now, and, undoubtedly, the abuse of power of those in authority was surely as frequent among the Greeks as among us. Still, Diogenes universalizes a small number of occurrences and turns them into the norm, and even alters ordinary speech—a 'policeman' becomes a 'public thief'—to accentuate his point. This is, however, the undeniable mark of his Cynicism, for, as he himself said, it is necessary to "set the note a bit too high" in order to compel us to sing his tune, and recognize and denounce evil and vice whenever and wherever we find it. His παρρησία, then, was not only an absolute commitment to a systematic unmasking of deceptions and bursting of illusions, but also a rhetorical game, played in all seriousness, to dissipate, even if only slightly, the suffocating τῦφος of his contemporaries and, in fact, of all subsequent generations.

His example was imitated and emulated by many among the late Cynics and even by some of the Stoics. Like him, they were committed to 'calling things by their right name', for which reason we find them 'spitting out the truth'—at least what *they* saw as the truth—everywhere and without any concern about the consequences.[20] We hear repeatedly that during Roman times the Cynics were often flogged, thrown in prison, and exiled for their public indecencies, but we are justified in suspecting that it was for their freedom of speech that they were punished, particularly, as Dio Cassius tells us (*Historia Romanorum* LVI), for publicly insulting imperial magistrates. The list of Cynics harshly treated by the Roman authorities is long, but there should be nothing surprising in this, for how else could they have dealt with those whose primary aim was to undermine the foundations of the greatest enemy of human freedom, the State? How could have an ordinary emperor endured for long the presence of a barking Cynic at his side, reminding him of his tarantula-like character and of his worthlessness as a human being? Only an emperor of the moral and intellectual stature of Marcus Aurelius, who as a Stoic philosopher was ideologically related to the Cynics, could have tolerated such behavior, as in fact he did when Peregrinus Proteus abused him in public. As for the rest of those in power among the Romans, we can rest assured that they dealt harshly with the Cynics, who practiced so freely what Diogenes called "the most beautiful thing in the world," namely, freedom of speech (D.L. VI, 69), and who saw themselves as witnesses of the truth, as Seneca reports of Demetrius (*Epist.* XX),[21] willingly accepting even execution rather than the silence demanded by the State. Among the Stoics, the notable example of Helvidius Priscus comes to mind. This remarkable man, a Roman senator and the son-in-law of the distinguished Stoic philosopher Thrasea Paetus, practiced what he must have learned from the Cynics, especially from Demetrius. After Thrasea Paetus was forced to commit suicide by Nero in A.D. 66, Helvidius Priscus turned decisively toward Cynicism and a few years later openly challenged the imperial authority of Vespasian, doing on the floor of the Roman senate what the Cynics did in the streets: spitting out the truth, he called the emperor's claim to be the sole authority in Rome by its right name, that is, a manifestation of madness, for which he was summarily executed in A.D. 75. By his martyrdom, he paid a fitting homage to Diogenes' legacy.

Undoubtedly, genuine Cynicism did not become extinct with the end of classical times, and the legacy of Diogenes, ultimately a profound human reaction in the presence of the persistent and permeating irrationality of human behavior, has remained alive. Examples of Cynic-like men and women can be adduced, people who either by temperament, or on account of powerful philosophical influences, or because of painful circumstances, have turned themselves into rebellious dogs in the midst of a human world that gives every indication of being a mistake. Such people, some well known like Henry Thoreau, Bertrand Russell, and Michel Foucault, and others—the majority—anonymous and unnoticed, have been and are regulars in the Army of the Dog, an army that as long as human beings remain immersed in τῦφος cannot be disbanded. Faithful to the building blocks of Cynicism with which Diogenes sought to build his philosophy of protest, and attached to the concepts that lurk behind his sayings and antics, such modern Cynics maintain alive the flame of his lamp, identifying and denouncing deception wherever they find it, unmasking the delusions that render human life disoriented and turbulent, speaking out against the confusions that infect the human mind, and, in sum, making sure that the man in the tub is not altogether forgotten or transformed into what he was not.[22]

For through a curious linguistic transformation, Diogenes' Cynicism has come to mean in modern times something fundamentally different from what it was. In modern languages, Cynicism has undergone a radical metamorphosis and has become *cynicism*,[23] and the ancient Cynics have been replaced by hordes of *cynical* characters, who are as distant from Diogenes as those "less-than-human" creatures against whom he directed his Cynic rhetoric. Cynicism, then, in its modern ordinary sense has acquired a meaning that is not even a faint reflection of its ancient classical meaning, for which reason Bertrand Russell, as we saw in chapter 1, was correct in insisting that modern cynical people have nothing in common with Diogenes.[24] Writing at the end of the nineteenth century, Émile Tardieu noted that cynicism "stands for everything that is ugly and repulsive in the human heart," and characterized a cynic as an individual who is immersed in egoism, who is not ashamed of his selfishness, and who is even proud of his carelessness for society and for every person except himself. Cynicism, argued Tardieu, is a mode of consciousness that promotes contempt for human nature and is the great supporter of every imaginable kind of immoral instinct. Akin to nihilism, cynicism leads individuals and nations to abandon all moral values and to drown in a fetid sea of intellectual and ethical moroseness and pessimism.[25] As such, then, cynicism is ultimately a manifestation of cultural decadence. The theme of cultural decadence reappears clearly in one of the most perceptive studies of cynicism in recent years, Peter Sloterdijk's *Kritik der zynischen Vernunft*,[26] where cynicism is understood as the manifestation of "the twilight of false consciousness" (*"Dämmerung des falschen Bewusstsein"*).

Modern cynicism, while related historically to the Cynicism of Diogenes and other classical Cynics, represents a new cultural phenomenon that is disseminated throughout all areas of human concern and activity. We find it in international and national affairs, in politics and education, in art and music, in religion and theology, and in philosophy, where it constitutes, as it were, its very deathbed. It unambiguously announces to the world, not only that God and the gods are dead, but also that all ideals and aspirations are defunct. All values and all styles of life stand, from its point of view, exactly on the same level of worth or worthlessness. The modern cynic, accordingly, has undertaken and succeeded in an all-out iconoclastic campaign to tear down all vertical valuations, and has placed all things on one horizontal level of intellectual and spiritual mediocrity. He has pushed Diogenes' selective anti-intellectualism to an extreme that would have left him baffled and distressed. Not the least among his accomplishments, we may add, has been the fundamental alteration of the very meaning of the word that gave its name to Diogenes' philosophy and style of life. Almost as if taking revenge on what Diogenes stood for, the new cynic has transformed the meaning of Cynicism into its very opposite. Instead of clarity of mind, he extols irrationality; instead of the commitment to 'saying it all', he strives at covering up all things under a mantle of euphemistic deceptions; instead of self-sufficiency, he proclaims the need to belong to the State, to be a spokesperson for mystifying ideologies, and to glorify and worship what has come to be known among us as 'celebrities'; instead of strength of character, he advocates the enfeeblement of everyone; and instead of the asceticism of Diogenes and Antisthenes, he preaches undiluted hedonism. For these are the virtues inherent in modern cynicism.

This depressing assessment of the stage to which cultural evolution—or rather devolution—has taken us twenty-three centuries after Diogenes' death is not altogether misguided, for undeniable manifestations of intellectual vacuity and irrational excess abound everywhere. Surely, such forms of decadence have always existed in human communities, as Diogenes' own war against *his* social and political world demonstrates. One only has to recall the cynicism of Thrasymachus of Chalcedon, the Sophist who defined the purpose of human life in terms of the success brought about by naked power. The unscrupulous and low-life politicians of Diogenes' own time give testimony of the fact that then, too, cynicism in its modern sense was a common phenomenon.

Nevertheless, the difference is that among us this new cynicism seems to have become dominant and all-inclusive, for the mentality and style of life of its adherents have been enthroned as the norm or the standard. The *revolt* of the masses, foreseen by Ortega y Gasset in 1927, has become the *triumph* of the masses, the victory of what he called *el hombre masa*—the mass man,[27] that is, the clearest specimen of modern cynicism, for whom nothing is sacred or holy and nothing is worth his respect, and for whom truth and falsity are empty linguistic games, and appearance and reality are indistinguishable. Equipped with the tools of technology and proud of the achievements of science that he enjoys but does not understand, the mass man views himself, his culture, and his country as the highest plateau of human evolution. Forgetful of anything that cannot be turned into a source of immediate advantage for himself, the new cynic marches blindly into the future in a state of emotional and irrational intoxication that is precisely what the Cynics called τῦφος.

To counterbalance the onslaught of modern cynicism that as an epidemic appears to be destined to rule over all human affairs, it is necessary to resurrect from his Corinthian grave the man in the tub, who, transformed into a dog, lived among the classical Greeks practicing his uncompromising Cynicism, teaching them by word and by deed the necessity of returning to their true human nature and, above all, the art of recognizing the gap that separates appearance from reality. His legacy, mostly confined today to scholarly journals and found in occasional newspaper cartoons and editorials, and kept alive by only very few marginal individuals, could serve as a source of light that, like the flame of his lamp, may succeed in dissipating the cloud of confusion—the inveterate τῦφος—in which we are immersed. Every century, every culture, and every community needs a Diogenes, and ours, it seems, needs him with great urgency. What is also needed, however, is not only a Diogenes in our midst, but the courage to withstand his presence and the clarity of mind to understand and actualize his message.

Notes

1. Sallustius, the last representative of classical Cynicism, was a Syrian philosopher about whom only secondary information is available. While living in Alexandria, he exemplified a rigorous and uncompromising asceticism. He insisted that the pursuit of philosophy as a speculative study is not only difficult but impossible, for which reason he, like Diogenes, urged others to abandon so futile an endeavor.

2. Stoicism derived its name from the Stoa (ἡ Ποικιλὴ Στοά), a painted colonnade in ancient Athens on the north side of the marketplace, where Zeno and other Stoic philosophers were in the habit of lecturing and conversing. Zeno was the first head (προστάτης) of the school.

3. A. A. Long, "The Socratic Tradition: Diogenes, Crates, and Hellenistic Ethics," in *The Cynic Movement in Antiquity and Its Legacy*. Edited by R. Bracht Branham and M. O. Goulet-Cazé (Berkeley: University of California Press, 1996), p. 28.

4. J. Ferrater Mora, "Cyniques et stoïciens." *Revue de Métaphysique et de Morale* 62 (1957), p. 20.

5. Ibid., p. 23.

6. J. Ferguson, *Moral Values in the Ancient World* (London: Methuen & Co., 1959), p. 108.

7. In the *Euthyphro* (3c), Socrates says to Euthyphro: "I have a benevolent habit of pouring out myself to everybody, and would even pay for a listener."

8. A useful listing of Cynic philosophers, with brief biographical comments, is found in M. O. Goulet-Cazé, "A Comprehensive Catalogue of Known Cynic Philosophers," in *The Cynic Movement in Antiquity and Its Legacy*. Edited by R. Bracht Branham and M. O. Goulet-Cazé (Berkeley: University of California Press, 1996), pp. 389-413. The author divides her catalogue into eight sections: (1) eighty-three Cynics whose historical authenticity is certain; (2) fourteen Cynics whose names are unknown; (3) ten persons whose relationship with Cynicism is uncertain; (4) thirty-one Cynics mentioned in the *Cynic Epistles*; (5) thirteen probably fictional Cynics who appear in various literary works; (6) a certain Nabal who is mentioned in *1 Kings* 25:3 as a dog-like man (*kéléb* in Hebrew and *kunikos* in the Septuagint translation); (7) four non-Cynic individuals known as 'dogs'; and (8) various literary works whose titles include the word 'dog' possibly in a Cynic sense.

9. For a documented discussion of the late Cynics, see L. E. Navia, *Classical Cynicism: A Critical Study* (Westport, Conn.: Greenwood Press, 1996), pp. 119-192.

10. For a description of Jesus as a Hellenistic Cynic, see R. N. Ostling et al., "Who Was Jesus?" *Time* 132 (August 15, 1988), pp. 37-42. In this article, Burton Mack is quoted referring to Jesus as a "rather normal cynic-like figure" and as "the epitome of a cross-cultural mix" in which Hellenistic and Roman cultural trends, including Cynicism, collided with Jewish thought and traditions. Jesus' behavior and preaching, according to Mack, reflected the typical Cynic rebelliousness against the prevailing social malaise. For comments on the relationship between the Essene traditions connected with the community at Qumran and the Cynics, see C. M. Tuckett, "A Cynic *Q*?" *Biblica* 70 (1989), pp. 349-376. A discussion of the possible presence of Cynic elements in certain Gospel passages (e.g., *Luke* 10:2-16 and 6:27-28), see L. E. Vaage, "*Q*: The Ethos and Ethics of an Itinerant Intelligence" (Ph.D. diss. Claremont Graduate School, 1987).

11. The outward resemblance between the Cynics, especially those of Roman times, and Christian mendicant monks has been noticed by numerous historians and classical scholars. See, for instance, W. Durant, *The Life of Greece* (New York: Simon and Schuster, 1939), where Antisthenes is referred to as "a Franciscan without theology" (p. 506), and where Cynicism after Diogenes is described as "a religious order without religion" (p. 509). The scholarly and popular literature that has recognized more than an apparent relationship between Cynicism and Christianity is extensive and varied. See, for instance, J. Ferguson, *Background of Christian Origins* (Grand Rapids, Mich.: William B. Eerdmans Publishing Company, 1993), pp. 327-333, and F. G. Downing, "Cynics and Early Christianity," in *Le Cynisme ancien et ses prolongements. Actes du Colloque International du CNRS*. Edited by M. O. Goulet-Cazé and R. Goulet (Paris: Presses Universitaires de France, 1993), pp. 281-302, where the author notes that "Cynicism as a sect seems to have been for the early Christians both a model and an ally, while also a most important rival, having too much in common with the newer movement to be other than disturbing" (p. 285). The author also observes that "a Galilean peasant such as Jesus of Nazareth" could have been acquainted with, and influenced by, the Cynic community at Gadara, only thirty-five kilometers from

Nazareth (ibid.). The idea that Cynic ideas may have influenced Jesus during his formative years is also emphasized by Downing in *Jesus and the Threat of Freedom* (London: SMC, 1987), pp. 126ff. We are not unjustified, argues Downing, in referring to Jesus as a Cynic preacher. For further comments on the influence of Cynicism on the development of Christianity, see F. Gasco Lacalle, "Cristianos y cínicos. Una tificación del fenómeno cristiano durante el siglo II." *Memorias de Historia Antigua* 7 (1986), pp. 111-119, where the author calls attention to the fact that Christian apologists often made use of the same rhetorical means employed by the Cynics.

12. For a discussion of the idealization of the early Cynics, principally Diogenes, in Roman times, see M. Billerbeck, "Le Cynisme idéalisé d'Épictète à Julien," in *Le Cynisme ancien et ses prolongements. Actes du Colloque International du CNRS*. Edited by M. O. Goulet-Cazé and R. Goulet (Paris: Presses Universitaires de France, 1993), pp. 319-338. Julian, the author notes, "defends a sublime kind of Cynicism, tinted with an element of religiosity" and presents to us "the man of Sinope as a paradigm of a philosophy that is both divine and universal" (p. 319).

13. Lucian's treatment of the late Cynics in general and of Peregrinus in particular has been subjected to criticism in many scholarly works. In most of them, there is the sense that, as Gomperz put it (*Greek Thinkers*, Vol. 2, p. 152), Lucian displayed "more zeal than wit," and that the portrait of the Cynics that emerges from his satirical accounts is unduly distorted and grossly exaggerated. See in this regard, for instance, J. Bernays, *Lucian und die Kyniker* (Berlin: Verlag von Wilhelm Harts, 1879).

14. For a discussion of this idea among the late Cynics—an idea traceable to Diogenes—see D. Ingalls, "Cynics and *pasupatas*: The Seeking of Dishonor." *Harvard Theological Review* 55 (1962), pp. 281-298.

15. For a documented discussion of the significance of τῦφος, see F. Decleva Caizzi, "Τῦφος. Contributo all storia di un concetto." *Sandalion* 3 (1980), pp. 53-66.

16. In Hippocratic medical writings, typhus is described as a disease caused by vapors from swamps and putrid water. Among other things, typhus was known to be responsible for a delirium-like condition in which the afflicted person utters unintelligible sounds.

17. The Greek term for truth, ἀλήθεια, conveys an idea that is not obvious in the English word. The meaning of the Greek word ἀλήθεια can be rendered as 'unhiddenness' or 'uncovering', or, more precisely, 'bringing back to memory'.

18. J. Swift, *Gulliver's Travels* (New York: The Heritage Press, 1940), p. 264. In Swift's work, we hear about an extraordinary race of intelligent horses, the Houyhnhnms, whose language an ordinary Yahoo like Gulliver finds difficult to understand, because of its lack of words or phrases to express "the Thing-which-is-not." These horses, accordingly, are unable to deceive one another because their language prevents them from lying. For comments on the parallelism between Swift and the Cynics, particularly Antisthenes, see Navia, *Classical Cynicism*, p. 64.

19. During the fifth and fourth centuries B.C., Scythian archers were used in Athens as policemen, as we learn, for instance, from Aristophanes' *Acharnians* 703-706.

20. Diogenes' definition of philosophy as the art of calling things by their right names reminds us of a component in Confucius' approach to the issue of right living. Like Diogenes, Confucius insisted that only through the systematic 'rectification of names' can we begin to clear the mind of its confusions and take the first steps toward the attainment of virtue and happiness. For a discussion of Confucius' call for the 'rectification of names', especially in the context of Socrates' insistence on the necessity of avoiding inaccurate language (*Phaedo* 115e), see W. E. Steinkraus, "Socrates, Confucius, and the Rectification of Names." *Philosophy East and West* 30 (1980), pp. 261-264.

21. For a discussion of the Cynics' conception of themselves as 'witnesses for the truth', see A. Delatte, "Le sage-témoin dans la philosophie stoïco-cynique." *Bulletin de la Classe de Lettres de l'Académie de Belgique* 39 (1953), pp. 166-186.

22. The name of Diogenes has come to be associated with modes of behavior that are as removed from him as one can imagine. In modern medical geriatrics, for instance, there is a family of symptoms known as 'the Diogenes syndrome' that refers to the behavior of senile people who are incontinent, neglect themselves, and do not obey any rules. For comments on this syndrome, see B. V. Reifler, "The Diogenes Syndrome: Of Omelettes and Souffles." *Journal of the American Geriatrics Society* 44 (1966), pp. 1484-1486.

23. I use the capitalized words 'Cynicism' and 'Cynic' when referring to the classical Cynics, and the words 'cynicism', 'cynic', and 'cynical' when referring to modern cynics. For a discussion of the transformation in meaning of the word 'Cynic', see J. Fellsches, "Zynismus," in *Europäische Enzyklopädie zu Philosophie und Wissenschaften*. Edited by H. J. Sandkühler. (Hamburg: Felix Miner Verlag, 1990), Vol. 4, pp. 1008-1010. I have ignored, as not being especially enlightening, the very common use of the terms 'cynical' and 'cynicism', in which a sense of distrust and suspicion concerning people's behavior in general and the operations of governments in particular is implied.

24. B. Russell, *A History of Western Philosophy* (New York: Simon & Schuster, 1972), pp. 231ff.

25. É. Tardieu, "Le Cynisme: Étude psychologique." *Revue Philosophique de la France et de l'Étranger* 57 (1904), pp. 1-28.

26. P. Sloterdijk, *Kritik der zynischen Vernunft* (Frankfurt/Main: Suhrkamp, 1983), Vol. 1, pp. 33ff.

27. J. Ortega y Gasset, *La rebelión de las masas* (Madrid: Revista de Occidente, 1927).

Appendix

Diogenes Laertius: *The Life of Diogenes of Sinope*

[VI, 20] Diogenes was a native of Sinope,[1] son of Hicesias,[2] a banker.[3] Diocles[4] relates that he went into exile because his father was entrusted with the money of the state and adulterated the coinage. But Eubulides[5] in his book on Diogenes says that Diogenes himself did this and was forced to leave home along with his father. Moreover, Diogenes himself actually confesses in his *Pordalus* that he adulterated the coinage.[6] Some say that having been appointed to supervise the workmen, he was persuaded by them, and that he went to Delphi or to the Delian oracle in his own city to ask Apollo whether he should do what he was urged to do. When the god gave him permission to alter the political 'currency',[7] not understanding what this meant, he adulterated the state coinage, and when he was detected, according to some he was banished, while according to others he voluntarily left the city for fear of the consequences.

[21] One version is that his father entrusted him with the money and he debased it, in consequence of which the father was imprisoned and died, while the son fled, came to Delphi, and inquired, not whether he should falsify the coinage, but what he should do to gain the greatest reputation; and that then it was that he received the oracle. On reaching Athens, he came under the influence of Antisthenes. Being rejected by him, because he never welcomed disciples, Diogenes wore him out by sheer persistence. Once, when Antisthenes stretched out his staff against him, Diogenes offered his head with the words, "Strike, for you will find no wood hard enough to keep me away from you, so long as I think that you have something to say."[8] From that time on he was his disciple, and, exile as he was, set out upon a simple life.

Reprinted by permission of the publishers and the Loeb Classical Library from *Diogenes Laertius: Lives of Eminent Philosophers*, Vol. II. Translated by R. D. Hicks (Cambridge, Mass.: Harvard University Press, 1925). Edited and annotated by L. E. Navia.

[22] According to Theophrastus in the Megarian dialogue,[9] after watching a mouse running around in the marketplace, not looking for a place to lie down, not afraid of the dark, and not seeking any of the things considered dainties, Diogenes discovered the means of adapting himself to circumstances.[10] He was the first, some say, to fold his cloak in half because he was obliged to sleep in it as well, and he carried a wallet[11] to hold his food, and used any place for any purpose, either for eating, or for sleeping or conversing. Then he would say, pointing to the portico of the temple of Zeus and the Hall of Processions, that the Athenians had provided him with places to live in.

[23] He did not lean upon a staff[12] until he grew old, but afterwards he would carry it everywhere, not indeed in the city, but when walking along the road with it and with his wallet, as we learn from Olympiodorus,[13] Polyeuctus the orator, and Lysanias[14] the son of Aeschrio. Once he wrote to someone to try and procure a cottage for him, but when this man took a long time in complying with his request, Diogenes took for his abode the tub in the Metroön,[15] as he himself explains in his letters. In the summer, he used to roll in it over hot sand, while in the winter he would embrace statues covered with snow, seeking every means to accustom himself to hardship.

[24] He was great at pouring contempt on his contemporaries. The school of Euclides[16] he called bilious, Plato's lectures a waste of time,[17] the performances at the Dionysian festival great peepshows for fools, and the demagogues the mob's lackeys. He also used to say, when he saw physicians, philosophers, and ship pilots, that he deemed man to be the most intelligent of all animals, but, when he saw interpreters of dreams and diviners and all those who went to them, he would argue that man was the most stupid among all animals. He would constantly say that for the right conduct of life we only need reason or a halter.[18]

[25] One day, observing Plato eating olives at a costly banquet, "How is it," he noted, "that you, a philosopher who sailed to Sicily for the sake of these delicacies, now, when they are in front of you, do not seem to enjoy them?"[19] "By the gods," replied Plato, "there also for the most part I lived on olives and other things." "Why then," said Diogenes, "did you have to go to Syracuse? Was it that Attica did not grow olives at that time?" Favorinus in his *Miscellaneous History*,[20] however, attributes this to Aristippus.[21] Again, another time he was eating dried figs when he encountered Plato and offered him a share of them. When Plato took and ate them, Diogenes remarked, "I said that you might share them, not that you should eat all of them."

[26] One day, when Plato had invited to his house some friends coming from Dionysius, Diogenes entered the house and trampling on the carpets said, "I trample upon Plato's vainglory," to which Plato replied, "How much pride, Diogenes, you expose to view by pretending not to be proud!" Others tell us that what Diogenes said was, "I trample upon the pride of Plato," to which Plato

retorted, "Yes, Diogenes, with another kind of pride." Sotion, however, in his fourth book makes the Cynic address this remark to Plato himself.[22] Once Diogenes asked Plato for wine and for some dried figs, upon which Plato sent him a whole jar of wine. "If someone asks you how many two and two make, will you answer," asked Diogenes, "twenty? So, it seems that you neither give what you are asked nor answer as you are questioned." Thus he scoffed at him as one who talked without end.[23]

[27] When he was asked where in Greece he found good men, he replied, "Good men, nowhere; but good boys in Sparta." One day, when he was discoursing in earnest and no one paid attention to him, he began whistling, and as people gathered around him, he reproached them for coming in all seriousness to hear nonsense, but slowly and disdainfully when the subject was serious. He would say that men strive in digging trenches and kicking to outdo one another, but that no one strives to become a good and true man.[24]

[28] He would wonder why the grammarians insist on investigating the ills of Odysseus, while remaining unconcerned about their own shortcomings[25]; or why musicians should tune the strings of the lyre, while leaving the dispositions of their souls discordant; or why the mathematicians should gaze at the sun and the moon, while overlooking matters nearby; or why the orators should make a fuss about justice in their speeches, while never being willing to practice it; or why the avaricious should cry out against money, while remaining excessively attached to it. He also used to condemn those who would praise honest men for being superior to money, while themselves envying the very rich. He was moved to anger that men should sacrifice to the gods to ensure health, while in the middle of the sacrifice would feast to the detriment of their health.[26] He was astonished to see that slaves, when they saw that their masters were gluttons, would not steal some of their food.

[29] He would praise those who were about to marry and refrained, those who intending to go on a voyage never set sail, those who wanting to become engaged in politics did not do such a thing, those who spoke about raising a family and did not do so, and those who were ready to live with potentates but never went near them. He used to say, moreover, that we ought to stretch out our hands to our friends with the fingers open and not closed. In his *Sale of Diogenes*, Menippus[27] recounts how, when pirates captured and put Diogenes for sale, he was asked what was his occupation, to which he replied, "To govern men." He told the crier to give notice that in case anybody wanted to purchase a master for himself, he should buy him. Then, when he was asked to sit, he remarked, "It makes no difference, for in whatever position the fish lie, they still find purchasers."

[30] He said that he found it amazing that before we buy a jar or dish, we inspect its quality, but if it is a man [a slave], we are satisfied simply to look at him. To Xeniades,[28] the man who purchased him, he said: "You must obey me, although

I am a slave, for if a physician or a steersman were in slavery, they would obey him." Eubulus in his book entitled *The Sale of Diogenes* tells us that this is how Diogenes trained the sons of Xeniades. After their other studies, he taught them to ride, to shoot with the bow, and to sling stones and hurl javelins. Later, when they reached the wrestling school, he would not permit the master to give them full athletic training, but only so much as to heighten their color and keep them in good condition.

[31] The boys learned by heart many passages from the poets and the historians, and from the writings of Diogenes himself, and were trained to develop a clear and sharp memory. In the house, too, he taught them to wait upon themselves and to be content with simple food and to drink water. He would make them cut their hair short and wear it unadorned, and go lightly clad, barefoot, silent, and not looking about them in the streets. He would also take them out hunting. For their part, they had a great respect for him and made requests from their parents on his behalf. Eubulus also informs us that Diogenes grew old in the house of Xeniades, and that upon his death he was buried by his sons.

[32] Xeniades once asked him how he wished to be buried, to which he replied, "On my face." "Why?" asked Xeniades. Diogenes replied, "Because after a short time, down is bound to be converted into up." Possibly, this was a reference to the fact that the Macedonians had recently risen from a humble position to political supremacy. Once someone took him into a magnificent house and warned him not to spit, whereupon, after clearing his throat, Diogenes discharged the phlegm on the man's face, arguing that he could not find a more despicable receptacle for it. Some writers associate this incident with Aristippus. One day he shouted out for men to come to listen to him, and when people gathered around him, he began to strike everyone with his staff, saying, "I called for men, not for scoundrels." Hecaton[29] in the first book of his *Anecdotes* recounts this incident. Alexander is reported to have said, "Had I not been Alexander, I would have liked to have been Diogenes."

[33] The word 'disabled', according to Diogenes, ought to be applied, not to the deaf or the blind, but to those who have no wallet.[30] Once, he made his way into a party of young revelers with his head half shaven, as Metrocles relates in his *Anecdotes*,[31] and was roughly handled by them. Afterwards, he entered on a tablet the names of those who had struck him and went around with the tablet hung from his neck, until he had secured universal ridicule, blame, and discredit upon them. He described himself as a dog of the sort which all men praise, but, he added, no one among his admirers had the courage to go out hunting with him.[32] When someone boasted that he had succeeded in vanquishing men at the Pythian games,[33] Diogenes replied, "You defeat slaves, but I defeat human beings."

[34] To those who said to him, "You are an old man and you should take a rest," he replied, "What? If I were running in the stadium, should I slacken my

pace when approaching the goal? Should I not rather attempt to run even faster?"[34] Once, when he was invited to a dinner, he said that he would not go, for on a previous occasion the host had failed to express to him the appropriate gratitude. He would walk barefoot on the snow and do similar things. Even more, he even attempted to eat raw meat, but found himself unable to digest it. Once he found Demosthenes the orator lunching at an inn, and when he retired within, Diogenes remarked, "Now you will really find Demosthenes inside the tavern." When some strangers expressed their desire to see Demosthenes, Diogenes said, stretching out his middle finger, "There goes the demagogue of Athens."[35]

[35] Someone dropped a loaf of bread and was ashamed to pick it up. Then, Diogenes, wishing to teach him a lesson, tied a rope to the neck of a wine jar and proceeded to drag it across the Ceramicus.[36] He was in the habit of saying that he followed the example of the trainers of choruses. For they, too, set the note a bit too high to insure that the singers hit the right note. Most people, he would argue, are so nearly mad that a finger makes all the difference: if you go along with your middle finger stretched out somebody is bound to think that you are mad, but if it is the little finger, nobody would call you mad. Very valuable things are bartered, he said, for things of no value, and vice versa: a statue can bring in three thousand drachmas, whereas a quart of barley flour is sold for two copper coins.

[36] To Xeniades, the man who purchased him, he once said, "Come, see that you obey orders," and when Xeniades answered him by quoting the line, "Backward the streams flow to their fonts," Diogenes asked, "If you had been ill and had purchased a physician, would you then still say to him 'Backward the streams flow to their fonts', instead of obeying him?"[37] Someone once wanted to study under him. Diogenes gave this man a large fish to carry and told him to follow him. In shame, the man threw the fish away and left. Later, when Diogenes met him again, he laughed and said, "A tunny has broken the friendship between you and me!" Diocles, however, gives us another version: someone said to Diogenes, "Tell us what to do," upon which he took him aside and gave him a large piece of cheese, worth half an obol, to carry.[38] As the man declined, Diogenes remarked, "A piece of cheese worth only half an obol has destroyed the friendship between us."

[37] One day, observing a child drinking out of his hands, Diogenes drew away the cup from his wallet with these words: "A child has given me a lesson in plainness of living." He also threw away his bowl when on another occasion he saw a child, who had broken his plate, picking up his lentils with the hollow part of a piece of bread.[39] He would also reason along these lines: "All things belong to the gods. The wise are friends of the gods, and friends own everything in common. Therefore, all things belong to the wise." One day he saw a woman kneeling before the gods in an ungraceful position, and, according to Zoïlus of Perga,[40] wishing to liberate her from her superstitions, he approached her and said, "Are you not afraid,

my good woman, that a god may be standing behind you? For the gods are present everywhere and they may put you to shame."

[38] He dedicated to Asclepius a certain quarrelsome man, who, whenever people fell on their faces, would run up to them and bruise them.[41] All the curses of tragedy, he would say, had befallen him, and he described himself as

> A homeless exile, to his country dead.
> A wanderer who begs for his daily bread.[42]

He claimed, however, that he was able to oppose courage to fortune, nature to convention, and reason to passion. Once, when he was sunning himself in the Craneum,[43] Alexander came to him and, standing close to him, said, "Diogenes, ask of me whatever you want!" His replied was, "Stand out of my light!"[44] Someone was once reading aloud for a very long time, and when he was nearing the end of his lecture, he pointed to a space in the roll with no writing on it. Diogenes then exclaimed: "Cheer up, my men! There is land in sight!"

[39] To someone who had proven conclusively by means of an argument that he had horns, Diogenes, approaching him and touching his forehead, said, "Well, for my part, I do not see any horns." In a similar way, when someone declared that there was no such a thing as motion, he got up and started to walk around.[45] A certain man was once discoursing on astronomical phenomena, which prompted Diogenes to ask him, "How many days has it taken you to come down from the sky?" A eunuch of bad character had inscribed on his door the words, "Let nothing evil enter!" Diogenes asked him, "How is it, then, that the master of the house is allowed to enter?" When he had anointed his feet with an unguent, he affirmed that whereas unguents passed from the head into the air, when applied to the feet they go directly to the nostrils. The Athenians urged him to become initiated into the Mysteries, and told him that those who have been initiated enjoy special privileges in the other world. "It would be ridiculous," said Diogenes, "if Agesilaus and Epaminondas are condemned to lie in the mire, while certain people of no account will live in the Isles of the Blessed just because they were initiated."[46]

[40] When mice crept on the table, he addressed them thus: "See now that even Diogenes keeps parasites." When Plato called him a dog, Diogenes replied, "Quite true, for I come back over and over again to those who have sold me." As he was leaving the public baths somebody asked him if many men were bathing, to which he replied, "No." To another who asked him if there were many bathers he replied, "Yes." Plato had defined man as a biped and featherless animal, for which he was applauded. Diogenes plucked a chicken and brought it into the lecture hall, saying, "Behold Plato's man!" Because of this, 'having broad nails' was added to the definition.[47] To someone who asked him what was the proper time to have lunch, Diogenes replied, "If you are a rich man, whenever you want; if you

are a poor man, whenever you can."

[41] At Megara, he saw the sheep protected by leather jackets, while children went bare. "It might be better," he noted, "to be a Megarian's ram than his son." To someone who was brandishing a beam at him and cried, "Look out," he replied, "What, are you intending to strike me again?" He used to call demagogues the lackeys of the people and the crowns awarded to them the efflorescence of fame. He lit a lamp in broad daylight and said, as he went about, "I am looking for a man." One day he got a thorough drenching where he stood, and, when the bystanders pitied him, Plato remarked that if they really pitied him, they should move away from him, alluding to his vanity. When someone struck him with his fist, Diogenes exclaimed, "By Hercules! How could I have forgotten to put on a helmet when I walked out?"

[42] Again, when Midias assaulted him and went on to say, "Here are three thousand drachmas to your credit," the next day Diogenes put on a pair of boxing gloves and gave the man a thrashing, saying, "Here are three thousand blows to *your* credit."[48] When Lysias the druggist asked him if he believed in the gods, "How can I not believe in them," Diogenes answered, "when I have in my presence a godforsaken wretch like you?" Some writers, however, attribute this to Theodorus.[49] Seeing a man perform religious purifications, Diogenes said, "Unhappy man, don't you know that it is as impossible to get rid of errors of conduct by sprinklings as to correct mistakes of grammar?"[50] He would usually rebuke people concerning their prayers, declaring that they only pray for those things that appear good in their eyes, not for things that are truly good.

[43] As for those who were excited over their dreams, he would say that they did not care for what they did in their waking hours, but were concerned about the dreams and visions of their sleeping hours. At Olympia, when the herald proclaimed Dioxippus the victor over other men, Diogenes objected, saying that whereas Dioxippus was victorious over slaves, he himself was the conqueror of men. Still he was loved by the Athenians, for when some youth broke up his tub, they gave the boy a flogging and furnished Diogenes with another tub. Dionysius the Stoic[51] says that after the battle of Chaeronea, Diogenes was seized and dragged off to Philip, and that, when asked who he was, he replied, "A spy on your insatiable greed." For this answer he was admired and set free.[52]

[44] Once, when Alexander sent a letter to Antipater at Athens through a certain Athlios, Diogenes, who was present, said, "The wretched son of a wretched father to a wretched man through another wretched man."[53] When Perdiccas threatened to put him to death unless he came to him, Diogenes said, "There is nothing surprising in this, for a beetle or a tarantula would do precisely the same."[54] He added that he would have expected the threat to be that Perdiccas would be happy without his company. He would often insist loudly that the gods had given to human beings the means to live well and happily, but that they had ignored this

fact and had chosen to require honey cakes, unguents, and other similar things. Hence, he once said to a man whose shoes were being put on by his servant, "You have not attained complete happiness unless your servant wipes out your nose as well; but that will come when you have lost the use of your hands."

[45] Once he saw the officials of a temple leading away a man who had stolen a bowl that belonged to the temple's treasure, and said, "The big thieves are leading away the little thief." Noticing one day that a young man was throwing stones at a cross,[55] he said to him, "Well done, for some day you will come to the gallows." When some boys gathered around him and said, "Let's be careful, lest he may bite us," Diogenes answered, "Don't be afraid, boys, dogs don't eat garbage."[56] To someone who was proud of wearing a lion's skin his words were, "Stop wearing the trappings of courage." When someone was extolling the good fortune of Callisthenes,[57] commenting on the splendor that he shared in the company of Alexander, Diogenes remarked, "Not quite so, but rather his ill fortune; for he breakfasts and dines only when Alexander thinks fit."

[46] Once, being short of money, he told his friends that he was not asking them for alms, but for the repayment of what belonged to him. One day, having behaved indecently in the marketplace, he remarked that he wished that it were as easy to relieve his hunger by rubbing his empty belly. When he saw a young man getting ready to dine with satraps, he dragged him off, took him to his friends, and begged them to keep strict watch over him. When an effeminately attired youth asked Diogenes a question, he said to him that he would not answer him unless he took off his clothes and showed him whether he was a man or a woman. To another youth who was playing throwing wine from a cup into a basin, Diogenes remarked, "The better you play at this sort of thing, the worse off you will be."[58] At a feast certain people kept throwing bones at him, as they would have done to a dog. Diogenes played a dog's trick and urinated on them.

[47] He would speak of rhetoricians, orators, and those seeking to become celebrities, as "three times human," meaning by this, "three times wretched."[59] There was an ignorant rich man whom Diogenes used to call "the sheep with the Golden Fleece." Once, when he saw the sign 'For sale' on the house of a profligate, he said to the house, "I knew that after so much overindulgence you would throw up your owner." To a young man who complained about the number of people who annoyed him by their attentions, he said, "Cease hanging out a sign of invitation."[60] He said about a certain public bath that was dirty, "When people bathe here, where are they to go to get clean?" There was a stout musician whom everybody despised, except Diogenes who would praise him. When asked why, he said, "Because despite his big size, he insists on playing the flute and has not yet become a brigand."

[48] He greeted with these words a certain musician who was invariably deserted by his audience: "Hail you, rooster!" When the musician asked him why

he called him so, Diogenes replied, "Because you manage to make everyone get up." As a young man was delivering a speech, Diogenes, having filled the front of his cloak with lupines,[61] began to eat them, standing in front of him. When the audience turned to look at Diogenes, he said that he was greatly surprised that everyone should ignore the orator just to look at him. A very superstitious man once said to him, "With one blow I can break your head in half," to which Diogenes replied, "And I, by a sneeze from the left, can make you tremble."[62] When Hegesias once asked him to lend him one of his writings, Diogenes said to him, "You are a fool, Hegesias, because you choose painted figs instead of real figs, and pass over true training and opt for written rules."[63]

[49] When someone reproached him of having been exiled, his reply was, "It was precisely through that, you miserable creature, that I became a philosopher."[64] Again, when someone reminded him that the people of Sinope had sentenced him to exile, he replied, "And I condemned them to stay in Sinope." When he saw an Olympic victor tending sheep, he accosted him and said, "Too quickly, my friend, have you left Olympia for Nemea."[65] Once, when someone asked him why athletes are so stupid, he replied, "Because they are built of pork and beef." When he was begging alms from a statue, someone asked him why he did so, to which he answered, "To get practice in being refused." When he begged for alms—as was at first his custom because of his poverty—he would use these words, "If you have already given to someone else, why not also to me? If you have not given any alms, why not begin with me?"

[50] "What kind of bronze," they asked him, "is the best to make a statue of a tyrant?" He replied, "That of which Harmodius and Aristogiton were molded."[66] "How did Dionysius treat his friends?" someone wanted to know from him. "Like purses," he replied, "for as long as they are full, he hangs them up, but when they are empty, he throws them away."[67] To a man who was recently married and had posted on his door this sign:

> The son of Zeus, victorious Hercules,
> Dwells here. Let nothing evil enter!

Diogenes remarked, "After the war, there will be an alliance." The love of money, he would insist, is the mother-city of all evils. When a certain spendthrift was eating olives in a tavern, he said to him, "If you had had your lunch in this way, you would not be dining in this fashion."

[51] He called good men the images of the gods, and love the business of the idle. To the question, "What is the most wretched thing in life?" he replied, "To grow old without any resources." Again, to the question, "Which among the beasts has the most terrible bite?" he answered, "Of those that are wild, a sycophant,[68] and of those that are tame, a flatterer." Seeing two badly painted centaurs, he asked,

"Which of these two is Chiron?"[69] He compared flattering speech to honey with which people choke, and he referred to the stomach as man's Charybdis.[70] When he heard that a certain Didymon, the flute-player, had been caught in adultery, his comment was, "His name is sufficient to have him hanged."[71] To the question, "Why is gold pale?" his answer was, "Because it has so many thieves plotting against it."[72] Once, when he saw a woman carried in a litter, he observed that the cage was not in keeping with its contents.

[52] One day, when he saw a runaway slave sitting on the brink of a well, he said to him, "Take care, my lad, lest you may fall in."[73] Again, when he saw a boy stealing clothes at the baths, he asked him, "Is it for a little unguent or for a new cloak?" Observing some women hanged from an olive-tree, he remarked, "I wish that every tree bore similar fruit." To a highway robber who approached him he said:

> What art thou doing here, my gallant?
> Dost thou come perchance to plunder the dead?[74]

When asked whether he had a house cleaner or a servant to wait on him, he replied, "No." "But if you should die," they inquired, "who will carry you to burial?" "Whoever wants to keep my house," he answered.[75]

[53] Noticing a handsome young man lying in an indecent position, he nudged him and shouted, "Up, man, up, lest some enemy may thrust a dart into your back!" To someone who was feasting lavishly he said:

> Short-lived thou shalt be, my son, by what thou buyest.[76]

As Plato was discoursing about Ideas and using nouns such as 'tablehood' and 'cuphood', Diogenes said, "I see tables and cups, but your tablehood and cuphood I cannot see anywhere." "That," replied Plato, "is easily explainable, for you have eyes to see the visible tables and cups, but not the understanding by which the ideal tablehood and cuphood can be discerned."[77]

[54] Someone once asked him [Plato], "What sort of man do you consider Diogenes to be?" His answer was, "A Socrates gone mad."[78] To someone who wanted to know what is the right time to get married, he answered, "For a young man, not yet; for an old man, never at all."[79] When asked how he would like to be struck, he answered, "Wearing a helmet." When he encountered a youth who was elaborately dressed, he said to him, "If it is for the sake of men, you are a fool; if for the sake of women, you are a scoundrel." One day he noticed that a young man was blushing, and he said to him, "Have courage, my boy, for that is the color of virtue." Once, after listening to a couple of lawyers disputing among themselves, he condemned both of them, saying that while one of them had stolen from the other, the other had not lost anything that was his. When asked what is the best

kind of wine, he replied that it is always the wine for which other people pay. When they told him that many people laughed at him, he replied, "I am not laughed down."

[55] Someone once affirmed that life is something evil, but Diogenes corrected him in these words: "Not life itself, but living an evil life."[80] When they advised him to go in pursuit of his runaway slave, he replied, "That would be absurd, for if Manes can live without Diogenes, why cannot Diogenes get along without Manes?"[81] Once, when he was eating olives he found a piece of cake among them. He took the piece and threw it away, saying, "Stranger, take away yourself from the prince's path."[82] Again, on a similar occasion he said, "He lashed an olive."[83] When asked what kind of dog he was, he answered, "When hungry, a Maltese; when full, a Molossian—two breeds which most people praise, although for fear of fatigue they do not venture to go hunting with them.[84] Thus, you cannot stand my company, because you are afraid of the discomforts."

[56] "Do wise men eat cakes?" he was asked, to which he replied, "Yes, cakes of all kinds, just like other men."[85] "Why do people give alms to beggars and not to philosophers?" they asked him. "Because," he said, "people fear one day being lame or blind, but never expect to become philosophers." Once, he was begging a miserly man who was slow in responding. Diogenes then said to him, "My friend, I am asking you for some food, not for money for my funeral expenses." When they reproached him one day for having counterfeited the currency, he replied, "That belongs to another time—when I was just as you are now. For your part, however, you will never be as I am now." To a man who reproached him for the same offence, Diogenes made a more scurrilous remark.

[57] When he visited Myndus[86] and noticed that, though a small town, its gates were huge, he shouted, "Men of Myndus, close your gates, lest your city should run away." When he saw that they had caught a certain man stealing a purple robe, he quoted this line:

Fast gripped by purple death and forceful fate.[87]

Craterus once invited him to go and visit him, but Diogenes replied, "No, I would rather live on a few grains of salt in Athens than enjoy the sumptuous food at Craterus' table."[88] He approached Anaximenes the rhetorician,[89] who was a fat man, and said, "Why don't you let us beggars have a piece of your belly? It will be a great relief for you and a benefit for us." Again, when this man was making a speech, Diogenes distracted the audience by holding in his hands some salt fish. As this annoyed the speaker, Diogenes remarked, "An obol's worth of fish has disrupted Anaximenes' lecture."

[58] When they scolded him for eating in the marketplace, he said, "Well, it was in the marketplace that I felt hungry."[90] Some writers maintain that the following anecdote should be associated with Diogenes: When Plato saw him

washing lettuces, he approached him and quietly said to him, "If you had paid your respects to Dionysius, you would not be washing lettuces now," to which with equal calmness Diogenes replied, "If you had washed lettuces, Plato, you would not have had to pay your respects to Dionysius." Someone once told him that most people laughed at him, to which Diogenes countered, "Donkeys, I am sure, probably laugh at them, but since I do not care about donkeys, I could not care less about them either." Observing a young man studying philosophy, he said, "Well done, Philosophy, for you manage to divert admirers of physical charms to the real beauty of the soul!"

[59] When someone expressed astonishment at the votive offerings found in Samothrace, Diogenes' comment was, "There would surely be many more, if those who were not saved had set up their offerings."[91] There are some, however, who attribute this remark to Diagoras of Melos.[92] To a handsome young man, who was on his way to a dinner, Diogenes said, "You will come back as a worse man." The young man came back the next day and said to Diogenes, "I went and I am not worse for it," to which Diogenes replied, "Not Chiron, but Eurytion."[93] When he was asking for alms from a bad-tempered man, who said to him, "I will give you, but only if you can persuade me." "If I could have persuaded you of anything," said Diogenes, "I would have persuaded you to hang yourself." Returning once from Sparta, someone asked him, "Where are you going to and where are you coming from?" Diogenes replied, "I am coming from where men live to where women dwell."[94]

[60] As he was on his way back from Olympia, someone asked him if there had been a great crowd there, to which Diogenes answered, "Yes, a great crowd, but hardly any who could be called human." He compared libertines with fig-trees that grow on a cliff, whose fruit is not enjoyed by anybody but is eaten by ravens and vultures. When Phryne set up a statue of Aphrodite in Delphi, they say that Diogenes wrote on it the following inscription: "From the licentiousness of Greece."[95] Alexander once came to him and, standing in front of him, said, "I am Alexander the great king," to which Diogenes replied, "And I am Diogenes the Dog!"[96] When asked what he had done to deserve being called a dog, he said, "I brown-nose those who give me alms, I yelp at those who refuse, and I set my teeth on those who are rascals."

[61] As he was gathering figs from a tree, the gardener told him that a man had recently hanged himself from that very tree. Diogenes commented, "I will therefore have to cleanse it." Once he saw an Olympic victor casting repeated glances at a prostitute. Diogenes then said about him, "Look, here is a ram ready for battle, who is now fascinated and caught by the neck by a vulgar prostitute!" He would compare courtesans with deadly honeyed poison. Once, as he was eating in the marketplace, people gathered around him and began shouting, "Dog! Dog!" "You are the stupid dogs," he cried, "when you just gather around me to see me

eat!" When two cowards among the crowd hid from him, he shouted at them, "Don't panic, you fools, dogs don't eat garbage."[97]

[62] Once he came upon a stupid wrestler who had taken up medicine, and he said to him, "What is the meaning of this? Have you decided to practice the art of revenge on the wrestling rivals who formerly beat you?" When he saw the child of some prostitute throw stones at a crowd, Diogenes shouted to him, "Take care that you don't hit your father!" Once, a boy showed him a dagger that an admirer had given him. Diogenes then said to him, "A pretty blade with an ugly handle." When some people praised someone who had given him a gift, he said to them, "You have no praise for me, although I am the one who deserves it." To someone who had given him a cloak and said that he wanted it back, Diogenes remarked, "If it was a gift, now it is mine; but if it was a loan, I am still using it." A certain fraudulent youth once told him that he was carrying gold in his pocket, to which Diogenes said, "And I suppose that you sleep with it under your pillow."

[63] When asked what he had gained from philosophy, his answer was, "This at least, if nothing else, to be prepared for all sorts of things." To the question, "Where do you come from?" his reply was, "I am a citizen of the world."[98] Certain parents were sacrificing to the gods, praying that a son be born to them. "But you," said Diogenes to them, "forget to sacrifice to ensure what kind of person your son might turn out to be?" They once asked him for a subscription for a club. His comment was, "Go and rob other people, and keep your hands off Hector!" He called the mistresses of kings queens, for, according to him, they tell kings what to do.[99] When the Athenians gave Alexander the title of 'Dionysus', he declared, "They might as well call me 'Sarapis'."[100] To someone who reproached him for going to dirty places, he said that even the sun visited cesspools without being defiled.[101]

[64] When he was once dining in a temple and was served pieces of bread with dirt on them, he threw them away, saying that nothing dirty should enter a temple. To the man who said to him, "You don't know anything, though you are a philosopher," he replied, "Even if I am a pretender to wisdom, that in itself is philosophy." When someone brought his son to him, saying that he was highly gifted and of excellent character, Diogenes commented, "If that is so, what need can he have of me?" Those who speak about great things but fail to do them, he compared with harps, for a harp, he said, had neither hearing nor perception. Once, when he was entering a theater, meeting face to face those who were coming out, someone asked him why, "Because," he said, "this is what I have practiced all my life."

[65] When he saw a young man behaving effeminately, "Are you not ashamed," said Diogenes, "that your own intentions about yourself should be worse than those of nature? For nature made you a man, but you are forcing yourself to play the role of a woman." Observing that a foolish man was tuning a psaltery, he

said, "Are you not ashamed to give this wood concordant sounds, while you yourself fail to harmonize your soul with life?" To someone who protested that he was ill adapted for the study of philosophy, he said, "Why then do you live, if you do not care to live well?" To someone who despised his father he said, "Are you not embarrassed to despise him to whom you owe it that you can be so proud of yourself?" Noticing a handsome young man chattering in an unbecoming manner, he said to him, "Are you not ashamed to draw a dagger of lead from an ivory scabbard?"

[66] When they reproached him for drinking in a tavern, he replied, "Well, I also get my hair cut in a barber's shop." As he was criticized for accepting a cloak from Antipater, he replied: "The choice gifts of the gods are not to be spurned."[102] When someone shook a beam at him and said, "Look out!" Diogenes struck the man with his staff and added, "Look out!" To a man who was urgently pressing his suit to a courtesan, he said, "Why, miserable man, are you at such pains to gain your suit, when it would be better for you to lose it?" When he came upon a man with perfumed hair, he remarked to him, "Beware, lest the sweet scent on your head cause an ill smell in your life." He once said that bad men obey their lusts as servants obey their masters.

[67] When asked why footmen are so called, he answered, "Because they have the feet of men, but souls such as you, my questioner, have." Once, when he asked a spendthrift for a mina,[103] the man inquired why he would ask others only for an obol, to which Diogenes replied, "Because I expect to receive from others again, but I suspect that receiving anything from you again is something that lies in the hands of the gods." Someone reproached him for begging while Plato never did. "Oh yes," said Diogenes, "he surely begs, but when he does, 'he holds his head down, so that no one can hear him'."[104] When he came upon a bad archer, he sat beside the target with these words, "In this way I will never get hit." He affirmed that lovers derive their pleasures from their misfortunes.

[68] When asked whether death was an evil thing, he replied, "How can it be something evil, if when it comes to us we are not aware of it?" As Alexander, standing in front of him, asked him, "Are you not afraid of me?" Diogenes responded, "Why, what are you, a good thing or a bad thing?" Alexander replied, "A good thing!" Diogenes then said, "Who could possibly be afraid of something good?" According to him, education is a controlling grace to young people, consolation to the old, wealth to the poor, and an ornament to the rich. When Didymon,[105] who was a rascal, was treating some girl's eye, Diogenes remarked to her, "Beware, lest the oculist ruin the pupil, instead of curing your eye." Someone told him that his own friends were plotting against him, to which Diogenes replied, "What is to be done then, if you have to treat enemies and friends alike?"

[69] "What is the most beautiful thing in the world?" he was asked, to which he answered, "Freedom of speech."[106] When he entered a school for boys

and found that there were more statues of the Muses than pupils, he said to the schoolmaster, "By the help of the gods, you seem to have plenty of students." It was his custom to do everything in public, even the works of Demeter and those of Aphrodite.[107] He would argue in the following way: "If eating is not something absurd, then it is not absurd to eat in the marketplace." After behaving indecently in public, he remarked that he wished that it were just as easy to banish hunger by rubbing one's belly. Enumerating many other sayings attributed to him would be interminable.

[70] He used to affirm that training was of two kinds, mental and physical, the latter being that by which, through constant exercise, we form perceptions that secure freedom of movement for doing virtuous deeds. Half this training, he would add, is incomplete without the other, because good health and strength are essential things, both for the body and for the soul. He would adduce indisputable evidence to show how easily we arrive at virtue through gymnastic training, for in the manual arts and other arts, we can see that craftsmen develop extraordinary manual skills through practice. Take the case of flute-players and of athletes: what surprising skills they acquire by their own incessant toil! If they had transferred their efforts to the training of the mind, it is certain that their labors would not have been unprofitable or ineffective.

[71] He maintained, moreover, that nothing in life has any chance of succeeding without strenuous practice, which is capable of overcoming any obstacles. Accordingly, instead of useless toils, men should choose those that nature recommends and that lead to a happy life. Yet, so great is people's madness that they choose to be miserable. For even the despising of pleasure is itself most pleasurable, when we are accustomed to it; and just as those who are accustomed to a life of pleasure feel disgust when they pass over to the opposite experience, so those whose training has been of the opposite kind derive more pleasure than from the pleasures themselves. This was the gist of his conversations, and it was plain that he acted accordingly, truly adulterating or defacing the ordinary 'currency', and allowing convention far less authority than he allowed natural right, and asserting that the manner of his life was the same as that of Hercules, who preferred liberty to anything else.

[72] He maintained that all things are the property of the wise, and to prove this, he used arguments such as this: All things belong to the gods; the gods are friends to the wise; friends share all property in common; therefore, all things are the property of the wise. Again, concerning law: it is impossible for society to exist without law, for without a city no benefit can be derived from what is civilized. But the city is civilized and there is no advantage in law without a city. Therefore, law is something civilized. He would ridicule good birth and fame, and all other similar distinctions, calling them the showy ornaments of vice. The only true commonwealth, he would insist, is that which is as wide as the universe. He

advocated a community of wives, recognizing no other form of marriage than the union of the man who lives freely with a consenting woman. For this reason, he thought, children, too, should be held in common.

[73] He saw no impropriety either in stealing anything from a temple or in eating the flesh of any animal, and believed that there was nothing impious even in eating human flesh, mentioning in this last regard the customs of certain foreign nations. According to right reason, as he put it, all the elements are contained in all things and pervade everything.[108] There is meat in bread and vegetables are found in bread, and all other bodies find their way into other bodies in the form of vapor through certain invisible passages and particles, as he affirms in the *Thystes*—if the tragedies attributed to him are really his and not the work of his friend Philiscus of Aegina or of Pasiphon the son of Lucian, who, according to Favorinus in his *Miscellaneous History*, wrote them after Diogenes' death.[109] Diogenes also held that we should neglect music, geometry, astronomy, and other similar studies, as useless and unnecessary endeavors.

[74] He became an expert in disputations, as is evident from what has been said above. When he was sold as a slave, he endured his tribulations most nobly. When on a voyage to Aegina, he was captured by pirates under the command of a certain Scirpalus,[110] and was transported to Crete, where he was put up for sale. When the auctioneer asked him in what he was proficient, he replied, "In governing people." He then pointed to a certain man from Corinth who was wearing a fine purple on his robe, and said, "Sell me to this man, because he needs a master." This is how Xeniades came to buy him.[111] Taking him to Corinth, then, Xeniades made him the teacher of his children and entrusted the management of his household to him. Diogenes administered it in so excellent a manner that Xeniades used to say constantly, "A good spirit has entered my house."

[75] Cleomenes in his work entitled *Concerning Pedagogues* says that Diogenes' friends wanted to ransom him, for which he called them simpletons, for, he said, lions are not the slaves of those who feed them, but rather those who feed them are at the mercy of the lions. Fear, he added, is the mark of the slave, whereas wild beasts make human beings afraid of them. The man had in fact a wonderful gift of persuasion, so that he could easily vanquish any opponent in argument. A certain Onesicritus of Aegina[112] sent a son of his named Androsthenes to learn from Diogenes. The youth became his disciple and stayed with him. Onesicritus then sent his older son, a youth named Philiscus, to look for his other son, but he, too, chose to stay with Diogenes.

[76] At last, the father went in search of his sons, but he, too, became attracted by the pursuit of philosophy and joined the circle—so magical was the spell which the discourses of Diogenes exerted. There were others who also joined him—Phocion the Honest,[113] Stilpo the Megarian,[114] and many other men of prominence in political affairs.

Diogenes is said to have been nearly ninety years old at the time of his death. There are several accounts about the way in which he died. Some say, for instance, that after eating a raw octopus, he was seized with colic and died. Others say that he killed himself by voluntarily holding his breath, and such was the opinion of Cercidas of Megalopolis (or of Crete),[115] who in his meliambics left us these lines:

> He who once was a citizen of Sinope,
> That famous man, who carried a staff,
> Doubled his cloak, and lived in the open air,
> [77] Soared aloft with his lips
> Tightly pressed against his teeth, holding his breath within.
> For in truth he was rightly named Diogenes,[116]
> A true-born son of Zeus, a hound of heaven.

There is yet another version of his death in which we learn that, while trying to divide an octopus among some dogs, he was so severely bitten on the sinew of his foot that he died. His friends, however, according to Antisthenes in his *Successions of Philosophers*,[117] insisted that his death was the result of self-suffocation. He happened to be living in the Craneum, the gymnasium outside Corinth. When, as was their custom, his friends came to him in the morning, they found him wrapped in his cloak, and thought that he was asleep, although they knew that he was by no means a drowsy or somnolent type. When they drew aside the cloak, however, they found that he was dead. They assumed that his death had been a deliberate act on his part to escape from the burden of life.

[78] They say that after his death a quarrel arose among his disciples about who was in charge of burying him, and that on this account they came to blows. However, when their fathers and men of influence arrived and prevailed upon them, they buried him beside the gate leading to the Isthmus. Subsequently, his fellow-citizens honored him with bronze statues, on which they inscribed these lines:

> Even bronze groweth old with time, but thy fame, Diogenes, not all
> Eternity shall take away. For thou alone didst point out to mortals the
> lesson of self-sufficiency, and the path for the best and easiest life.[118]

[79] We, too, have written these lines in his honor:

> — Tell us, Diogenes, what fate took you to the world below?
> — The savage tooth of a dog![119]

Some say that shortly before his death, he left instructions that he should just be thrown out and left unburied, so that wild beasts could feed on him, or that he should be thrust into a ditch and sprinkled with dust. According to some, however, his instructions were that they should throw him into the river Ilissus, so that he could be rendered useful to his disciples.[120]

Demetrius in his work *On Men of the Same Name* maintains that Diogenes died in Corinth precisely on the same day that Alexander died in Babylon.[121] He was already an aged man in the 113th Olympiad.[122]

[80] The following writings are attributed to him. Dialogues: *Cephalion, Ichthyas, Jackdaw, Pordalus, The Athenian Demos, Republic, Art of Ethics, On Wealth, On Love, Theodorus, Hypsias, Aristarchus, On Death*, and *Letters*. Seven tragedies: *Helen, Thyestes, Hercules, Achilles, Medea, Chrysippus*, and *Oedipus*.

Sosicrates[123] in the first book of his *Successions* and Satyrus[124] in the fourth book of his *Lives* allege that Diogenes left nothing in writing, and Satyrus adds that the poorly written tragedies are works by his friend Philiscus of Aegina. Sotion in his seventh book affirms that these are the only genuine works that belong to Diogenes: *On Virtue, On Love, The Mendicant, Tolmaeus, Pordalus, Casandrus, Cephalion, Philiscus, Aristarchus, Sisyphus, Ganymedes, Anecdotes*, and *Letters*.

[81] There have been five other men named Diogenes. First, a natural philosopher from Apollonia, whose treatise begins with these lines: "At the outset of every investigation, I believe that one should insure that the foundation is laid down with unquestionable certainty." Second, a man from Sicyon, who wrote *An Account of the Peloponnesus*. Third, Diogenes of Sinope. Fourth, a Stoic philosopher from Seleucia, also known as the Babylonian, because of the proximity of Seleucia to Babylon. Fifth, an author from Tarsus, who wrote a work on poetical problems.

According to Athenodorus in the eighth book of his *Walks*, Diogenes had a well-groomed appearance, because of his use of unguents.[125]

Notes

1. Sinope was a Greek town of Milesian ancestry, situated at the midpoint of the southern coast of the Euxine (Black Sea). The democracy established there by Pericles in 444 B.C. was still in existence at the time of Diogenes' birth (c. 410 B.C.). In ancient times, Sinope was a prosperous seaport, especially famous for its coinage. In present-day Turkish Sinop, significant archeological ruins of its Hellenic heritage can still be seen, including the foundations of the temple of Serapis (Sarapis), which belong to Diogenes' time.

2. The name of Diogenes' father is known also from other sources. Coins that bear his name have been found in various sites.

3. The word used by the biographer, τραπεζίτης, means 'banker', 'money-changer', and, by extension, 'someone associated with the minting of currency'.

4. Diocles of Magnesia (first century B.C.) was an associate of the Cynic poet Meleager of Gadara. He is repeatedly mentioned by Diogenes Laertius, for which reason Nietzsche viewed some of the biographies of the latter as summaries of Diocles' own works.

5. Eubulides of Miletus was a dialectician of the fourth century B.C.

6. The word παραχάραξις can be understood in various ways such as the defacement of currency, or the counterfeiting of coins, or the adulteration of money.

7. The reported words of the oracle were Παραχάραττειν τὸ νόμισμα, that is, "Deface the currency," 'currency' understood, obviously, in the sense of 'values' or 'customs'.

8. Cf. Aelian, *Hist. Var.* X, xvi; Saint Jerome, *Adv. Jovin.* II, xiv, 345.

9. Theophrastus (c. 372-288 B.C.) was a Peripatetic philosopher and a disciple of Aristotle.

10. Cf. Plutarch, *Moralia* 77e-78a; Aelian, *Hist. Var.* XIII, xxvi. The phrase "to adapt oneself to the circumstances" occurs frequently in Cynic writings and expresses an important Cynic principle. Teles of Megara (VI), for instance, speaks of destiny as a sort of playwright who creates characters in varying circumstances. Our response to the whimsical creations of destiny should be to learn to adapt ourselves to them. The saying attributed to Bion of Borysthenes, a third century B.C. Cynic, reflects well this response: "Adapt yourself to conditions as sails to the wind."

11. The Cynic wallet (πήρα) was a leathern wallet or knapsack that the Cynics carried with much pride. Crates, Diogenes' associate, named his Cynic republic Πήρα.

12. The Cynic staff or walking stick (βάκτρον), like the wallet, was part of the Cynic 'uniform'. It symbolized the royal scepter that by nature belonged to the Cynics, and was a reminder of the legendary maze (ῥόπαλον) of Hercules . For comments on the significance of Hercules' maze for the Cynics, see B. R. Voss, "Die Keule der Kyniker." *Hermes* 95 (1967), pp. 441-446.

13. Olympiodorus was an Athenian magistrate and an influential political figure of the early third century B.C.

14. Possibly, the Alexandrian philologist and teacher of Eratosthenes (second century B.C.).

15. The Metröon was a temple dedicated to the Great Mother (the Mother of the Gods), situated at the western end of the Athenian Agora. Diogenes' tub (πίθος) appears to have been a large barrel-like container made of clay. Resting sideways, it provided shelter and a place to sleep. Sources other than Diogenes Laertius give testimony about Diogenes' tub, for instance, Seneca, Lucian, and Juvenal. In Aristophanes' *Knights* (792), we hear that tubs were used in Athens as shelter by homeless people.

16. An associate of Socrates, who founded the Megarian school of philosophy.

17. Here, as in other passages of Diogenes Laertius, we come upon a pun that can only be appreciated in the original Greek: the school (σχολή) of Euclides is full of χολή (bile—a euphemism?), and Plato's teaching (διατριβή) is nothing but a κατατριβή (a waste of time).

18. The word used by Diogenes Laertius is βρόχος that can be translated as a halter or bridle, or as a noose for hanging. Both meanings can be read into the text: if we do not have the necessary clarity of mind (λόγος) to live well, we need either a rope to hang ourselves or at least a halter to aid us to control our impulses. Plutarch (*De stoic. repugn.* xiv, 1039e-f) ascribes this saying to Antisthenes. In Diogenes Laertius (VI, 86), we find a similar saying attributed to Crates: "If you cannot extinguish in yourself the fire of passion, then hang yourself." Here, too, the same word is used (βρόχος), allowing for the possibility of a double meaning.

19. As we learn from his *Seventh Letter*, Plato visited the court of Dionysius II in Syracuse on two occasions (367 and 361 B.C.). Earlier, around the year 387 B.C., Plato had visited Dionysius I also for the purpose of converting him to a philosophical mode of life.

20. Favorinus (c. A.D. 80-150) was an influential rhetorician and polyhistor. The non-extant *Miscellaneous History* mentioned by Diogenes Laertius was an encyclopædic twenty-four volume work that dealt with a multitude of biographical and historical themes.

21. Aristippus of Cyrene was the founder of the Cyrenaic school of philosophy.

22. Sotion of Alexandria (second century B.C.) was a Peripatetic philosopher.

23. In Stobaeus (III, xxxvi, 21), we find a variation of this anecdote: "Diogenes once asked Plato to send him three dried figs out of his own garden. Plato, however, sent him, not three, but a full barrel of them. 'Ah!,' exclaimed Diogenes, 'this man is in the habit of giving a thousand answers when someone asks him just one question!'"

24. It was the practice among athletes to dig trenches with their bare hands and cover themselves with mud in preparation for their competitions.

25. A similar remark is attributed in Stobaeus (III, vi, 52) to Bion of Borysthenes.

26. Cf. Stobaeus III, xviii, 30.

27. Menippus of Gadara (third century B.C.) was one of the most influential among the Greek Cynics. Of the thirteen books attributed to him by Diogenes Laertius (D.L. VI, 101), nothing has survived, except for a few fragments. His non-extant *The Sale of Diogenes*, from which the story of the abduction of Diogenes by pirates seems to have originated, appears to have been the model on which Lucian constructed his *Sale of Creeds*.

28. There is no reliable information concerning Xeniades. It is possible that he may have been the philosopher mentioned by Sextus Empiricus in *Adv. math.* (VII, 53).

29. Hecaton of Rhodes (second century B.C.) was a Stoic philosopher.

30. A pun on the Greek words ἀναπήρους (disabled) and πήρα (wallet). The sense of this apophthegm is this: those who do not have the necessary courage to become Cynics are truly crippled or disabled.

31. Metrocles of Maroneia (early third century B.C.) was an associate of Crates of Thebes and the brother of Hipparchia.

32. The ancient references to Diogenes as a dog are innumerable. In Stobaeus, for example, we come upon this line: "Diogenes used to say that other dogs bite only their enemies, whereas he himself bites also his friends in order to save them" (III, xiii, 44). In

the *Gnomologium Vaticanum* (194), we are told that when Polyxenus the Sophist became angry when people would refer to Diogenes as a dog, the philosopher said to him, "You, too, Polyxenus, can call me a dog, for 'Diogenes' is just a name that I have been given, but in reality I am a dog."

33. The Pythian games were celebrated every eight years in Delphi in honor of Apollo.

34. Cf. *Gnom. Vat.* 202.

35. As in subsequent ages, pointing at someone with one's middle finger was an insult among the Greeks.

36. The Ceramicus was an Athenian neighborhood, situated below the Acropolis, on the northwestern side of the Agora, and inhabited mostly by artisans and manual workers.

37. The phrase "Backward the streams flow to their fonts" comes from Euripides' *Medea* (413). It was used in antiquity in the sense that things are upside down or that the world is topsy-turvy. For instance, when Julian complains that the Cynics of his time had reversed and vitiated the teachings of the original Cynics, he quotes Euripides' line (*Or.* VI).

38. An obol (ὀβολός) was a coin of little value, equivalent to a penny.

39. In Seneca (*Epist.* XXX, 14), Diogenes, who rejected all artefacts, is contrasted with Daedalus, who was believed to have invented the saw. After seeing a boy drink out of his hands, Diogenes is described saying to himself, as he crawls back into his tub and gets ready to fall asleep, "What a fool I have been, carrying with me all sorts of unnecessary things!"

40. Possibly, Zoïlus of Amphipolis, a Cynic philosopher (fourth century B.C.), who was famous for his attacks on Homer.

41. In 'dedicating' a man to Asclepius, the god of medicine, Diogenes' meaning is that he presents him to the god as a pious gift. The sense is, of course, sarcastic: he 'dedicates' to Asclepius a man who inflicts pain on others and makes them sick.

42. In *Gnom. Vat.* 201, these lines are rendered thus: "Poor, homeless, living day by day, but regardless of my condition, always ready to fight, even against the Great King, to secure my happiness."

43. A gymnasium outside the Corinthian walls, where Diogenes is said to have died. Its name (κρανίον) means 'skull', the same as the Aramaic word '*golgotha*' that was the name of the hill where Jesus was executed (*Matt.* 27:22; *Mark* 15:22; *John* 19:17).

44. See Cicero, *Tusc. disp.* V, xxxii, 92; Plutarch, *Alexander* xiv.

45. The denial of the reality of motion was a thesis advanced by Parmenides of Elea and Zeno, his disciple. For them, motion was only a sensory illusion, because nothing ever moves. In Sextus Empiricus (*Hyp. Pyrrh.* III, 66), Diogenes' empirical rejection of the Eleatic thesis is described in these terms: "Once an argument was advanced in the presence of a Cynic [presumably Diogenes] against the reality of motion. He, without uttering a single word, simply got up and began to walk about, showing thereby that motion does in fact exist."

46. Agesilaus (444-360 B.C.) was a Spartan king and Epaminondas (d. 362 B.C.) was a Theban commander. Both were men whose moral characters and virtuous lives greatly impressed tradition. Diogenes' point, therefore, is this: if such men, who were not initiated into the Mysteries, do not gain eternal bliss, do unworthy human beings deserve it just because they have been initiated?

47. This anecdote reveals the traditional Cynic dislike for definition. Antisthenes had already rejected the value of any definition that involves predication, and had spoken of ostensive definition, that is, 'pointing' to an object, as the only valid kind of definition. By securing a featherless chicken and *showing* it to Plato's audience, Diogenes sought to show the inadequacy of predication.

48. Midias was a wealthy Athenian, known for his violent outbursts.

49. Theodorus of Cyrene was a mathematician, famous for his radical atheism.

50. Sprinkling water or powder was a practice in religious ceremonies.

51. Dionysius of Heraclea (c. 328-248 B.C.) was a Stoic philosopher who in his old age adopted the view that pleasure is the goal of human life. He starved himself to death.

52. In the battle of Chaeronea in northern Boeotia, the Macedonians, under Philip, defeated the Athenians and the Thebans in 338 B.C.

53. Antipater (397-319 B.C.) was a Macedonian commander, who ruled over the Athenians during the Macedonian hegemony. Diogenes' comment about Alexander's letter to Antipater involves a sarcastic pun. The name of the messenger was Athlios, whose name (Ἄθλιος) literally means 'wretched'.

54. Perdiccas III was the king of Macedonia from 364 to 359 B.C. The report of Diogenes Laertius concerning Perdiccas' invitation to Diogenes is important, because, if historically genuine, it indicates that already before the middle of the fourth century B.C., Diogenes had already attained sufficient fame to be recognized by Perdiccas. L. Paquet (*Les Cyniques Grecques: Fragments et Témoignages*, p. 73) suggests that the Perdiccas mentioned in this passage is the officer of Alexander's army, who commanded a brigade of Macedonian infantry, and who, upon the death of the emperor, inherited the supreme command of his armies. The text of Diogenes Laertius does not clarify which Perdiccas is mentioned.

55. The word used by Diogenes Laertius is σταυρός, which means 'cross' or 'stake'—as used for executions.

56. More precisely, 'beetroot' (τεύτλιον). This word was used among the Greeks as an insult for effeminate men and for transvestites.

57. Callisthenes was a historian and a nephew of Aristotle, who accompanied Alexander in his campaigns. He was executed in 327 B.C. for refusing to pay homage to Alexander.

58. This game was known as κότταβος. It involved throwing wine from a cup into a metal basin. Diogenes' point is clear: the more wine falls into the basin, the more wine will the player drink.

59. A pun on the similarities of these two expressions.

60. A possible meaning of Diogenes' remark is that the young man should not expose himself in public.

61. Lupine is a plant of the pea family. Its seeds are still used for food in certain parts of Europe, mostly among the poorer classes.

62. Sneezing, when someone sneezes on one's left, was viewed in antiquity as a bad omen. For comments on this subject, particularly in relation to Socrates, see Plutarch, *On the Sign of Socrates* (518a).

63. Possibly, Hegesias of Cyrene (d. 283 B.C.), who was a Cyrenaic philosopher, famous for his advocacy of suicide. His lectures in Alexandria are reported to have caused a wave of suicides, for which reason he was expelled from that city.

64. See Plutarch, *Moralia* 467c.

65. Nemea was a valley on the northern borders of the Argolid. The sense of Diogenes' remark is this: "You have too quickly given up athletic competitions for a shepherd's occupation."

66. Harmodius and Aristogiton are known for their attempt to kill Hippias, an Athenian tyrant, in 514 B.C. Although their plot was unsuccessful, the overthrow of the tyrant three years later was believed to have been made possible by their attempted tyrannicide. Their endeavor to free the Athenians earned for them great fame, and statues in their honor were erected in various places and it was agreed that no slave could bear their names. What Diogenes suggests is that the best material for the statue of a tyrant is the material out of which killers of tyrants are made, for such men are indeed real men.

67. Probably, Dionysius II, who became king of Syracuse in 367 B.C. It was he who invited Plato and other philosophers to his court. Allegedly a weak and dissolute man, he was the victim of Diogenes' vitriolic attacks, when in his old age he retired to Corinth, where Diogenes himself was living, as we learn from Plutarch (*Timoleon* XV).

68. A sycophant was a private citizen who made his living by prosecuting accused persons in court. Sycophants are, therefore, the ancestors of modern state prosecutors.

69. A pun on the name Χείρων (Chiron) given to one of the Centaurs, which, as an adjective, means 'the worse'.

70. In Greek mythology, Charybdis was a sea monster who lived in a cave in the Straits of Messina that separate Italy and Sicily. Charybdis personified a devastating whirlpool that would swallow the sea three times each day. Likewise, the stomach is a whirlpool that, if uncontrolled, destroys the lives of human beings.

71. A pun on the name Δίδυμος (Didymon) that, as an adjective, means 'double' or 'twofold'. Even in his name, Diogenes suggests, Didymon revealed his duplicity and his uncontrolled sexuality, for his name is also related to the Greek word for testicles.

72. See *Gnom. Vat.* 172.

73. A pun on the phrase 'fall in', which could mean *literally* 'fall in' or 'be brought before the authorities'.

74. Homer, *Iliad* X, 343, 387.

75. Cf. *Gnom. Vat.* 200.

76. Homer, *Iliad* V, 40; XVIII, 95.

77. In this encounter between Diogenes and Plato, we come across an example of the opposition between Cynicism, with its emphasis on the concrete and the individual, on the one hand, and, on the other, Platonism, with its postulation of a transcendent world of Ideal Forms, far more real than the world disclosed by ordinary sense perception.

78. Although the Greek text does not make it explicit, the question is clearly addressed to Plato. This is confirmed by Aelian (*Hist. Var.* XIV, xxxiii).

79. A similar statement was attributed to Thales: "When his mother tried to force him to marry, he replied that it was too soon, and when later in life she pressed him again, he said that it was already too late" (D.L. I, 26).

80. See Stobaeus (IV, liii, 26).

81. See Aelian, *Hist. Var.* XIII, xxviii. In Seneca (*De tranquil. animi* viii, 7), this anecdote is also recounted. Seneca ascribes these words to Diogenes: "Concern yourself with your own business, Oh Fate, for there is nothing in Diogenes that belongs to you. My slave has fled from me! What can I say now, but that it is I who have been liberated!" For a discussion of this anecdote, see J. García González, "Diógenes y el esclavo. Una propuesta de interpretación." *Soladitas* 2 (1981), pp. 51-68. García González argues that this anecdote, like other stories about Diogenes, should not be viewed as based on actual biographical incidents, but as a symbolic description of certain philosophical ideas. 'Manes' and 'Diogenes', argues the author, are simply generic names through which a philosophical point is conveyed.

82. Euripides, *Phoenicians* 40.

83. Homer, *Iliad* V, 366; VIII, 45.

84. Molossian dogs, originally from Molossia, a province in northwestern Greece, were widely used for hunting. Precise information about the Maltese and Molossian breeds is unavailable.

85. In *Gnom. Vat.* 188, a different sense is given to Diogenes' reply: "Wise men," he says, "have a taste for everything, but *not* like other people."

86. A Greek city on the southwestern coast of Asia Minor, founded by Dorian colonists.

87. Homer, *Iliad* V, 83.

88. Craterus (c. 370-321 B.C.) was a Macedonian commander, who was regarded as among the best soldiers in Alexander's army.

89. Anaximenes of Lampsacus (c. 380-320 B.C.) was a historian and rhetorician.

90. Among the ancient Greeks, eating in public places, as in the marketplace, was regarded as a gross breach of manners.

91. Samothrace was an island in the northeastern Aegean Sea, famous, among other things, for a sanctuary where religious mysteries were celebrated and where enormous quantities of votive offerings were kept.

92. Diagoras of Melos (fifth century B.C.) was a lyric poet and a disciple of Democritus. According Cicero (*De natura deorum* I, ii, 63), he was renowned for his uncompromising atheism. Anecdotes about Diagoras were occasionally transferred to Diogenes. For a discussion of this matter, see M. Winiarczyk, "Diagoras von Melos und Diogenes von Sinope." *Eos* 64 (1976), pp. 177-184.

93. See note 69. In Greek mythology, Eurytion was a centaur, notorious for his drunkenness and misbehavior.

94. A similar remark is attributed to Antisthenes. We can assume that both Antisthenes and Diogenes felt admiration for the strictness and rigor of Spartan customs, which were often contrasted with the laxity and softness of those of the Athenians (cf. Stobaeus, I, xiii, 25). In this passage of Diogenes Laertius, Diogenes says that he is returning from "the men's quarters" (ἐκ τῆς ἀνρωδωνίτιδος) to "the women's quarters" (εἰς τὴν γυναικωνῖτιν).

95. Phryne was a famous Theban courtesan, whose activities made her extremely wealthy. She was reportedly the mistress of Praxiteles, the sculptor, who used her as a model for his statue of Aphrodite of Cnidus. A gilded statue of Phryne by Praxiteles was found at Delphi.

96. Here we come upon a statement in which Diogenes gives himself the appellation 'Dog', the title by which he was known in ancient times and which gave his mode of life its name, 'Cynicism' (from κύων and the genitive κυνικός). In Aristotle (*Rhetoric* 1411a24), we encounter the most ancient authentication of Diogenes' title, when he is referred to simply as ὁ κύων.

97. See note 56.

98. If Diogenes Laertius' report is historically genuine, this is the first instance of the word 'cosmopolitan' (κοσμοπολίτης), literally, 'a citizen of the cosmos'. By this term Diogenes did not mean that he belonged to a universal human community, as might have been the sense given to this term by the Stoics, but that he did not belong to *any* established or existing human nation. Diogenes felt estranged from *every* human commonwealth, and it is in this sense that he could have called himself 'a citizen of the world'. For a discussion of this issue, see H. C. Baldry, *The Unity of Mankind in Greek Thought* (Cambridge: Cambridge University Press, 1965), pp. 110ff.

99. See Stobaeus, IV, xxi, 15.

100. Sarapis (or Serapis) was an Egyptian deity, who was conceived of as a healer and a worker of miracles. There is evidence that the cult of Sarapis was in vogue in Sinope during Diogenes' time, as can be seen from archeological remains found in modern Sinop.

101. In Cicero (*Moralia* 5c), we are that Diogenes was in the habit of speaking of the usefulness of visiting brothels: "There you will learn," he would say, "that there is no difference between those things for which we must pay with money and those things that can be obtained for nothing."

102. Homer, *Iliad* III, 65.

103. A mina was a unit of currency equivalent to about one hundred drachmas.

104. Homer, *Odyssey* I, 157; IV, 70.

105. See note 71.

106. The word used by Diogenes for 'freedom of speech' is παρρησία, a term that stands for one of the most important concepts of Cynicism. In Greek, the term comes from two words, πᾶς and ῥῆσις, that mean, respectively, 'all' and 'speaking' or 'speech'. Thus, παρρησία is not only freedom of speech in the sense of the right to speak freely, but the willingness '*to say it all*', that is, to speak the truth as one sees it, always and under all circumstances.

107. The phrase "the works of Demeter and those of Aphrodite" is a euphemistic way of referring to certain natural acts like eating, urinating, and the like, and to sexual activities.

108. The idea that all things contain elements of all things belongs to Anaxagoras (fifth century B.C.). The universe is composed of an infinity of 'seeds' (σπέρματα) that are found in all things. Hence, even a piece of bread contains 'pieces' of human flesh, and so on. It is conceivable that Diogenes may have been acquainted with Anaxagoras' ideas. For a discussion of Diogenes' debt to Anaxagoras, see M. Gigante, "Sul un insegnamento di Diogenes di Sinope." *Studi Italiani di Filologia Classica* 34 (1962), pp. 130-136.

109. Philiscus, a young associate of Diogenes, is mentioned also in VI, 75, where he is referred to as a son of Onesicritus. The tragedies sometimes attributed to Diogenes are sometimes believed to be the work of Philiscus. Pasiphon is possibly a philosopher from Eretria, to whom various spurious Socratic dialogues have been ascribed.

110. His name is given by Cicero as 'Harpalus' (*De natura deorum* III, xxxiv, 83).

111. See note 28.

112. Onesicritus of Astypalaea, an associate of Diogenes, accompanied Alexander in his campaigns and became his chief pilot, guiding the emperor's fleet from India to the mouth of the Tigris in 326 B.C. He left an account of Alexander's expedition.

113. Phocion was an Athenian general, who became renowned for his honesty.

114. Stilpo of Megara (c. 380-300 B.C.) was the third head of the Megarian school of philosophy and the teacher of Zeno of Citium.

115. Cercidas of Megalopolis (third century B.C.) was an important Cynic philosopher and poet, who combined in himself a variety of civic and personal virtues. Fragments of his meliambic poetry have survived in the Oxyrhynchus papyrus discovered in Egypt in 1906. Diogenes Laertius' reference to Crete as a possible birthplace of Cercidas does not make sense in light of present-day historical research. Comments on Cercidas' lines about Diogenes and in particular on his designation of him as one who "lived in the open air" (αἰθεριβόσκας) can be found in G. Giangrande, "Cercidas, fr. 1 Powell." *Revue des Études Anciennes* 86 (1984), pp. 213-216.

116. Diogenes' name, Διογένης, means 'God-sent' or 'coming from God'.

117. Antisthenes of Rhodes (second century B.C.).

118. *Anthologia Palatina* xvi, 334.

119. Ibid., vii, 116.

120. The Ilissus was one of the two main rivers of Attica that flowed outside the Athenian walls. As we learn from Pausanias (I, xx), it was from the Ilissus that Orithyia was carried off by Boreas, the god of the north wind. In times of distress, as when the Persians invaded Attica, the Athenians would seek the protection of Boreas. The Ilissus, therefore, was a sacred river from whom benefits could be expected as a result of propitiations and offerings. Ironically, then, Diogenes suggests that if his corpse is thrown into the river, his disciples will be rewarded by Boreas. The conversation between Socrates and Phaedrus reported by Plato (*Phaedrus* 229a) takes place outside the city walls by the Ilissus.

121. Demetrius of Magnesia (first century B.C.). The generally accepted year for the death of Diogenes, as well as for Alexander's death, is the year 323 B.C.

122. 324/321 B.C.

123. Sosicrates of Rhodes (unknown dates).

124. Satyrus of Callatis Pontica (third century B.C.) was a Peripatetic biographer who lived and wrote mostly at Oxyrhynchus in Egypt.

125. According to Epictetus, "Diogenes used to go about with a radiant complexion and would attract the attention of the common people by the very appearance of his body" (*Discourses* III, xxii, 88).

Bibliography

Alciati, A. *Emblemata cum commmentariis.* New York: Garland Publishing, 1976, 1004 pages.
Amelung, W. "Notes on Representations of Socrates and of Diogenes and Other Cynics." *The American Journal of Archaeology* 31 (1927), pp. 281-296.
Anastasi, R. "Diog. Laert. VI 72." In *Studi in onore di Quintino Cataudella.* 3 vols. Catania: Università di Catania, 1972, Vol. 2, pp. 367-370.
"Antisthène." *Dictionnaire des Sciences Philosophiques.* Edited by A. Franck. Paris: Librairie Hachette, 1885, pp. 76-77.
Babelon, J. "Diogène le Cynique." *Revue Numismatique* 18 (1914), pp. 14-19.
———. "La monnaie de Diogène." *Bulletin de la Société Nationale des Antiquaires de France* (1933), pp. 179-180.
Badian, E. "Alexander the Great and the Unity of Mankind." *Historia* 7 (1958), pp. 425-444.
Baldry, H. C. *The Unity of Mankind in Greek Thought.* Cambridge: Cambridge University Press, 1965, 223 pages.
Bannert, H. "Numismatisches zur Biographie und Lehre des Hundes Diogenes." *Litteræ Numismaticæ Vindobonenses* 1 (1979), pp. 49-63.
Bartalucci, A. "Una probabile ricostruzione dell'*Eracle* di Diogene di Sinope." *Studi Classici e Orientali* 19-20 (1970-1971), pp. 109-122.
Bayle, P. "Diogène." In *Dictionnaire historique et critique.* 2 vols. Paris: France Expansion, 1972-1973, Vol. 2.
Bayonas, A. C. "Travail manuel et esclavage d'après les Cyniques." *Rendiconti dell'Istituto Lombardo* 100 (1966), pp. 383-388.
Bell, D. O. "New Identifications in Raphael's School of Athens." *Art Forum* 77 (1995), pp. 4ff.
Billerbeck, M. *Die Kyniker in der modernen Forschung.* Amsterdam: B. R. Grüner, 1991, 324 pages.
———. "Le Cynisme idéalisé d'Épictète à Julien." In *Le Cynisme ancien et ses prolongements. Actes du Colloque International du CNRS.* Edited by M. O. Goulet-Cazé and R. Goulet. Paris: Presses Universitaires de France, 1993, pp. 319-338.
Billot, M. F. "Antisthène et le Cynosarges dans l'Athènes des Ve et IVe siècles." In *Le Cynisme ancien et ses prolongements. Actes du Colloque International du*

CNRS. Edited by M. O. Goulet-Cazé and R. Goulet. Paris: Presses Universitaires de France, 1993, pp. 69-116.

———. "Le Cynosarges. Histoire, mythes et archéologie." In *Dictionnaire des Philosophes Antiques.* Edited by R. Goulet. Paris: CNRS Éditions, 1994, Vol. 2, pp. 917-966.

Boegehold, A. L. "An Apophthegm of Diogenes the Cynic." *Greek, Roman and Byzantine Studies* 9 (1968), pp. 58-60.

Bracht Branham, R. "Diogenes' Rhetoric and the *Invention* of Cynicism." In *Le Cynisme ancien et ses prolongements. Actes du Colloque International du CNRS.* Edited by M. O. Goulet-Cazé and R. Goulet. Paris: Presses Universitaires de France, 1993, pp. 445-473.

Bracht Branham, R. and M. O. Goulet-Cazé, editors. *The Cynic Movement in Antiquity and Its Legacy.* Berkeley: University of California Press, 1996, 456 pages.

Brancacci, A. "Érotique et théorie du plaisir chez Antisthène." In *Le Cynisme ancien et ses prolongements. Actes du Colloque International du CNRS.* Edited by M. O. Goulet-Cazé and R. Goulet. Paris: Presses Universitaires de France, 1993, pp. 35-55.

———. "La filosofia di Pirrone e le sue relazioni con il cinismo." In *Lo scetticismo antico. Atti del Convegno organizzato dal Centro di Studi del Pensiero antico del CNR.* Edited by G. Giannantoni, Rome: Bibliopolis, 1981, pp. 213-242.

———. "Le orazioni diogeniane di Dione Crisostomo." In *Scuole socratiche minori e filosofia ellenistica.* Edited by G. Giannantoni. Bologna: Il Mulino, 1977, pp. 141-171.

———. Οἰκεῖος λόγος. *La filosofia del linguaggio di Antistene.* Naples: Bibliopolis, 1990, 302 pages.

Brandenberg, A. *Diogenes: The Story of the Greek Philosopher.* Englewood Cliffs, N.J.: Prentice-Hall, n.d., 28 pages.

Braun, R. "Diogène le Cynique et le credo d'Ovide." *Annales de la Faculté des Lettres et Sciences Humaines de Nice* No. 35, 1979, pp. 223-233.

Brochard, V. "Diogène le Cynique." In *La Grande Encyclopédie. Inventaire Raisonné des Sciences, des Lettres et des Arts.* Paris: H. Lamirault et Cie, n.d., Vol. 14, p. 601.

Browning, R. "How It Strikes a Contemporary." In *Robert Browning: The Poems.* Edited by J. Pettigrew. Supplemented and Completed by T. J. Collins. 2 vols. New Haven, Conn.: Yale University Press, 1981, Vol. 1, pp. 605-607.

Buora, M. "L'incontro tra Alessandro e Diogene. Tradizione e significato." *Atti dell'Istituto Veneto di Scienze, Lettere ed Arti* 132 (1973-1974), pp. 247ff.

Bury, J. B. *A History of Greece to the Death of Alexander the Great.* New York: The Modern Library, n.d., 885 pages.

Butler, F. G. "Who Are King Lear's Philosophers? An Answer with Some Help from Erasmus." *English Studies* 67 (1986), pp. 511-524.

Bywater, I., and J. G. Milne. "Παραχάραξις." *The Classical Review* 54 (1940), pp. 10-12.

Calogero, G. "Diogene di Sinope." In *Enciclopedia Italiana di Scienze, Lettere ed Arti.* 36 vols. Rome: Istituto dell' Enciclopedia Italiana, 1950, Vol. 12, pp. 928-929.

Capelle, W. "De cynicorum epistulis." Ph.D. diss. University of Göttingen, 1896, 62 pages.

Castera, C. *Le Livre de Diogène*. Paris: L'Enseigne du Pot Cassé, 1950, 408 pages.
Chappuis, C. *Antisthène*. Paris: August Durand, Libraire, 1854, 195 pages.
Chilson, R. "Diogenes' Lantern." *Analog Science Fiction/Science Fact* 109 (1989), pp. 134-147.
Chroust, A. H. "The Antisthenian Elements in the Two Apologies of Xenophon." In *Socrates: Man and Myth; The Two Socratic Apologies of Xenophon*. Notre Dame, Ind.: University of Notre Dame Press, 1957, pp. 101-163.
"Cínicos." In *Diccionario de Filosofía*. Buenos Aires: Editorial Sudamericana, 1971, Vol. 1, p. 291.
Clay, D. "Picturing Diogenes." In *The Cynic Movement in Antiquity and Its Legacy*. Edited by R. Branham and M. O. Goulet-Cazé. Berkeley: University of California Press, 1996, pp. 366-388.
Comenius, J. A. *Diogenes lebt!* Edited by H. Below. Weinheim: Deutscher Theaterverlag, 1990, 93 pages.
———. *Diogenes the Cynic Back from the Grave*. Translated by M. C. Mittelstadt. New York: Czechoslovak Society of Arts and Sciences in America, 1970, 73 pages.
Comte-Sponville, A. *Valeur et vérité. Études cyniques*. Paris: Presses Universitaires de France, 1994, 282 pages.
Cools, G. "Diogène, sa vie, son oeuvre." *La Connaissance Hellénique* No. 2, 1980, pp. 3-7; ibid., No. 7, 1981, pp. 3-5.
Davenport, G. *Herakleitos and Diogenes*. San Francisco: Gray Fox Press, 1979, 1981, 59 pages.
Decleva Caizzi, F. *Antisthenis fragmenta*. Milan: Istituto Editoriale Cisalpino, 1966, 145 pages.
———. "Τῦφος. Contributo alla storia di un concetto." *Sandalion* 3 (1980), pp. 53-66.
Delatte, A. "Le sage-témoin dans la philosophie stoïco-cynique." *Bulletin de la Classe de Lettres de l'Académie de Belgique* 39 (1953), pp. 166-186.
Diderot, D. "Cynique." In *Encyclopédie ou Dictionnaire Raisonné des Sciences, des Artes et des Métiers*. 37 vols. Stuttgart: Frommann, 1966, Vol. 4, p. 599.
Diels, H. "Aus dem Leben des Kynikers Diogenes." *Archiv für Geschichte der Philosophie* 7 (1894), pp. 313-316.
"Diogène le Cynique." In *Dictionnaire des Sciences Philosophiques*. Edited by A. Franck. Paris: Librairie Hachette, 1885, pp. 403-405.
Dodds, E. R. *The Greeks and the Irrational*. Berkeley: University of California Press, 1951. 327 pages.
Doloff, S. "'Let me talk with this philosopher': The Alexander Paradigm in *King Lear*." *The Huntington Library Quarterly* 54 (1991), pp. 253-255.
Donawerth, J. "Diogenes the Cynic and Lear's Definition of Man, *King Lear* III. iv. 101-109." *English Language Notes* 15 (1977), pp. 10-14.
Donzelli, G. B. "Del παραχάραττειν τὸ νόμισμα." *Siculorum Gymnasium* 11 (1958), pp. 96-107.
———. "Del 'tieste' di Diogene di Sinope, in Diog. Laert., VI, 73." *Studi di Filologia Classica* 37 (1965), pp. 241-258.
———. "Un'ideologia 'contestaria' del secolo IV a.C." *Studi Italiani di Filologia Classica* 42 (1970), pp. 225-251.
Dorandi, T. "La *Politeia* de Diogène de Sinope et quelques remarques sur sa pensée

politique." In *Le Cynisme ancien et ses prolongements. Actes du Colloque International du CNRS*. Edited by M. O. Goulet-Cazé and R. Goulet. Paris: Presses Universitaires de France, 1993, pp. 57-68.

Doribal, G. "L'image des cyniques chez les Pères grecs." In *Le Cynisme ancien et ses prolongements. Actes du Colloque International du CNRS*. Edited by M. O. Goulet-Cazé and R. Goulet. Paris: Presses Universitaires de France, 1993, pp. 419-443.

Döring, K. "Die Kyniker, eine antike Protestbewegung." *Der altsprachliche Unterricht* 28 (1985), pp. 19-38.

Downing, F. G. "Cynics and Christians." *New Testament Studies* 30 (1984), pp. 584-593.

———. *Cynics and Christian Origins*. Edinburgh: T. & T. Clark, 1992, 377 pages.

———. "Cynics and Early Christianity" In *Le Cynisme ancien et ses prolongements. Actes du Colloque International du CNRS*. Edited by M. O. Goulet-Cazé and R. Goulet. Paris: Presses Universitaires de France, 1993, pp. 281-302

———. "The Social Contexts of Jesus the Teacher," *New Testament Studies* 33 (1987), pp. 439-451.

Dudley, D. R. *A History of Cynicism from Diogenes to the 6th Century A.D.* Cambridge, 1937; Chicago: Aries Press, 1980, 224 pages.

Duhomme, F. *La lanterne de Diogène*. Paris: Marchant, 1846, 35 pages.

Durant, W. *The Life of Greece*. New York: Simon and Schuster, 1939, 754 pages.

Duverne, R. *Diogène; ou, Le Gros Lot*. Niort: H. Boulord, Éditeur, 1933, 45 pages.

Düwell, K. *Ich sehe hier Diogenes*. Vienna: Europäischer Verlag, 1975, 80 pages.

Eisler, R. "Sur les portraits anciens de Cratès, de Diogène et d'autres philosophes cyniques." *Revue Archéologique* 33 (1931), pp. 1-13.

Emeljanow, V. E. "The Letters of Diogenes." Ph.D. diss. Stanford University, 1968, 262 pages.

———. "A Note on the Cynic Short-Cut to Happiness." *Mnemosyne* 18 (1965), pp. 182-184.

Esclapez, R. "Montaigne et les philosophes cyniques." *Bulletin de la Société des Amis de Montaigne* 5-6 (1986), pp. 59-76.

Ewald, O. "Zur Psychologie des Cynikers." *Logos* 5 (1915), pp. 330-337.

Fellsches, J. "Zynismus." In *Europäische Enzyklopädie zu Philosophie und Wissenschaften*. Edited by H. J. Sandkühler. Hamburg: Felix Miner Verlag, 1990, Vol. 4, pp. 1008-1010.

Ferguson, J. *Background of Christian Origins*. Grand Rapids, Mich.: William B. Eerdmans Publishing Company, 1993, 612 pages.

———. *Moral Values in the Ancient World*. London: Methuen & Co., 1958, 256 pp.

Ferrater Mora, J. "Cyniques et stoïciens." *Revue de Métaphysique et de Morale* 62 (1957), pp. 20-36.

Flynn, T. R. "Foucault and the Politics of Postmodernity." *Nous* 23 (1989), pp. 187-198.

———. "Foucault as Parrhesiast: His Last Course at the Collège de France," in *The Final Foucault*. Edited by J. Bernauer and D. Ramussen. Cambridge, Mass.: MIT Press, 1991, pp. 102-118.

Fritz, K. von. "Antistene e Diogene. Le lore relazioni reciproche e la loro importanza per la setta cinica." *Studi Italiani di Filologia Classica* 5 (1927), pp. 133-149.

———. "Cynics." In *The Oxford Classical Dictionary*. Edited by M. Cary et al. Oxford:

The Clarendon Press, 1949, p. 248.
———. "Quellenuntersuchungen zum Leben und Philosophie des Diogenes von Sinope." Leipzig: Dietrich, 1925, 97 pages. *Philologus* Supp. 18, No. 2 (1926).
García González, J. "Diógenes y el esclavo. Una propuesta de interpretación." *Soladitas* 2 (1981), pp. 51-68.
García Gual, C. *La secta del perro*. Madrid: Alianza, 1987, 151 pages.
Gardner, P. "Diogenes and Delphi." *The Classical Review* 7 (1873), pp. 437-439.
Gasco Lacalle, F. "Cristianos y cínicos. Una tificación del fenómeno cristiano durante el siglo II." *Memorias de Historia Antigua* 7 (1986), pp. 111-119.
Gerhard, G. A. "Zur Legende vom Kyniker Diogenes." *Archiv für Religionswissenschaft* 15 (1912), pp. 388-408.
Giangrande, G. "Diogenes' Apophthegm from Herculaneum in the Light of the Ancient *topoi*." *Museum Philologum Londiniense* 8 (1987), pp. 67-74.
Giannantoni, G. "Tradizioni cinici e problemi di datazione nelle orazioni diogeniane di Dione Crisostomo." *Elenchos* 1 (1980), pp. 92-100.
Giannaras, A. "Plato und K. Popper zur Kritik der politischen Philosophie Platons." *Philosophia* 3 (1973), pp. 208-255.
Giannattasio Andria, R. "Diogene Cinico nei papiri ercolanesi." *Bolletino del Centro Internazionale per lo Studio dei Papiri Ercolanesi* 10 (1980), 129-151.
Gigante, M. "Su un insegnamento di Diogenes di Sinope." *Studi Italiani di Filologia Classica* 34 (1962), pp. 130-136.
———. "Sul pensiero politico di Diogene di Sinope." *La Parola del Passato* 16 (1961), pp. 454-455.
Gill, J. E. "Theriophily in Antiquity: A Supplementary Account." *The Journal of the History of Ideas* 30 (1969), pp. 401-412.
Gillespie, C. M. "The Logic of Antisthenes." *Archiv für Geschichte der Philosophie* 26 (1913), pp. 479-500; 27 (1914), pp. 17-38.
Gladisch, A. *Einleitung in das Verständniss der Weltgeschichte*. Posen, 1841, pp. 356-377.
Goettling, C. W. "Diogenes der Cyniker oder die Philosophie des griechischen Proletariats." In *Gesammelte Abhandlungen aus dem classischen Alterthume*. Halle, 1851, pp. 251-277.
Gomperz, T. "The Cynics." In *Greek Thinkers: A History of Ancient Philosophy*. Translated by G. G. Berry. 4 vols. London: John Murray, 1905, 1964, Vol. 2, pp. 139-169; Vol. 3, pp. 285-290.
Goulet, R. "Dioclès de Magnésie." In *Dictionnaire des Philosophes Antiques*. Paris: CNRS Éditions, 1994, Vol. 2, pp. 775-776
Goulet-Cazé, M. O. *L'Ascèse cynique. Un commentaire de Diogène Laërce VI 70-71*. Paris: J. Vrin, 1986, 292 pages.
———. "Le livre VI de Diogène Laërce. Analyse de sa structure et réflexions méthodologiques." In *Aufstieg und Niedergang der römischen Welt*. Berlin-New York: W. de Gruyter, 1990, Vol. 2, pp. 3880-4048.
———. "Les premiers Cyniques et la religion." In *Le Cynisme ancien et ses prolongements. Actes du Colloque International du CNRS*. Edited by M. O. Goulet-Cazé and R. Goulet. Paris: Presses Universitaires de France, 1993, pp. 117-159.
———. "Un syllogisme stoïcienne sur la loi dans la doxographie de Diogène le Cynique à propos de Diogène Laërce VI 72." *Rheinisches Museum für Philologie* 115

(1982), pp. 214-240.

———. "Who Was the First Dog?" In *The Cynic Movement in Antiquity and Its Legacy*. Edited by R. Branham and M. O. Goulet-Cazé. Berkeley: University of California Press, 1996, pp. 414-416.

Goulet-Cazé, M. O., and R. Goulet, editors. *Le Cynisme ancien et ses prolongements. Actes du Colloque International du CNRS*. Paris: Presses Universitaires de France, 1993, 612 pages.

Goulet-Cazé, M. O., D. Gutas, and M. C. Hellmann. "Diogène de Sinope, surnommé le Chien." In *Dictionnaire des Philosophes Antiques*. Edited by R. Goulet. Paris: CNRS Éditions, 1994, Vol. 2, pp. 812-823.

Green, P. *Alexander to Actium: The Historical Evolution of the Hellenistic Age*. Berkeley: University of California Press, 1990, 1993, 970 pages.

Grube, G.M.A. "Antisthenes Was No Logician." *Transactions and Proceedings of the American Philological Association* 81 (1950), pp. 16-27.

Guérin, R. *La confession de Diogène*. Paris: Gallimard, 1947, 314 pages.

Gutas, D. "Sayings by Diogenes Preserved in Arabic." In *Le Cynisme ancien. Actes du Colloque International du CNRS*. Edited by M. O. Goulet-Cazé and R. Goulet. Paris: Presses Universitaires de France, 1993, pp. 475-518.

Guthrie, W.K.C. *A History of Greek Philosophy*. 4 vols. Cambridge: Cambridge University Press, 1980.

———. *Socrates*. London: Cambridge University Press, 1977, 200 pages.

Hammarskjöld, D. *Markings*. Translated by L. Sjöberg and W. H. Auden. New York: Alfred A. Knopf, 1971, 222 pages.

Hammerstädt, J. Γοήτων φώρα. *Die Orakelkritik des Kyniker Oenomaus*. Frankfurt am Main: Athenaeum, 1988, 328 pages.

Hansen, P. A. "Diogenes at Venice." *Zeitschrift für Paryrologie und Epigraphik* 82 (1990), pp. 198-200.

Häusle, H. *Sag mir, o Hund—Wo der Hund begraben liegt. Das Grabepigram für Diogenes von Sinope. Eine komparative literarisch-epigraphische Studie zu Epigrammen auf theriophore Namenstrager*. Hildesheim: G. Olms, 1989, 74 pages.

Hedrick, D. K. "'It is no novelty for a prince to be a prince': An Enantiomorphous Hamlet." *Shakespeare Quarterly* 35 (1984), pp. 62-76.

Hegel, G.W.F. *Lectures on the History of Philosophy*. Translated by E. S. Haldane. 3 vols. London: Routledge and Kegan Paul, 1963.

Henne, D. "Cynique (École)." In *Dictionnaire des Sciences Philosophiques*. Edited by A. Franck. Paris: Librairie Hachette, 1885, pp. 334-335.

Herakleitos and Diogenes. Bolinas, Calif.: Grey Fox Press, 1979, 59 pages.

Herding, K. "Diogenes als Bürgerheld." *Boreas* 5 (1982), pp. 232-254.

Hermann, H. A. *Abhandlung über den Cyniker Diogenes*. Heilbronn: H. Guldig, 1860, 37 pages.

Hock, R. F. "Simon the Shoemaker as an Ideal Cynic." *Greek, Roman and Byzantine Studies* 17 (1976), pp. 41-53.

Höistad, R. *Cynic Hero and Cynic King: Studies in the Cynic Conception of Man*. Uppsala: C.W.K. Gleerup, 1948, 233 pages.

———. "Cynicism." In *Dictionary of the History of Ideas*. Edited by P. P. Wiener. 4 vols. New York: Charles Scribner's Sons, 1973, Vol. 1, pp. 627-634.

Humphreys, S. C. "The Nothoi of Kynosarges." *The Journal of Hellenic Studies* 94 (1976), p. 89.
Ingalls, D. "Cynics and *pasupatas*: The Seeking of Dishonor." *Harvard Theological Review* 55 (1962), pp. 281-298.
Innes, D. R. *The Lamp of Diogenes and Other Poems*. Boston, 1935.
James, W. *The Varieties of Religious Experience: A Study in Human Nature*. New York: The Modern Library, 1929, 526 pages.
Joël, K. "Die Auffassung der kynischen Sokratik." *Archiv für Geschichte der Philosophie* 20 (1907), pp. 1-24, 147-170.
Jouan, F. "Le Diogène de Dion Chrysostome." In *Le Cynisme ancien et ses prolongements. Actes du Colloque International du CNRS*. Edited by M. O. Goulet-Cazé and R. Goulet. Paris: Presses Universitaires de France, 1993, pp. 381-397.
Kant, I. *Immanuel Kant's Critique of Pure Reason*. Translated by N. K. Smith. London: Macmillan & Co., 1961, 681 pages.
Katridis, J. T. "A Cynic Homeromastix." *Serta Turyaniana: Studies in Greek Literature and Paleography in Honor of Alexander Turyn*. Edited by J. L. Heller. Urbana: University of Illinois Press, 1974, pp. 361-373.
Kelly, E. and L. E. Navia, editors. *The Fundamental Questions: A Selection of Readings in Philosophy*. Dubuque, Iowa: Kendall/Hunt Publishing Company, 1997, 591 pages.
Kidd, I. G. "Cynics." In *The Encyclopedia of Philosophy*. Edited by P. Edwards. 4 vols. New York: Macmillan Publishing Co., 1967, Vol. 1, pp. 284-285.
———. "Diogenes of Sinope." In *The Encyclopedia of Philosophy*. Edited by P. Edwards. 4 vols. New York: Macmillan Publishing Co., 1967, Vol. 1, pp. 409-410.
Kindstrand, J. F. "The Cynics and Heraclitus." *Eranos* 82 (1984), pp. 149-178.
———. "Diogenes Laertius and the *Chreia* Tradition." *Elenchos* 7 (1986), pp. 219-243.
Krueger, D. "The Bawdy and Society: The Shamelessness of Diogenes in Imperial Rome." *The Cynic Movement in Antiquity and Its Legacy*. Edited by R. Branham and M. O. Goulet-Cazé. Berkeley: University of California Press, 1996, pp. 222-239.
———. "Cynics, Christians, and Holy Fools: The Late Antique Context of Leontius of Neapolis' 'Life of Symeon the Fool'." Ph.D. diss. Princeton University, 1992, 346 pages.
———. "Diogenes the Cynic Among the Fourth Century Fathers." *Vigiliæ Christianæ* 47 (1993), pp. 29-49.
Lacaris, C. "Del tonél de Diógenes, o del repudio del desarrollo." *Revista de Filosofía* (Costa Rica) 12 (1974), pp. 123-126.
Lalande, A. "Cynisme." In *Vocabulaire technique et critique de la Philosophie*. Paris: Presses Universitaires de France, 1972, pp. 200-201.
Lana, I. "Tracce di dottrine cosmopolitiche in Grecia prima del cinismo." *Rivista di Filologia e d'Istruzione Classica* 29 (1951), pp. 193-216, 317-338.
Larre, J. P. *Diogène, ou, La science du bonheur*. Helette: Éditions Harriet, 1997, 207 pages.
Láscaris, C. C. "Los perros filósofos de Platón." *Actas del Primer Congreso Español de Estudios Clásicos* (Madrid, 1956). Madrid: Publicaciones de la Sociedad de Estudios Clásicos, 1958, pp. 338-342.
Laurenti, R. "Il 'filosofo ideale' secondo Epitteto." *Giornale di Metafisica* 17 (1962), pp.

501-513.
Lebek, W. D. "Dichterisches über den 'Hund' Diogenes." *Zeitschrift für Papyrologie und Epigraphik* 22 (1976), pp. 293-296.
Lenaerts, J. "Fragment d'Analecta sur Diogène (P. Osl. III,177)." *Chronique d'Égypte* 49 (1974), pp. 121-123.
Lewes, G. H. "The Cynics—Antisthenes and Diogenes." In *The Biographical History of Philosophy from Its Origins in Greece Down to the Present Day*. 2 vols. New York: D. Appleton and Company, 1883; Westmead, England: Gregg International Publishers, 1970, Vol. 1, pp. 177-185.
Lindsay, B. "A Lamp for Diogenes: Leadership Giftedness and Moral Education." *Roeper Review* 11 (1988), pp. 8-11.
Lipsey, R. "Diogenes, the Hound." *Parabola* 10 (1989), pp. 50-59.
Livrea, E. "La morte di Diogene cinico." In *Filologia e forme litterarie. Studi offerti a Francesco della Corte*. Edited by S. Boldrini et al. 5 vols. Urbino: Università degli Studi di Urbino, 1987, Vol. 1, pp. 427-433.
Livsay, J. L. "Some Renaissance Views of Diogenes the Cynic." In *Joseph Quincy Adams: Memorial Studies*. Edited by J. G. McManaway, G. E. Dawson, and E. E. Willowghby. Washington, D.C.: The Folger Shakespeare Library, 1948, pp. 447-455.
Long, A. A. "Cynics." In *Encyclopedia of Ethics*. Edited by L. C. Becker and C. B. Becker. 2 vols. New York: Garland Publishing, 1992, Vol. 1, pp. 234-236.
———. "The Socratic Tradition: Diogenes, Crates, and Hellenistic Ethics." In *The Cynic Movement in Antiquity and Its Legacy*. Edited by R. Branham and M. O. Goulet-Cazé. Berkeley: University of California Press, 1996, pp. 28-46.
López Cruces, J. L. "El epitafio de Diógenes de Sinope y Cerc. fr. 54 Livrea (Consideraciones en torno a un estudio reciente sobre el tema)." *Epos* 7 (1991), pp. 609-614.
Lovejoy, A. O., and G. Boas. *Primitivism and Related Ideas in Antiquity*. New York: Octagon Books, Inc., 1965, 482 pages.
Luz, M. "Cynics as Allies of Scepticism." In *Scepticism: Inter-Disciplinary Approaches. Proceedings of the Second International Symposium on Philosophy and Inter-Disciplinary Research. September 27-31, 1988*. Athens: The Ministry of Culture, 1990, pp. 101-114.
Lyly, J. *Campaspe; Sappho and Phao*. New York: Manchester Press, 1991, 307 pages.
Lynch, G. E. "Diogenes." In *Dictionary of Greek and Roman Biography and Mythology*. London: John Murray, 1853, pp. 1021-1022.
Machado, A. "Un loco." In *Obras. Poesía y Prosa*. Buenos Aires: Editorial Losada, 1964, pp. 139-140.
MacDowell, D. M. "Bastards as Athenian Citizens." *The Classical Quarterly* 26 (1976), pp. 88-91.
Malherbe, A. J. *The Cynic Epistles: A Study Edition*. Missoula, Mont.: Scholars Press, 1977, 334 pages.
Martin, R. P. "The Scythian Accent. Anacharsis and the Cynics." In *The Cynic Movement in Antiquity and Its Legacy*. Edited by R. Branham and M. O. Goulet-Cazé. Berkeley: University of California Press, 1996, pp. 136-155.
Mauthner, F. *Mrs. Socrates*. Translated by J. W. Hartmann. New York: International

Publishers, 1926, 254 pages.
McEvilley, T. "Diogenes of Sinope (c.410-c.320 B.C.): Selected Performance Pieces." *Art Forum* 21 (March 1983), pp. 58-59.
McGovern, J. T. *Diogenes Discovers Us*. Freeport, N.Y.: Books for Libraries Press, 1967, 304 pages.
McKirahan, V. T. "The Socratic Origins of the Cynics and Cyrenaics." In *The Socratic Movement*. Edited by P. A. Vander Waerdt. Ithaca, N.Y.: Cornell University Press, 1994, pp. 367-391.
Meilland, J. M. "L'anti-intellectualisme de Diogène le Cynique." *Revue de Théologie et de Philosophie* 3 (1983), pp. 233-246.
Mesk, J. "Die Anklagerede des Polykrates gegen Sokrates." *Wiener Studien* 32 (1911), pp. 56-84.
Messina, G. "L'uomo e la felicità nel pensiero ellenistico." *Civiltà Cattolica* 107 (1956), pp. 598-609.
Miralles, C. "Los cínicos. Una contracultura en el mundo antiguo." *Estudios Clásicos* (Madrid) 14 (1970), pp. 347-377.
Moles, J. "The Career and Conversion of Dio Chrysostom." *The Journal of Hellenic Studies* 98 (1978), pp. 79-122.
———. "Le cosmopolitisme cynique." In *Le Cynisme ancien et ses prolongements. Actes du Colloque International du CNRS*. Edited by M. O. Goulet-Cazé and R. Goulet. Paris: Presses Universitaires de France, 1993, pp. 259-280.
———. "The Woman and the River: Diogenes' Apophthegm from Herculaneum and Some Popular Misconceptions About Cynicism." *Apeiron* 17 (1983), pp. 125-130.
Monterroso, A. "Diógenes también." In *Cuentos*. Madrid: Alianza Editorial, 1986, pp. 39-50
More, P. E. "Diogenes of Sinope." In *Hellenistic Philosophies*. Princeton, N.J.: Princeton University Press, 1923, pp. 260-303.
Muckensturm, C. "Les gymnosophistes étaient-ils des cyniques modèles?" *Le Cynisme ancien et ses prolongements. Actes du Colloque International du CNRS*. Edited by M. O. Goulet-Cazé and R. Goulet. Paris: Presses Universitaires de France, 1993, pp. 225-239.
Muhll, P. von der. "Interpretationen biographischer Überlieferung." *Museum Helveticum* 23 (1966), pp. 234-239.
Mullach, F.G.A. *Fragmenta Philosophorum Græcorum*. 3 vols. Paris: Firmin-Didot, 1857-1865, 1928. Darmstadt: Scientia Verlag, 1968, Vol. 2, pp. 261-395.
Müller, K. O. In *A History of the Literature of Ancient Greece*. Translated by G. C. Lewis and J. W. Donaldson. 3 vols. London: Longman, Green, and Co., 1884.
Museler, E. *Die Kynikerbriefe*. Paderborn: F. Schoningh, 1994, 2 vols.
Natorp, P. "Diogenes von Sinope." In *Paulys Realencyclopädie der classischen Altertumswissenschaft*. Stuttgart: Alfred Druckenmüller Verlag, 1903, 1958. Vol. 5, pp. 765-773.
Navia, L. E. *Classical Cynicism: A Critical Study*. Westport, Conn.: Greenwood Press, 1996. 227 pages.
———. "The Epigenes." In *The Socratic Presence: A Study of the Sources*. New York: Garland Publishing, 1993, pp. 317-343.

———. "The Meaning and Origin of Philosophy." In *The Fundamental Questions: A Selection of Readings in Philosophy*. Edited by E. Kelly and L. E. Navia. Dubuque, Iowa: Kendall/Hunt Publishing Company, 1997, pp. 1-33.

———. *The Philosophy of Cynicism: An Annotated Bibliography*. Westport, Conn.: Greenwood Press, 1995, 213 pages.

———. "The Problem of the Will in the Philosophy of Schopenhauer." Ph.D. diss. New York University, 1972, 258 pages.

———. "A Reappraisal of Xenophon's *Apology*," in *New Essays on Socrates*. Edited by E. Kelly. Lanham, Md.: University Press of America, 1984, pp. 47-65.

———. "Schopenhauer's Concept of Character." *The Journal of Critical Analysis* 5 (1974), pp. 85-91.

———. *The Socratic Presence: A Study of the Sources*. New York: Garland Publishing, 1993, 403 pages.

Navia, L. E. and E. L. Katz. *Socrates: An Annotated Bibliography*. New York: Garland Publishing, 1988, 536 pages.

Ner, H. *Les Paraboles Cyniques*. Paris: Éditions Athéna, 1922, 246 pages.

Niehues-Pröbsting, H. *Der Kynismus des Diogenes und der Begriff des Zynismus*. Munich: W. Fink, 1979, 320 pages.; Frankfurt: Suhrkamp, 1988, 389 pages.

———. "Die Kynismus-Rezeption der Moderne: Diogenes in der Aufklärung." In *Le Cynisme ancien et ses prolongements. Actes du Colloque International du CNRS*. Edited by M. O. Goulet-Cazé and R. Goulet. Paris: Presses Universitaires de France, 1993, pp. 519-555.

Nietzsche, F. W. *Beitrage zue Quellenkunde und Kritik des Laertius Diogenes*. Basel, 1870, 36 pages.

———. *Thus Spake Zarathustra*. Translated by T. Common. In *The Philosophy of Nietzsche*. New York: The Modern Library, 1954, pp. 21-368.

Onfray, M. *Cynismes. Portrait du philosophe en chien*. Paris: B. Grasset, 1990, 215 pages.

Orsini, G. R. *I filosofi cinici. Storia e sistema*. Turin: Chiantore, 1920, 318 pages.

Ortega y Gasset, J. *La rebelión de las masas*. Madrid: Revista de Occidente, 1927, 315 pages.

Orth, E. "Ein Fragment des Kynikers Diogenes." *Philologische Wochenschrift* 44 (1926), pp. 843-847.

Ostling, R. N. et al. "Who Was Jesus?" *Time* 132 (August 15, 1988), pp. 37-42.

Packmohr, A. "De Diogenis Sinopensis apophthegmatis quæstiones selectæ." Ph.D. diss. University of Münster, 1913.

Paquet, L. *Les Cyniques grecs. Fragments et témoignages*. Ottawa: Éditions de l'Université d'Ottawa, 1975, 1988, 365 pages.

Paton, W. R. *The Greek Anthology*. London: William Heinemann, 1925, Vol. 2.

Penna, R. "San Paolo (*1 Cor.* 7:29b-31a) e Diogene il Cinico." *Biblica* 58 (1977), pp. 237-245.

Perry, B. E. *Secundus the Silent Philosopher*. Ithaca, N.Y.: Cornell University Press, 1964, 160 pages.

Petzl, G. "Der begrabene Hund und andere veroneser Fälschungen." *Zeitschrift und Epigraphik* 84 (1990), pp. 79-80.

Philippson, P. "Verfasser und Abfassungszeit der sogenannten Hippokratesbriefe." *Rheinisches Museum für Philologie* 77 (1928), pp. 318-319.

Pinski, D. *Aleksander un Dyogenes. Veltgeshikhtlekhe Tragedye.* Vilne: B. Kletskin, 1930, 179 pages.
Pizzagalli, A. M. "Influssi buddhistica nella leggenda di Alessandro." *Rendiconti dell'Istituto Lombardo* 76 (1942-1943), pp. 154-160.
Polansky, R. M. "The Tale of the Delphic Oracle in Plato's *Apology.*" *Ancient World* 2 (1979), pp. 83-85.
Popper, K. *The Open Society and Its Enemies.* 2 vols. New York: Harper Torchbooks, 1963.
Praechter, K. "Zur kynischen Polemik gegen die Bräuche bei Totenbestattung und Totenklage." *Philologus* 57 (1898), pp. 504-507.
Raaflaub, K. A. "Democracy, Oligarchy, and the Concept of the 'Free Citizen' in Late Fifth Century Athens." *Political Theory* 11 (1933), pp. 517-544.
Radt, S. L. "Zu Plutarchs *Vita Alexandri.*" *Mnemosyne* 20 (1967), pp. 120-126.
Rahn, H. "Die Frömmigkeit der Kyniker." *Paideuma* 7 (1959-1961), pp. 280-292.
Rankin, H. D. "Οὐκ ἔστιν ἀντιλέγειν." In *The Sophists and Their Legacy.* Edited by G. B. Kerferd. Wiesbaden: Steiner, 1981, pp. 25-37.
———. *Sophists, Socratics and Cynics.* London: Croom Helm, 1983, 263 pages.
———. "That It Is Impossible to Say 'Not' and Related Topics in Antisthenes." *International Logic Review* 10 (1979), pp. 51-98.
Reifler, B.V. "Diogenes Syndrome: Of Omelettes and Souffles." *Journal of the American Geriatrics Society* 44 (1966), pp. 1484-1486.
Reinach, T. "Sur le classement chronologique des monnaies de Sinope." *Revue des Études Grecques* 39 (1926), pp. xlv-xlvi.
Rhodes, P. J. "Bastards as Athenian Citizens." *The Classical Quarterly* 28 (1978), pp. 89-92.
Rich, A.N.M. "The Cynic Conception of αὐτάρκεια." *Mnemosyne* 9 (1956), pp. 23-29.
Rieger, D. *Diogenes als Lumpensammler. Materialen zu einer Gestalt der französischen Literatur des 19. Jahrhunderts.* Munich: Wilhelm Fink Verlag, 1982, 140 pages.
Riley, W. *Men and Morals: The Story of Ethics.* New York: Frederick Ungar Publishing Co., 1960, 425 pages.
Ritter, H., and L. Preller. *Historia Philosophiæ Græcæ-Romanæ ex fontium locis contexta.* Gotha: F. A. Perthes, 1913, 606 pages.
Robin, L. *La pensée grecque et les origines de l'esprit scientifique.* Paris: La Renaissance du Livre, 1923, 480 pages.
Romm, J. "Cynicism Before the Cynics?" in *The Cynic Movement in Antiquity and Its Legacy.* Edited by R. Branham and M. O. Goulet-Cazé. Berkeley, Cal.: University of California Press, 1996, pp. 121-135.
Rosenthal, F. "Witty Retorts of Philosophers and Sages from the *Kitab al-Ajwibah al-Muskitah* of Ibn Abi 'Awn." *Græco-Arabica* (Athens) 4 (1991), pp. 179-221.
Roucaute, Y. "Diogène le Cynique." In *Dictionnaire des Philosophes.* Edited by D. Huisman. 2 vols. Paris: Presses Universitaires de France, 1993, Vol. 1, 760-761.
Roy, P. "Antisthenes' Affairs with Athenian Women: Xenophon, *Symposium* iv, 38." *Liverpool Classical Monthly* 10 (1985), pp. 132-133.
Rudberg, G. "Diogenes the Cynic and Marcus Aurelius." *Eranos* 47 (1949), pp. 7-12.
———. "Zum Diogenes-Typus." *Symbolæ Osloenses* 15 (1936), pp. 1-18.
———. "Zur Diogenes-Tradition." *Symbolæ Osloenses* 14 (1935), pp. 22-43.

Russell, B. *A History of Western Philosophy*. New York: Simon & Schuster, 1972, 896 pages.
Sandbach, F. H. "Diogenes." In *Encyclopædia Britannica*. Chicago: Encyclopædia Britannica, Inc., 1960, Vol. 7, p. 394.
Sayre, F. *Diogenes of Sinope: A Study of Greek Cynicism*. Baltimore: J. H. Furst, 1938, 142 pages.
———. "Greek Cynicism." *The Journal of the History of Ideas* 6 (1945), pp. 113-118.
———. *Greek Cynicism and the Sources of Cynicism*. Baltimore: J. H. Furst, 1948, 49 pages.
———. *The Greek Cynics*. Baltimore: J. H. Furst, 1948, 112 pages.
Schaefer, M. "Diogenes als Mittelstoiker." *Philologus* 91 (1936), pp. 174-196.
Schmidt, S. *Diogenes. Studien zu seiner Ikonographie in der niederlandischen Emblematik und Malerei des 16. und 17. Jahrhunderts*. Hildesheim: Olms, 1993, 373 pages.
Schneider, M. W. "Browning's Spy." *Victorian Poetry* 17 (1979), pp. 384-388.
Schopenhauer, A. *Complete Essays of Schopenhauer*. Translated by T. B. Saunders. New York: Willey Book Company, 1942.
———. *The World as Will and Representation*. 2 vols. Translated by E.F.J. Payne. Indian Hills, Colo.: The Falcon's Wing Press, 1958.
Schulz-Falkenthal, H. "Bemerkungen zum Ideal des naturgemässen Lebens bei den älteren Kynikern." *Wissenschaftliche Zeitschrift der Martin Luther Universität* 26 (1977), pp. 51-60.
———. "Die Kyniker und ihre Erkenntnistheorie." *Klio* 58 (1976), pp. 534-542.
———. "Kyniker. Zur inhaltlichen Deutung des Namens." *Wissenschaftliche Zeitschrift der Martin Luther Universität* 26 (1977), pp. 41-49.
———. "Zum Arbeitsethos der Kyniker." *Wissenschaftliche Zeitschrift der Martin Luther Universität* 29 (1980), pp. 91-101.
———. "Zur Bewertung der älteren Kyniker." *Altertum* 24 (1978), pp. 160-166.
Schwartz, E. "Diogenes der Hund und Krates der Kyniker." In *Characterköpfe aus der antiker Literatur*. 2 vols. Leipzig: Teubner, 1906-1911, Vol. 2, pp. 1-23.
Seltman, C. T. "Diogenes of Sinope, Son of the Banker Hikesias." In *Transactions of the International Numismatic Congress 1936*. Edited by J.A.H. Mattingly and E.S.G. Robinson. London, 1938, 121 pages.
Servais, J. "Alexandre-Dionysos et Diogène-Sarapis. À propos de Diogène Laërce, VI,63." *L'Antiquité Classique* 28 (1958), pp. 98-106.
Sinko, T. "De perenni memoria Diogenis cognomine canis." *Meander* 15 (1960), pp. 86-99.
Sloterdijk, P. *The Critique of Cynical Reason*. Translated by M. Eldred. Minneapolis: University of Minnesota Press, 1987, 558 pages.
———. *Kritik der zynischen Vernunft*. 2 vols. Frankfurt/Main: Suhrkamp, 1983.
Srodes, J. "Mr. Diogenes, Call Your Office." *Financial World* 158 (June 27, 1989), pp. 24-26.
Stafford, K. *Stafford's Heauenly Dogge, or The Life and Death of That Great Cynicke Diogenes*. London, 1615, 112 pages.
Steiner, G. "Diogenes' Mouse and the Royal Dog: Conformity in Non-Conformity." *The Classical Journal* 72 (1976), pp. 36-46.
Steinkraus, W. E. "Socrates, Confucius, and the Rectification of Names." *Philosophy East*

and West 30 (1980), pp. 261-264.
Stevenson, R. L. "Diogenes at the Savile Club." In *The Works of Robert Louis Stevenson*. 32 vols. New York: Charles Scribner's Sons, 1925, Vol. 24, pp. 183-186.
———. "Diogenes in London." In *The Works of Robert Louis Stevenson*. 32 vols. New York: Charles Scribner's Sons, 1925, Vol. 24, pp. 177-183.
Stewart, Z. "Democritus and the Cynics." *Harvard Studies in Classical Philology* 63 (1958), pp. 179-191.
Stirner, Max. *The Ego and His Own: The Case of the Individual Against Authority*. Translated by S. T. Byington. New York: Libertarian Book Club, 1963, 366 pages.
Strohmaier, G. "Diogenesanekdoten auf Papyrus und in arabischen Gnomologien." *Archiv für Papyrusforschung und verwandte Gebiete* 22-23 (1973-1974), pp. 285-288.
———. "Τὸ κακὸν ὑπὸ κακοῦ. Zu einem weiberfeindlichen Diogenesspruch aus Herculaneum." *Hermes* 95 (1967), pp. 253-255.
Süpfle, G. "Zur Geschichte der cynischen Sekte." *Archiv für Geschichte der Philosophie* 4 (1891), pp. 414-423.
Swift, J. *Gulliver's Travels*. New York: The Heritage Press, 1940, 331 pages.
Symonds, J. A. *Studies of the Greek Poets*. New York: Harper & Brothers, 1917, Vol. 2.
Szarmach, M. "Les discourses diogéniques de Dion de Pruse." *Eos* 65 (1977), pp. 77-90.
Taki. "Athens Tea-Party." *The Spectator* 272 (April 2, 1994), p. 39.
Tardieu, É. "Le Cynisme: Étude psychologique." *Revue Philosophique de la France et de l'Étranger* 57 (1904), pp. 1-28.
Tarn, W. W. "Alexander, Cynics and Stoics." *American Journal of Philology* 60 (1939), pp. 41-70.
———. "Alexander the Great and the Unity of Mankind." *Makers of the Western Tradition: Portraits from History*. 2 vols. New York: St. Martin's Press, 1979, Vol. 1, pp. 73-80.
Taylor, E.M.M. "Lear's Philosopher." *Shakespeare Quarterly* 6 (1955), pp. 364-365.
Taylor, T. *Diogenes and His Lantern, or, A Hue and Cry after Honesty*. London: Lacy, 1850, 32 pages.
Tezas, C. A. "'Αρετή and κακία as Political Concepts in the Cynic Tradition." *Dodone* 15 (1986), pp. 65-84.
Thoreau, H. D. *On Civil Disobedience*. In *The Fundamental Questions: A Selection of Readings in Philosophy*. Edited by E. Kelly and L. E. Navia. Dubuque, Iowa: Kendal/Hunt Publishing Company, 1997, pp. 231-239.
Tsirikas, D. "Κριτικὰ εἰς Διογένους 'Επιστολάς." *Athena* 57 (1953), pp. 69-77.
Tuckett, C.M. "A Cynic *Q*?" *Biblica* 70 (1989), pp. 349-376.
Ucciani, L. *De l'ironie socratique à la dérision cynique. Éléments pour une critique par les formes exclués*. Paris: Les Belles Lettres, 1993, 270 pages.
Vaage, L. E. "*Q*: The Ethos and Ethics of an Itinerant Intelligence." Ph.D. diss. Claremont Graduate School, 1987, 616 pages.
Verleyen, C. *Diogenes and His Lantern*. New York: T. Y. Crowell Co., 1968, 23 pages.
Vexliard, A. "Diogène 'le Chien'; Socio-psychologie d'une doctrine philosophique naissante." *Arastirma* (Ankara) 2 (1964), pp. 93-106.
Vlastos, G. "The Socratic Elenchus." In *Oxford Studies in Ancient Philosophy*. 4 vols. Edited by J. Annas. Oxford: The Clarendon Press, 1983, Vol. 1, pp. 27-59.

Vogel, C. J. de. *Greek Philosophy*. 4 vols. Leiden: Brill, 1959.
Voss, B. R. "Die Keule der Kyniker." *Hermes* 95 (1967), pp. 441-446.
Weber, C. W. *Diogenes. Die Botschaft aus den Tonne*. Munich: Nymphenburger, 1987, 211 pages.
Wenley, R. M. "Cynics." In *Encyclopædia of Religion and Ethics*. New York: Charles Scribner's Sons, n.d., Vol. 4, pp. 378-383.
Wieland, C. M. *Socrates out of His Senses, or Dialogues of Diogenes of Sinope*. Translated by Wintersted. 2 vols. Newburgh, N.Y.: D. Denniston, 1797.
———. *Sokrates mainomenos, oder die Dialogen des Diogenes von Sinope aus einer alten Handschrift*. Leipzig: Dieterich, 1984.
Winiarczyk, M. "Diagoras von Melos und Diogenes von Sinope." *Eos* 64 (1976), pp. 177-184.
———. "Theodoros ὁ Ἄθεος und Diogenes von Sinope." *Eos* 69 (1981), pp. 37-42.
Xenakis, J. "Hippies and Cynics." *Inquiry* 16 (1973), pp. 1-15.
Zeller, E. "The Cynics." In *Socrates and the Socratic Schools*. Translated by O. J. Reichel. New York: Russell & Russell, 1962, pp. 285-337.

Index of Names

Academy (Academic), 4, 53
Acropolis (Athenian), 173 n. 36
Aegean Sea, 20, 176 n. 91
Aegina, 18, 20, 168
Aelian, 8, 21, 48, 52, 65, 86, 100 n. 31, 140, 171 n. 8, 171 n. 10, 176 n. 78, 176 n. 81
Aeschines, 87, 102 n. 48
Aeschrio, 154
Aesop, 78
Aetna (Mount), 141
Agesilaus of Sparta, 158, 174 n. 46
Alcibiades, 32
Alexander Severus, 6
Alexander the Great, 1, 8, 9, 10, 19, 20, 28, 29, 31, 38 n. 30, 38 n. 32, 46, 82, 83, 118, 122, 123, 124, 126, 127, 130 n. 24, 130 n. 27, 131 n. 28, 131 n. 29, 131 n. 30, 131 n. 31, 131 n. 32, 131 n. 33, 139, 156, 158, 159, 160, 164, 165, 166, 170, 174 n. 53, 174 n. 54, 174 n. 57, 176 n. 88, 178 n. 112, 179 n. 121
Alexandria (Alexandrian), 137, 149 n. 1, 171 n. 14, 175 n. 63
Amazon, 62
Amelung, W., 43 n. 75
American (America), 81
Anacharsis, 83, 84, 100 n. 30, 101 n. 34
Anaxagoras, 21, 130 n. 26, 178 n. 108
Anaximander, 9
Anaximenes of Lampsacus, 163, 176 n. 89
Anaximenes of Miletus, 9
Anchimolius, 53
Androsthenes of Aegina, 168
Antigonus Gonatas, 98 n. 11
Antipater of Macedonia, 10, 28, 159, 166, 175 n. 53
Antisthenes of Athens (Antisthenean), 6, 9, 13, 18, 19, 20, 21, 27, 41 n. 54, 41 n. 55, 42 n. 64, 52, 53, 54, 55, 58, 67 n. 15, 67 n. 19, 67 n. 21, 77, 80, 83, 84, 86, 87, 90, 91, 92, 93, 94, 95, 96, 97, 104 n. 61, 104 n. 62, 104 n. 63, 104 n. 64, 104 n. 66, 104 n. 67, 104 n. 68, 105 n. 71, 105 n. 72, 105 n. 73, 105

Included in this index are proper names, geographical and mythological names, and the names of philosophical schools and religious movements. The names of editors have not been included.

196 Index of Names

n. 75, 107, 108, 110, 111, 112, 113, 120, 137, 138, 140, 143, 144, 148, 150 n. 11, 151 n. 18, 153, 172 n. 18, 174 n. 47, 177 n. 94
Antisthenes of Rhodes, 32, 169, 178 n. 117
Anytus, 105 n. 72
Aphrodite, 51, 61, 164, 167, 178 n. 107
Aphrodite of Cnidus, 177 n. 95
Apollo (Apollonian), 11, 14, 15, 16, 17, 18, 23, 39 n. 43, 40 n. 46, 153, 173 n. 33
Apollonius of Tyana, 75, 98 n. 8
Arabia (Arabic), 8, 25, 27, 29, 31, 32, 38 n. 29, 39 n. 33, 42 n. 66, 46, 48, 50, 56, 122, 130 n. 24
Aramea (Aramaic), 173 n. 43
Arctonnesus, 101 n. 35
Argolid, 175 n. 65
Argonauts, 53
Argos (ship), 53
Aristippus, 19, 66 n. 4, 87, 102 n. 49, 154, 156, 172 n. 21
Aristocrates, 53
Aristogiton, 161, 175 n. 66
Ariston of Chios, 54
Aristophanes (Aristophanic), 22, 143, 144, 151 n. 19, 171 n. 15
Aristotle (Aristotelian, Aristotelianism), 7, 8, 47, 49, 53, 54, 74, 91, 115, 117, 121, 122, 126, 171 n. 9, 174 n. 57, 177 n. 96
Artaxerxes, 100 n. 27
Asclepius, 158, 173 n. 41
Asia Minor, 9, 18, 176 n. 86
Aspasia, 26, 43 n. 67
Assyria, 43 n. 70
Athena, 143
Athenaeus of Naucratis, 8, 33, 50, 52
Athenodorus, 31, 170
Athens (Athenian), 1, 8, 9, 10, 11, 13, 14, 18, 19, 20, 21, 22, 23, 27, 29, 32, 38 n. 32, 41 n. 55, 41 n. 57, 43 n. 67, 43 n. 75, 46, 49, 52, 53, 67 n. 19, 69 n. 34, 70 n. 40, 76, 77, 79, 80, 83, 84, 85, 88, 90, 91, 93, 94, 96, 99 n. 11, 100 n. 31, 101 n. 41, 103 n. 53, 103 n. 59, 105 n. 72, 105 n. 75, 116, 130 n. 21, 133, 134, 137, 143, 149 n. 2, 151 n. 19, 153, 154, 157, 158, 159, 163, 165, 171 n. 13, 171 n. 15, 173 n. 36, 174 n. 48, 174 n. 52, 174 n. 53, 175 n. 66, 177 n. 94, 178 n. 113, 179 n. 120
Athlios, 159, 174 n. 53
Attica, 47, 154, 179 n. 120
Auden, W. H., 68 n. 30
Augias, 63
Augustine (Saint), 8, 50
Aulus Gellius, 7
Autolycus, 9

Babelon, J., 39 n. 36
Babylon (Babylonian), 8, 29, 124, 127, 170
Badian, E., 130 n. 27, 131 n. 28
Baldry, H. C., 131 n. 28, 131 n. 34, 177 n. 98
Bannert, H., 12, 39 n. 36
Bayle, P., 2
Bayonas, A. C., 43 n. 74
Bell, D. O., 43 n. 75
Bernays, J., 151 n. 13
Berry, G. G., 37 n. 9
Billerbeck, M., 151 n. 12
Billot, M. F., 53, 67 n. 19, 67 n. 20
Bion of Borysthenes, 54, 65, 67 n. 21, 71 n. 47, 77, 98 n. 11, 171 n. 10, 173 n. 25
Boas, G., 67 n. 7, 129 n. 15, 129 n. 19
Boeotia, 174 n. 52
Bolivia, 135
Boreas, 179 n. 120
Borysthenes, 98 n. 11
Bracht Branham, R., 40 n. 52, 51, 63, 67 n. 8, 67 n. 13, 69 n. 35, 69 n. 37, 70 n. 41
Brancacci, A., 68 n. 29, 104 n. 67, 105 n. 75
Brochard, V., 36 n. 5, 110, 129 n. 13
Browning, R., 127, 132 n. 40
Buddha (Buddhist), 130 n. 24

Buora, M., 38 n. 30
Bury, J. B., 40 n. 47
Bywater, I., 40 n. 50

Callisthenes, 160, 174 n. 57
Carneades of Cyrene, 54
Cebes, 88
Censorinus, 8, 33
Centaur, 176 n. 69
Ceramicus, 157, 173 n. 36
Cercidas of Megalopolis, 7, 32, 33, 55, 74, 77, 98 n. 6, 109, 128 n. 10, 169, 178 n. 115
Ch'an, 81
Chaeronea, 159, 174 n. 52
Chappuis, C., 96, 105 n. 73
Charon, 35
Charybdis, 162, 175 n. 70
China (Chinese), 81, 141
Chiron (Centaur), 162, 164, 175 n. 69
Christianity (Christian), 30, 36 n. 2, 120, 137, 150 n. 11, 151 n. 11
Chroust, A. H., 90, 104 n. 62
Chrysippus, 30
Cicero, 7, 20, 32, 34, 51, 52, 135, 139, 173 n. 44, 177 n. 92, 177 n. 101, 178 n. 110
Clay, D., 37 n. 17
Clazomenae, 130 n. 26
Clement of Alexandria (Saint), 8, 52
Cleomenes, 168
Colophon, 16
Communism (communist), 79, 80
Comte-Sponville, A., 71 n. 50
Confucius, 152 n. 20
Corinth (Corinthian), 1, 2, 18, 19, 20, 21, 22, 23, 27, 34, 35, 46, 52, 70 n. 40, 75, 122, 126, 130 n. 24, 137, 149, 168, 169, 170, 173 n. 43, 175 n. 67
Craneum, 20, 22, 23, 158, 169, 174 n. 43
Craterus of Macedonia, 163, 176 n. 88
Crates of Thebes, 6, 25, 29, 37 n. 21, 42 n. 63, 43 n. 75, 55, 69 n. 34, 71 n. 46, 77, 90, 92, 95, 103 n. 60, 104 n. 61, 111, 123, 125, 128 n. 8, 133, 134, 136, 137, 138, 141, 142, 149 n. 3, 171 n. 11, 172 n. 18, 172 n. 31
Crete, 18, 20, 168, 178 n. 115
Critias, 9, 86, 88, 101 n. 41
Croesus, 15
Ctesias of Cnidos, 82, 100 n. 27
Cynosarges, 20, 52, 53, 54, 67 n. 19, 67 n. 20, 90, 93, 94
Cyrene (Cyrenaic), 4, 55, 102 n. 49, 137, 172 n. 21, 175 n. 63
Cyzicus, 84, 101 n. 35

Daedalus, 173 n. 39
D'Alembert, J., 81, 109
Dandamis, 83
Darius, 131 n. 32
Datames, 9, 13
Daumier, H., 4
Decleva Caizzi, F., 104 n. 68, 151 n. 15
Delatte, A., 152 n. 21
Delos (Delian), 14, 18, 153
Delphi (Delphic), 11, 12, 14, 15, 16, 17, 18, 19, 39 n. 42, 39 n. 43, 39 n. 44, 40 n. 46, 40 n. 47, 40 n. 52, 41 n. 52, 41 n. 53, 59, 86, 93, 153, 164, 173 n. 33, 177 n. 95
Demeter, 51, 61, 167, 178 n. 107
Demetrius of Magnesia, 8, 170, 179 n. 121
Demetrius of Rome, 75, 77, 98 n. 8, 139, 146
Democritus, 58, 177 n. 92
Demosthenes, 53, 123, 157
Diagoras of Melos, 164, 177 n. 92
Diderot, D., 2, 4, 37 n. 16, 76
Didymon, 162, 166, 175 n. 71
Diels, H., 18, 40 n. 51
Dio Cassius, 146
Dio Chrysostom, 7, 8, 16, 18, 20, 22, 27, 38 n. 30, 49, 50, 51, 57, 62, 63, 64, 70 n. 39, 75, 77, 110, 130 n. 24, 141, 146
Diocles of Magnesia, 7, 11, 37 n. 23, 153, 157, 171 n. 4
Diodorus Siculus, 19, 91
Diogenes Laertius (D.L.), 1, 2, 5, 6, 7, 8, 9, 10, 11, 13, 16, 18, 20, 21,

Index of Names

22, 23, 24, 25, 27, 29, 30, 31, 32, 33, 35, 37 n. 24, 37 n. 25, 38 n. 26, 38 n. 32, 41 n. 52, 42 n. 62, 42 n. 64, 45, 46, 47, 48, 50, 51, 52, 55, 56, 57, 60, 61, 65, 66 n. 4, 71 n. 46, 86, 90, 91, 92, 93, 94, 95, 97, 98 n. 11, 99 n. 19, 100 n. 30, 102 n. 46, 102 n. 50, 105 n. 72, 111, 115, 118, 119, 122, 123, 124, 125, 126, 130 n. 24, 130 n. 26, 133, 140, 143, 146, 153, 171 n. 4, 171 n. 15, 171 n. 17, 172 n. 18, 172 n. 20, 172 n. 27, 174 n. 54, 174 n. 55, 176 n. 79, 177 n. 94, 177 n. 98, 178 n. 115
Diogenes of Apollonia, 170
Diogenes of Seleucia, 170
Diogenes of Sicyon, 170
Diogenes of Tarsus, 170
Diomean (Athenian gate), 53
Dionysius I of Syracuse, 172 n. 19
Dionysius II of Syracuse, 19, 28, 154, 161, 164, 172 n. 19, 175 n. 67
Dionysius of Heraclea, 159, 174 n. 51
Dionysus (Dionysian), 38 n. 32, 154, 165
Dioxippus, 159
Diphilus of Sinope, 14
Dodds, E. D., 14, 39 n. 45
Dog Heads, 82, 99 n. 24, 100 n. 27
Doloff, S., 130 n. 24
Domitian, 77
Donaldson, J. W., 99 n. 13
Donzelli, G. B., 40 n. 50, 132 n. 38
Dorandi, T., 131 n. 35
Doria (Dorian), 176 n. 86
Doribal, G., 36 n. 2
Downing, F. G., 36 n. 2, 150 n. 11, 151 n. 11
Dudley, D. R., 13, 19, 39 n. 38, 41 n. 54, 50, 52, 67 n. 9, 67 n. 11, 108
Durant, W., 150 n. 11

Ecbatana, 131 n. 31
Eclectic (Eclecticism), 4

Egypt (Egyptian), 10, 38 n. 32, 123, 145, 177 n. 100, 178 n. 115, 179 n. 124
Eisler, R., 42 n. 63, 43 n. 75
Elea (Eleatic), 60, 69 n. 32, 174 n. 45
Emeljanow, V. E., 37 n. 19, 130 n. 22
Epaminondas of Thebes, 158, 174 n. 46
Ephesus, 101 n. 42
Epictetus, 1, 2, 7, 8, 25, 31, 33, 50, 55, 59, 92, 110, 111, 112, 127, 132 n. 39, 138, 139, 151 n. 12, 179 n. 125
Epicurus, 53
Erasmus, D., 97
Eratosthenes of Cyrene, 171 n. 14
Eretria, 178 n. 109
Essene, 150 n. 10
Eubulides of Miletus, 153, 171 n. 5
Eubulus, 156
Euclides of Megara, 154, 171 n. 17
Euphrates, 10
Euripides, 138, 173 n. 37, 176 n. 82
Europe, 175 n. 61
Eurytion (Centaur), 164, 177 n. 93
Eusebius of Caesarea, 8, 16, 40 n. 49, 67 n. 16
Euthyphro, 150 n. 7
Euxine (Black Sea), 9, 10, 83, 84, 170 n. 1

Favorinus, 154, 168, 172 n. 20
Fellsches, J., 66 n. 5, 152 n. 23
Ferguson, J., 129 n. 12, 150 n. 6, 150 n. 11
Ferrater Mora, J., 149 n. 4
Fichte, J. G., 103 n. 52
Flacelière, R., 39 n. 44
Flynn, T. R., 36 n. 7, 128 n. 11
Foucault, M., 2, 36 n. 7, 110, 128 n. 11, 129 n. 11, 147
France (French), 38 n. 28, 99 n. 15, 141
Francis of Assisi (Saint), 63
Franciscan, 150 n. 11
Fritz, K. von, 41 n. 56
Fronto, M. C., 7

Gadara (Gadarean), 66, 71 n. 48, 137, 150 n. 11

Index of Names

Galilean, 150 n. 11
Galilee (Sea of), 71 n. 48
García González, J., 176 n. 81
Garden (Athenian park), 53
Gardner, P., 41 n. 53
Gasco Lacalle, F., 151 n. 11
Giangrande, G., 42 n. 65, 178 n. 115
Giannantoni, G., 70 n. 39
Giganti, M., 132 n. 36, 178 n. 108
Gill, J. E., 67 n. 7
Gillespie, C. M., 104 n. 67
Gladisch, A., 83, 101 n. 32, 101 n. 38
Glaucus (physician), 131 n. 31
Goethe, J. W. von, 2
Goetling, C. W., 39 n. 33, 79, 80, 99 n. 18
Gomperz, T., 36 n. 9, 151 n. 13
Gorgias of Leontini, 91, 105 n. 71
Goulet, R., 37 n. 23
Goulet-Cazé, M. O., 37 n. 25, 129 n. 16, 150 n. 8
Great Mother (Mother of the Gods), 84, 101 n. 34, 171 n. 15
Greece (Greek), 6, 7, 9, 10, 13, 14, 15, 16, 17, 19, 23, 26, 29, 32, 35, 37 n. 13, 37 n. 14, 38 n. 28, 38 n. 29, 38 n. 32, 39 n. 33, 39 n. 44, 39 n. 45, 40 n 47, 41 n. 57, 41 n. 58, 42 n. 58, 43 n. 71, 43 n. 74, 49, 53, 65, 74, 79, 80, 81, 82, 83, 84, 85, 94, 99 n. 13, 100 n. 25, 100 n. 30, 101 n. 38, 105 n. 69, 115, 117, 123, 124, 125, 128 n. 4, 128 n, 7, 129 n. 14, 130 n. 24, 131 n. 30, 131 n. 31, 131 n. 32, 137, 141, 143, 145, 149, 150 n. 11, 151 n. 13, 151 n. 17, 155, 164, 170 n. 1, 171 n. 17, 172 n. 27, 172 n. 30, 173 n. 35, 174 n. 56, 175 n. 70, 175 n. 71, 176 n. 78, 176 n. 84, 176 n. 86, 176 n. 90, 177 n. 93, 178 n. 106
Gregory Nazianzen, 33
Grube, G.M.A., 104 n. 66
Gulliver, 144, 151 n. 18
Gutas, D., 38 n. 29, 42 n. 66

Guthrie, W.K.C., 89, 103 n. 55
Gymnosophist, 82, 83, 100 n. 29, 101 n. 32, 120, 124

Hades (Underworld), 28, 127
Hadrian, 95
Haldane, E. S., 67 n. 17, 128 n. 1
Hamlet, 130 n. 24
Hammarskjöld, D., 59, 68 n. 30
Hammerstädt, J., 40 n. 49
Harmodius, 161, 175 n. 66
Harpalus, 20, 178 n. 110
Häusle, H., 44 n. 80
Hecaton of Rhodes, 156, 172 n. 29
Hector, 165
Hedrick, D. K., 130 n. 24
Hegel, G.W.F., 52, 67 n. 17, 101 n. 38, 107, 127, 128 n. 1
Hegesias of Cyrene, 55, 58, 161, 175 n. 63
Heidegger, M., 74
Hellas (Hellenic), 83, 84, 101 n. 38
Hellenism (Hellenistic), 37 n. 21, 103 n. 60, 108, 111, 128 n. 8, 129 n. 18, 135, 137, 138, 149 n. 3, 150 n. 10, 171 n. 1
Helvidius Priscus, 146
Henne, D., 78, 99 n. 14
Hephaestion, 131 n. 31
Heraclitus, 86, 101 n. 42
Herculaneum, 25, 26, 42 n. 65, 43 n. 69
Hercules (Herculean), 9, 16, 35, 40 n. 48, 53, 59, 62, 63, 81, 82, 102 n. 46, 120, 122, 140, 141, 159, 161, 167, 171 n. 12
Herodotus, 15, 53, 100 n. 30, 101 n. 34
Hesiod, 141
Hicesias, 10, 11, 12, 13, 39 n. 35, 153
Hicks, R. D., 153
Hipparchia of Maroneia, 6, 25, 42 n. 63, 92, 172 n. 31
Hippias (Athenian tyrant), 175 n. 66
Hippias of Elis, 91
Hippocrates (Hippocratic), 150 n. 16
Hock, R. F., 100 n. 31
Höistad, R., 108, 130 n. 25
Homer, 21, 100 n. 31, 173 n. 40, 175 n. 74, 176 n. 76, 176 n. 83, 176

n. 87, 177 n. 102, 178 n. 104
Horace, 67 n. 21
Houyhnhnms, 151 n. 18
Hunayn Ibn-Ishaq, 8, 26, 56
Hyrcania (Hyrcanian), 34, 44 n. 79

Ibn-Abi 'Awn, 123
Ibn-Hindu, 8, 26, 27, 31, 116, 145
Ilissus, 34, 179 n. 120
India, 10, 29, 34, 81, 82, 83, 100 n. 27, 101 n. 32, 120, 123, 124, 178 n. 112
Ingalls, D., 100 n. 28, 151 n. 14
Ionia (Ionian), 9
Isles of the Blessed, 158
Isocrates, 39 n. 34, 100 n. 31, 123
Isthmus (Isthmian), 19, 62, 64, 70 n. 39, 70 n. 40, 169
Italy, 175 n. 70

James, W., 40 n. 46
Jerome (Saint), 8, 22, 33, 67 n. 16, 92, 116, 171 n. 8
Jesus, 2, 36 n. 2, 39 n. 33, 63, 64, 70 n. 43, 75, 76, 137, 150 n. 10, 150 n. 11, 151 n. 11, 173 n. 43
Jew (Jewish), 137, 150 n. 10
John the Baptist (Saint), 66
Jordan, 71 n. 48
Jouan, F., 70 n. 39
Julian, 2, 8, 29, 51, 55, 111, 115, 137, 138, 140, 151 n. 12, 171 n. 15, 173 n. 37
Juvenal, 7, 171 n. 15

Kant, I., 61, 69 n. 33, 103 n. 52
Katridis, J. T., 100 n. 31
Kindstrand, J. F., 38 n. 26, 101 n. 42

Lakulisa, 82
Lalande, A., 66 n. 5
Latin, 38 n. 28, 38 n. 29
Leuctra, 91
Lewes, G. H., 37 n. 13, 107, 108, 128 n. 4
Lewis, G. C., 99 n. 13
Libanius, 102 n. 50, 105 n. 71
Lipsey, R., 36 n. 6

Livrea, E., 43 n. 77
Livsay, J. L., 36 n. 3
Long, A. A., 37 n. 21, 38 n. 27, 38 n. 31, 39 n. 41, 94, 103 n. 60, 104 n. 61, 104 n. 65, 108, 128 n. 8, 129 n. 17, 129 n. 19, 149 n. 3
Lovejoy, A. O., 67 n. 7, 129 n. 15, 129 n. 19
Lucian of Samosata, 7, 8, 22, 28, 79, 111, 127, 130 n. 24, 135, 137, 138, 151 n. 13, 171 n. 15, 172 n. 27
Luke (Evangelist), 70 n. 43
Luz, M., 102 n. 45
Lyceum, 53
Lydia (Lydian), 15
Lysanias, 154
Lysias (druggist), 159

Macedonia (Macedonian), 8, 10, 19, 22, 29, 47, 98 n. 11, 123, 124, 130 n. 24, 131 n. 32, 156, 174 n. 52, 174 n. 53, 174 n. 54, 176 n. 88
Machado, A., 87, 102 n. 47
Mack, B., 150 n. 10
Malherbe, A. J., 37 n. 19
Malta (Maltase), 45, 163, 176 n. 84
Manes, 163, 176 n. 81
Marcus Aurelius, 7, 118, 146
Martin, R. P., 83, 84, 100 n. 30, 101 n. 37
Matthew (Evangelist), 70 n. 43
Massachusetts, 42 n. 58
Mauthner, F., 42 n. 64
Maximus of Tyre, 7, 17, 23, 24, 25, 77
McEvilley, T., 69 n. 36, 100 n. 25
Media, 131 n. 31
Megara (Megarian), 154, 159, 171 n. 16, 178 n. 114
Meilland, J. M., 68 n. 24
Meleager of Gadara, 7, 55, 67 n. 22, 171 n. 4
Meletus, 102 n. 50, 105 n. 72
Melmoth, S., 99 n. 20
Memphis, 38 n. 32
Menedemus of Gadara, 6

Menippus of Gadara, 6, 33, 41 n. 56, 77, 155, 172 n. 27
Meno, 97
Mesk, J., 102 n. 50
Messina (Straits of), 175 n. 70
Messina, G., 129 n. 18
Metrocles of Maroneia, 6, 32, 156, 172 n. 31
Metroön, 22, 84, 154, 171 n. 15
Mexico (Mexican), 81
Midas, 28, 43 n. 71
Midias, 159, 174 n. 48
Miletus (Milesian), 9, 10, 43 n. 67, 85, 101 n. 35, 117, 170 n. 1
Milne, G., 41 n. 50
Moles, J., 42 n. 65, 43 n. 69
Molossia (Molossian), 45, 163, 176 n. 84
Monimus of Syracuse, 6, 29, 54, 77
Monterroso, A., 50, 67 n. 10
Mubassir Ibn-Fatik, 8, 25, 39 n. 33, 46, 73
Muhtasar Siwan al-hikma, 26, 31, 32, 118, 120
Mullach, F.G.A., 38 n. 28
Müller, K. O., 77, 99 n. 13
Muntahab Siwan al-hikma, 27, 46
Muses, 167
Myndus, 18, 163

Nabal, 150 n. 8
Nakhov, I. M., 99 n. 17
Navia, L. E., 42 n. 63, 43 n. 72, 67 n. 21, 67 n. 22, 71 n. 47, 71 n. 48, 98 n. 5, 98 n. 6, 98 n. 7, 98 n. 8, 98 n. 12, 100 n. 29, 101 n. 39, 102 n. 51, 102 n. 52, 150 n. 9, 151 n. 18, 153
Nazareth, 137, 151 n. 11
Nemea (Nemean), 59, 141, 161, 175 n. 65
Ner, H., 70 n. 44
Nero, 146
Niehues-Pröbsting, H., 36 n. 4, 41 n. 52
Nietzsche, F. W., 4, 7, 37 n. 24, 130 n. 20, 171 n. 4

Odysseus, 155

Oedipus, 49
Oenomaus of Gadara, 16, 17, 40 n. 49
Olympia (Olympic), 18, 33, 65, 121, 140, 159, 161, 164
Olympiodorus, 154, 171 n. 13
Onesicritus of Astypalaea, 6, 29, 54, 82, 83, 100 n. 29, 124, 168, 178 n. 109, 178 n. 112
Oriental, 10, 41 n. 57, 83, 101 n. 38
Orithyia, 179 n. 120
Ortega y Gasset, J., 148, 152 n. 27
Ostling, R. N., 150 n. 10
Ovid, 109
Oxythynchus, 178 n. 115, 179 n. 124

Palestine (Palestinian), 71 n. 48
Paphygonia, 9
Paquet, L., 38 n. 28, 67 n. 14, 174 n. 54, 175 n. 54
Paris (Parisian), 37 n. 10, 78, 128 n. 11, 135
Parium, 77
Parmenides, 69 n. 32, 173 n. 45
Pasion, 39 n. 34
Pasiphon, 168, 178 n. 109
Pasupatas, 82, 100 n. 28, 151 n. 14
Paul (Saint, Pauline), 128 n. 9, 137
Pausanias, 35, 53, 179 n. 120
Payne, E.F.J., 98 n. 1
Pera (Πήρα), 125, 141, 142, 171 n. 11
Perdiccas (Alexander's officer), 175 n. 54
Perdiccas III of Macedonia, 28, 47, 159, 174 n. 54
Peregrinus Proteus, 33, 77, 111, 138, 146, 151 n. 13
Pergamum, 137
Pericles, 9, 13, 14, 43 n. 67, 143, 170 n. 1
Peripatetic, 171 n. 9, 172 n. 22, 179 n. 124
Perry, B. E., 105 n. 69
Persia (Persian), 9, 12, 13, 18, 44 n. 79, 49, 83, 100 n. 27, 123, 131 n. 32, 145, 179 n. 120
Phaedrus, 68 n. 26, 179 n. 120
Philip II of Macedonia, 22, 28, 159, 174 n. 52

Philip V of Macedonia, 53
Philiscus of Aegina, 168, 170, 178 n. 109
Philo of Alexandria, 137
Philodemus of Gadara, 125, 131 n. 35
Philostratus, 75, 98 n. 8
Phocion the Honest, 29, 168, 178 n. 113
Phoenicia, 133
Phrygia, 101 n. 35
Phryne, 164, 177 n. 95
Pinski, D., 38 n. 30
Piraeus, 20
Pizzagalli, A. M., 130 n. 24
Plato (Platonic, Platonism), 6, 12, 14, 19, 20, 21, 24, 32, 41 n. 52, 41 n. 55, 42 n. 64, 43 n. 67, 45, 47, 53, 54, 55, 56, 57, 60, 61, 62, 68 n. 27, 68 n. 31, 70 n. 39, 74, 86, 87, 88, 89, 90, 91, 94, 96, 97, 100 n. 31, 101 n. 41, 102 n. 43, 102 n. 44, 102 n. 46, 102 n. 52, 103 n. 52, 103 n. 53, 103 n. 54, 103 n. 56, 103 n. 58, 105 n. 71, 105 n. 72, 109, 130 n. 21, 136, 142, 144, 145, 154, 155, 158, 159, 162, 163, 164, 166, 171 n. 17, 172 n. 19, 172 n. 23, 174 n. 47, 175 n. 67, 176 n. 77, 176 n. 78, 180 n. 120
Plutarch, 7, 8, 16, 19, 28, 38 n. 32, 48, 82, 91, 127, 130 n. 24, 131 n. 31, 131 n. 32, 171 n. 10, 172 n. 18, 173 n. 44, 175 n. 62, 175 n. 64, 175 n. 67
Polycrates, 87, 102 n. 50
Polyeuctus, 154
Polyxenus, 46, 66 n. 4, 173 n. 32
Pontus, 16, 23
Popper, K., 102 n. 52, 103 n. 52
Prasangika Madhyamika, 81, 100 n. 25
Praxiteles, 177 n. 95
Presocratic, 74, 84, 85, 86, 101 n. 39, 113, 117
Prodicus of Ceos, 91
Protagoras of Abdera, 85, 101 n. 40, 113, 114

Pyrrho of Elis (Pyrrhoist), 4, 66, 68 n. 29, 86, 95, 135
Pythagoras (Pythagorean), 6, 83, 85, 95
Pythia (Pythian), 11, 14, 15, 39 n. 43, 127, 156, 173 n. 33
Python, 39 n. 43

Qumran, 150 n. 10

Rahn, H., 129 n. 16
Rankin, H. D., 104 n. 66
Raphael (Raffaelo Santi), 43 n. 75
Reifler, B. V., 152 n. 22
Reinach, T., 39 n. 37
Rhodes, 65, 140
Rich, A.N.M., 130 n. 23
Rieger, D., 36 n. 10, 78, 99 n. 15
Riley, W., 129 n. 19
Robin, L., 129 n. 14
Rome (Roman), 2, 31, 32, 37 n. 14, 37 n. 25, 67 n. 21, 70 n. 39, 75, 77, 79, 107, 110, 111, 133, 135, 137, 138, 139, 146, 150 n. 10, 150 n. 11, 151 n. 12
Romm, J., 99 n. 24, 100 n. 27
Rousseau, J. J., 125
Roy, P., 105 n. 75
Rudberg, G., 79, 99 n. 16
Rumi (Maulana Jajal-uddin), 68 n. 30
Russell, B., 2, 36 n. 8, 147, 152 n. 24

Sahrastani, 31, 56, 59
Sahzazuri, 29
Sallustius, 133, 140, 149 n. 1
Samothrace, 164, 176 n. 91
Sarapis (Serapis), 10, 38 n. 32, 165, 170 n. 1, 177 n. 100
Sardanapalus, 28, 43 n. 70
Satyrus of Callias Pontica, 5, 170, 179 n. 124
Saunders, T. B., 98 n. 4
Sayre, F., 13, 21, 23, 37 n. 11, 37 n. 18, 37 n. 20, 39 n. 37, 39 n. 39, 40 n. 52, 41 n. 55, 41 n. 58, 42 n. 58, 42 n. 61, 43 n. 73, 52, 67 n. 15, 69 n. 37, 83, 93, 95, 98 n. 10, 101 n. 33, 104 n. 64,

105 n. 70, 128 n. 7
Schneider, M. W., 132 n. 40
Schopenhauer, A., 4, 28, 48, 73, 74, 97, 98 n. 1, 98 n. 3, 98 n. 4, 98 n. 5, 98 n. 7, 105 n. 74, 120, 132 n. 39
Schulz-Falkenthal, H., 43 n. 74, 99 n. 17
Scirpalus, 20, 168
Scythia (Scythian), 83, 84, 100 n. 30, 101 n. 34, 101 n. 37, 145, 151 n. 19
Secundus the Silent, 95, 105 n. 69
Seltman, C.T., 12, 39 n. 35
Seneca, 2, 7, 78, 115, 146, 171 n. 15, 173 n. 39, 176 n. 81
Servais, J., 38 n. 32
Sextus Empiricus, 8, 60, 97, 172 n. 28, 173 n. 45
Shakespeare, W., 130 n. 24
Shiva (Shivaite), 82
Sicily, 154, 175 n. 70
Simon the Shoemaker, 52, 67 n. 18, 83, 100 n. 31, 101 n. 31
Sinop, 10, 170 n. 1, 177 n. 100
Sinope (Sinopean), 9, 10, 11, 12, 13, 14, 17, 18, 19, 20, 21, 23, 29, 32, 35, 38 n. 32, 39 n. 37, 55, 66, 70 n. 39, 76, 77, 79, 83, 84, 93, 94, 124, 151 n. 12, 153, 161, 169, 170 n. 1, 177 n. 100
Sinova, 9
Sjöberg, L., 68 n. 30
Skepticism (skeptic), 4, 54, 68, 85, 86, 88, 91, 96, 135, 102 n. 45
Sloterdijk, P., 4, 37 n. 15, 55, 68 n. 23, 147, 152 n. 26
Smith, N. K., 69 n. 33
Socrates (Socratic), 5, 6, 9, 12, 14, 15, 20, 21, 24, 25, 26, 30, 31, 32, 34, 37 n. 21, 38 n. 27, 38 n. 31, 39 n. 41, 41 n. 52, 42 n. 64, 43 n. 67, 43 n. 68, 43 n. 75, 52, 53, 57, 66, 67 n. 15, 68 n. 26, 68 n. 31, 70 n. 39, 74, 75, 76, 80, 83, 84, 85, 86, 87, 88, 89, 90, 91, 92, 94, 95, 96, 97, 100 n. 31, 101 n. 40, 101 n. 41, 102 n. 43, 102 n. 46, 102 n. 48, 102 n. 49, 102 n. 50, 102 n. 51, 102 n. 52, 103 n. 52, 103 n. 53, 103 n. 54, 103 n. 55, 103 n. 56, 103 n. 57, 103 n. 58, 103 n. 59, 103 n. 60, 104 n. 61, 104 n. 63, 104 n. 64, 104 n. 65, 105 n. 68, 105 n. 71, 105 n. 72, 105 n. 76, 108, 110, 112, 113, 114, 120, 128 n. 8, 129 n. 17, 129 n. 19, 130 n. 21, 133, 134, 136, 144, 149 n. 3, 150 n. 7, 152 n. 20, 162, 171 n. 16, 175 n. 62, 179 n. 109, 179 n. 120
Sophist (Sophistical), 20, 21, 62, 85, 86, 91, 92, 94, 95, 101 n. 40, 102 n. 41, 102 n. 44, 113, 144, 148, 173 n. 32
Sosicrates of Rhodes, 5, 170, 179 n. 123
Sotion of Alexandria, 155, 170, 172 n. 22
Sparta (Spartan), 9, 18, 60, 65, 77, 141, 155, 164, 174 n. 46, 177 n. 94
Spartacus, 79
Statira, 131 n. 32
Steinkraus, W. E., 152 n. 20
Stilpo of Megara, 29, 168, 178 n. 114
Stirner, M., 126, 132 n. 37
Stoa, 53, 134, 149 n. 2
Stobaeus, 8, 23, 34, 52, 56, 64, 87, 172 n. 23, 172 n. 25, 172 n. 26, 172 n. 32, 176 n. 80, 177 n. 94, 177 n. 99
Stoicism (Stoic), 2, 30, 32, 54, 59, 65, 90, 104 n. 61, 108, 111, 113, 123, 125, 133, 134, 135, 136, 137, 138, 140, 146, 149 n. 2, 149 n. 4, 152 n. 21, 159, 172 n. 29, 174 n. 51, 177 n. 98
Strabo, 9
Strohmaier, G., 38 n. 29, 42 n. 65
Suidas, 8, 52
Susa, 131 n. 32
Swift, J., 144, 151 n. 18, 152 n. 18
Syracuse, 19, 154, 172 n. 19, 175 n. 67
Syria (Syrian), 149 n. 1

Syrkin, A., 82, 100 n. 26
Szarmach, M., 70 n. 39

Tacit, 38 n. 32
Tardieu, É., 147, 152 n. 25
Tarn, W. W., 123, 124, 131 n. 28, 131 n. 29, 131 n. 30, 131 n. 33
Tartarus, 141
Tatian, 33
Teles of Megara, 7, 19 , 171 n. 10
Tertullian, 8
Thales of Miletus, 9, 12, 15, 42 n. 62, 84, 85, 176 n. 79
Thebes (Theban), 49, 174 n. 46, 174 n. 52, 177 n. 95
Themistius, 8, 56
Theodorus of Cyrene, 59, 68 n. 31, 159, 174 n. 49
Theophrastus, 48, 154, 171 n. 9
Thompson, D. B., 100 n. 31
Thompson, H. A., 100 n. 31
Thoreau, H. D., 81, 99 n. 22, 147
Thrace (Thracian), 53, 77, 79, 91
Thracis, 16, 40 n. 48
Thrasea Paetus, 146
Thrasymachus of Chalcedon, 86, 102 n. 44, 148
Thucydides, 14
Tigris, 178 n. 112
Titus, 75, 77, 98 n. 8
Tuckett, C. M., 150 n. 10
Turkey (Turkish), 10, 170 n. 1
Typhon, 141

Ucciani, L., 105 n. 76
Ulysses, 53
Umm Qays, 71 n. 48

Utilitarianism (Utilitarian), 115

Vaage, L. E., 150 n. 10
Valladolid, 132 n. 40
Vespasian, 146
Vlastos, G., 103 n. 56
Voltaire, 2
Voss, B. R., 171 n. 12

Walden, 135
Walisa, 26
Wieland, C. M., 2
Wilde, O., 80, 99 n. 20
Winiarczyk, A., 68 n. 31, 177 n. 92

Xanthippe, 25, 42 n. 64
Xeniades, 20, 21, 155, 156, 157, 168, 172 n. 28
Xenophon, 12, 42 n. 64, 43 n. 68, 57, 70 n. 39, 75, 87, 88, 89, 90, 91, 94, 95, 97, 102 n. 50, 103 n. 54, 103 n. 58, 104 n. 62, 105 n. 71, 105 n. 75, 134

Yahoos, 151 n. 18

Zarathustra, 130 n. 20
Zen, 2
Zeno of Citium, 12, 30, 32, 53, 54, 90, 92, 104 n. 61, 133, 134, 135, 136, 149 n. 2, 178 n. 114
Zeno of Elea, 69 n. 32, 173 n. 45
Zeus, 17, 141, 154, 161, 169
Zoïlus of Amphipolis (Perga?), 52, 67 n. 18, 83, 100 n. 31, 157, 173 n. 40
Zopyrus, 32

Index of Subjects

Ἀγαμία (see Celibacy)
Ἀδιαφορία (see Indifference)
Ἀδοξία (dishonor, contempt for the opinions of others), 139
Agnosticism (agnostic), 91, 96
Ἀμαθία (see Ignorance)
Ἀναίδεια (see Shamelessness)
Anecdote (anecdotal reports, χρεῖα), 1, 5, 6, 7, 22, 23, 32, 34, 37 n. 26, 45, 46, 50, 57, 57, 58, 61, 62, 64, 69 n. 37, 70 n. 39, 90, 105 n. 72, 108, 110, 122, 134, 140, 143, 156, 163, 170, 172 n. 23, 174 n. 47, 176 n. 81, 177 n. 92
Animal (animalism), 3, 34, 47, 48, 49, 57, 58, 63, 68 n. 27, 75, 82, 107, 116, 117, 118, 119, 121, 126, 154, 158, 168
Anthropomorphism, 47
Anti-intellectualism, 21, 55, 58, 68 n. 24, 148
Ἀπάθεια (see Insensibility)
Apophthegm, 7, 25, 26, 43 n. 65, 56, 61, 69 n. 37, 172 n. 30
Ἀρετή (see Virtue)
Arrogance (μεγαληγορία), 75, 88, 95, 103 n. 54
Ἀρχή (see Element)
Asceticism (ascetic, ἄσκησις), 16, 20, 53, 60, 77, 81, 96, 105 n. 74, 120, 132 n. 40, 137, 138, 141, 148, 149 n. 1
Ἀσέβεια (see Impiety)
Ἄσκησις (see Asceticism)
Atheism (atheist), 59, 68 n. 31, 174 n. 49, 177 n. 92
Athlete (athletic), 18, 62, 63, 63, 65, 75, 121, 140, 141, 145, 156, 161, 167, 172 n. 24, 175 n. 65
Ἀτυφία (see Lucidity)
Αὐτάρκεια (see Self-sufficiency)

Begging (beggar), 23, 29, 30, 77, 107, 112, 137, 158, 161, 163, 166

Cannibalism, 21, 49, 116
Celibacy (ἀγαμία), 24, 27
Character, 2, 4, 5, 7, 9, 12, 17, 20, 33, 35, 45, 46, 50, 59, 62, 74, 75, 76, 77, 77, 78, 80, 89, 93, 96, 97, 98 n. 7, 103 n. 58, 113, 124, 125, 126, 129 n. 17, 134, 139, 140, 146, 147, 148, 158, 165, 174 n. 46, 42 n. 58, 43 n. 64
Child (children), 22, 24, 25, 38 n. 26, 42 n. 57, 47, 97, 157, 159, 165, 168
Chreia (χρεία, see Anecdote)

Cosmopolitanism (cosmopolitan, κοσμοπολίτης), 10, 23, 26, 42 n. 60, 123, 124, 125, 126, 131 n. 34, 132 n. 36, 138, 141, 177 n. 98
Currency (νόμισμα), 10, 11, 12, 13, 14, 17, 18, 19, 39 n. 36, 39 n. 37, 41 n. 52, 51, 76, 77, 93, 94, 109, 111, 112, 113, 120, 121, 127, 136, 139, 153, 163, 167, 170 n. 3, 171 n. 6, 171 n. 7, 177 n. 103
Custom (convention, νόμισμα), 6, 11, 13, 17, 18, 20, 24, 26, 28, 34, 41 n. 50, 44 n. 79, 46, 48, 50, 51, 62, 65, 66, 73, 78, 79, 82, 85, 86, 89, 93, 99 n. 17, 116, 117, 121, 127, 134, 135, 136, 138, 139, 142, 158, 161, 167, 168, 169, 171 n. 7, 178 n. 94
Cynicism (modern, cynical), 4, 37 n. 14, 47, 98 n. 3, 139, 140, 147, 148, 149, 152 n. 23

Death, 1, 2, 8, 9, 13, 16, 20, 27, 32, 33, 34, 35, 43 n. 67, 44 n. 77, 46, 47, 78, 90, 103 n. 59, 104 n. 63, 105 n. 68, 105 n. 71, 113, 114, 116, 124, 127, 128, 133, 135, 137, 141, 143, 148, 156, 159, 163, 166, 168, 169, 170, 174 n. 51, 174 n. 54, 179 n. 121
Definition, 56, 68 n. 27, 94, 104 n. 67, 143, 144, 152 n. 20, 158, 174 n. 47
Diatribe (diatribal, διατριβή), 55, 62, 67 n. 21, 105 n. 66, 109, 119, 143
Διατριβή (see Diatribe)
Diet, 30, 64, 120, 131
Dog (dog-like, κύων, κυνικός), 1, 3, 4, 6, 31, 33, 34, 35, 45, 46, 47, 48, 49, 50, 51, 52, 53, 54, 55, 64, 66, 75, 79, 80, 82, 94, 98 n. 3, 98 n. 8, 99 n. 24, 100 n. 27, 100 n. 31, 107, 110, 116, 117, 118, 119, 128 n. 10, 130 n. 24, 132 n. 40, 135, 136, 137, 139, 145, 147, 149, 150 n. 8, 156, 158, 160, 163, 164, 165, 169, 172 n. 32, 176 n. 84, 177 n. 96

Education, 11, 20, 21, 26, 56, 57, 65, 96, 120, 144, 145, 148, 166
Egoism, 4, 147
Ἔλεγχος (elenchus, elenchical), 88, 89, 103 n. 55, 103 n. 56
Element (ἀρχή), 84
Ἐλευθερία (see Freedom)
Εὐδαιμονία (see Happiness)
Exhibitionism, 3, 61, 64, 69 n. 36, 82, 88, 108

Φύσις (see Nature)
Freedom (free, ἐλευθερία), 2, 3, 13, 14, 19, 23, 24, 28, 30, 77, 78, 92, 93, 98 n. 5, 122, 125, 126, 129 n. 17, 134, 135, 139, 140, 146, 151 n. 11, 159, 167, 175 n. 66
Freedom of speech (παρρησία), 2, 3, 36 n. 7, 49, 110, 128 n. 11, 140, 143, 144, 145, 146, 166, 178 n. 106

Happiness (εὐδαιμονία), 16, 28, 30, 48, 55, 57, 58, 60, 82, 105 n. 68, 114, 115, 116, 119, 120, 126, 129 n. 17, 129 n. 18, 130 n. 22, 133, 140, 142, 145, 152 n. 20, 159, 160, 167, 173 n. 42
Hedonism, 86, 105 n. 75, 148
Humor, 61, 62, 69 n. 37

Iconography (works of art), 1, 31, 33, 44 n. 75
Ignorance (ignorant, ἀμαθία), 12, 21, 46, 56, 88, 114, 140, 160
Impiety (ἀσέβια), 103 n. 59, 43 n. 67
Incest, 49, 116
Indifference (ἀδιαφορία), 5, 24, 28, 34, 42 n. 57, 48, 49, 51, 78, 82, 85, 89, 90, 95, 96, 120, 133, 138, 139

Index of Subjects 207

Indifferentism, 61, 69 n. 33
Insensibility (ἀπάθεια), 140

Καρτερία (see Strength of character)
Κοσμοπολίτης (see Cosmopolitanism)
Κόσμος (see Universe)
Κύων, κυνικός (see Dog, dog-like)

Law (νόμος), 17, 24, 28, 49, 53, 66, 73, 76, 78, 79, 82, 83, 86, 88, 91, 96, 100 n. 29, 102 n. 43, 121, 126, 135, 139, 145, 167, 168
Λόγος (see Reason)
Lucidity (clarity of mind, ἀτυφία), 3, 26, 45, 64, 65, 66, 74, 81, 88, 89, 71 n. 49, 110, 114, 117, 118, 120, 136, 142, 144, 145, 148, 149, 167, 168, 172 n. 18

Madness (lunacy, mad, μανία), 21, 23, 51, 60, 64, 65, 74, 77, 86, 87, 88, 90, 97, 108, 109, 115, 125, 126, 131 n. 34, 132 n. 39, 136, 139, 141, 142, 144, 145, 146, 157, 162, 167
Marriage (married), 24, 25, 42 n. 63, 95, 97, 124, 131 n. 32, 145, 155, 161, 162, 168, 176 n. 79
Materialism (material, materialist), 4, 58, 59, 60, 61, 95, 96
Μεγαληγορία (see Arrogance)
Mendicant orders, 30, 137, 150 n. 11
Midwife (midwifery, μαῖα), 89, 103 n. 57
Misanthropy (misanthropic), 27
Misogyny (misogynist), 25, 26
Money (wealth), 10, 16, 28, 29, 39, 59, 64, 83, 92, 119, 121, 129 n. 17, 144, 145, 153, 155, 160, 161, 163, 166, 170, 170 n. 3, 171 n. 6, 174 n. 48, 177 n. 95, 177 n. 101

Nationalism (nation, nationality), 23, 73, 79, 80, 84, 155, 123, 124, 126, 131 n. 32, 134, 147, 148, 168, 177 n. 98
Natural law, 134, 135

Nature (natural, φύσις), 26, 30, 32, 46, 48, 50, 51, 57, 62, 63, 70 n. 42, 75, 77, 78, 80, 81, 84, 85, 86, 89, 105 n. 63, 109, 113, 114, 115, 116, 117, 118 119, 120, 121, 122, 126, 127, 129 n. 17, 129 n. 19, 133, 134, 135, 136, 140, 143, 145, 147, 149, 158, 165, 167, 178 n. 107
Nihilism (nihilistic), 4, 85, 102 n 44, 147
Nitrous oxide (N_2O), 40 n. 46
Νόμισμα (see Currency, Custom)
Νόμος (see Law)
Numismatics, 39 n. 36, 39 n. 37, 90

Obfuscation (confusion, smoke, τῦφος), 3, 18, 59, 60, 65, 70 n. 45, 84, 88, 89, 109, 120, 125, 136, 140, 141, 142, 147, 149, 152 n. 20
Optimism, 54, 74, 96
Oracle (oracular), 11, 12, 14, 15, 16, 16, 17, 18, 19, 23, 28, 39 n. 44, 40 n. 46, 40 n. 50, 40 n. 52, 53, 86, 93, 127, 133, 134, 153, 171 n. 7

Παραχάραξις, 11, 17, 41 n. 50, 99 n. 17, 127, 171 n. 6, 171 n. 7
Παρρησία (see Freedom of speech)
Patriotism (patriotic), 4, 42 n. 58, 126
Πενία (see Poverty)
Pessimism (pessimistic), 3, 73, 74, 98 n. 2, 147
Φιλανθρωπία (see Philanthropy)
Philanthropy (φιλανθρωπία), 136, 137, 140, 142
Pleasure, 16, 30, 60, 62, 65, 60, 62, 65, 88, 92, 96, 97, 105 n. 75, 115, 120, 140, 166, 167, 174 n. 51
Politics (political, politician), 3, 6, 8, 10, 11, 13, 14, 15, 20, 24, 26, 29, 43 n. 67, 47, 54, 63, 65, 78, 79, 81, 82, 85, 86, 87, 89, 90, 91, 92, 96, 102 n. 52, 120, 121, 122, 123, 126, 129 n. 17, 131 n. 30, 131 n. 35, 132 n. 36, 135, 138, 142, 143, 145,

148, 153, 155, 156, 169, 171 n. 13
Polytheism (polytheistic), 59, 84, 129 n. 16
Poverty (poor, penury, πενία), 28, 29, 59, 60, 63, 64, 70 n. 43, 78, 79, 80, 82, 88, 95, 96, 109, 115, 124, 134, 137, 138, 140, 145, 159, 161, 166, 173 n. 42, 175 n. 61
Primitivism (primitive), 4, 47, 58, 67 n. 7, 82, 116, 117, 125, 129 n. 15, 129 n. 19
Procreation, 24, 25, 97

Reason (λόγος), 3, 35, 74, 81, 84, 85, 88, 89, 117, 119, 120, 125, 127, 131 n. 31, 133, 134, 135, 142, 144, 154, 158, 168.
Religion (religious, religiosity), 4, 6, 16, 41 n. 52, 54, 59, 65, 85, 88, 91, 96, 101 n. 41, 103 n. 59, 110, 113, 114, 115, 129 n. 12, 129 n. 16, 138, 142, 148, 150 n. 11, 151 n. 12, 159, 174 n. 50, 176 n. 91

Self-sufficiency (independence, αὐτάρκεια), 3, 4, 23, 24, 35, 48, 84, 89, 96, 102 n. 52, 121, 122, 130 n. 23, 138, 139, 141, 148, 169
Shamelessness (impudence, ἀναίδεια), 3, 49, 50, 51, 79, 107, 118, 119, 127, 138, 139, 147
Slavery (slave), 41 n. 57, 44 n. 74, 53, 57, 65, 77, 79, 80, 91, 92, 93, 126, 134, 136, 155, 156, 159, 162, 163, 168, 176 n. 81
Speculative philosophy, 60, 61, 89, 94, 135, 145
Staff (stick, βάκτρον), 31, 34, 62, 92, 93, 104 n. 63, 112, 125, 136, 137, 138, 153, 154, 156, 166, 169, 171 n. 12
Strength of character (καρτερία), 16, 59, 81, 97, 120, 140, 141, 148
Successions (διαδοχαί), 6, 52, 80, 90, 99 n. 19, 104 n. 61, 134, 169, 170
Suicide, 32, 33, 78, 65, 111, 146, 175 n. 63

Theriomorphism, 47, 48, 49, 51, 67 n. 7, 116
Theriophily, 47, 48, 49, 67 n. 7
Tub (πίθος), 1, 4, 5, 22, 23, 30, 35, 49, 54, 60, 61, 64, 96, 98 n. 3, 116, 117, 118, 119, 135, 136, 147, 149, 154, 159, 171 n. 15, 173 n. 39
Τῦφος (see Obfuscation)
Typhus (typhoid fever), 142, 151 n. 16

Universe (κόσμος), 84, 85, 113, 117, 118, 123, 124, 130 n. 26, 145, 168, 178 n. 108

Virtue (virtuous, ἀρετή), 2, 3, 26, 30, 49, 50, 53, 55, 75, 82, 85, 89, 97, 103 n. 58, 105 n. 68, 116, 118, 120, 121, 129 n. 17, 133, 137, 138, 140, 148, 162, 167, 170, 174 n. 46, 178 n. 115

Wallet (πήρα), 31, 92, 104 n. 63, 112, 125, 141
War, 4, 6, 9, 11, 14, 23, 24, 26, 57, 65, 71 n. 46, 73, 77, 81, 84, 85, 126, 127, 143, 148, 161
Wife, 24, 25, 30, 42 n. 64, 43 n. 68, 98 n. 11
Woman, 24, 25, 26, 27, 42 n. 65, 43 n. 67, 43 n. 68, 47, 97, 98 n. 11, 103 n. 57, 105 n. 75, 124, 131 n. 32, 137, 145, 147, 157, 158, 160, 162, 164, 165, 168, 177 n. 94

About the Author

LUIS E. NAVIA is Professor of Philosophy at New York Institute of Technology. He has written extensively in philosophy and is the author of thirteen books. His most recent books are *The Socratic Presence: A Study of the Sources* (1993), *The Philosophy of Cynicism: An Annotated Bibliography* (Greenwood Press, 1995), and *Classical Cynicism: A Critical Study* (Greenwood Press, 1996).

**Recent Titles in
Contributions in Philosophy**

The Theory of Absence: Subjectivity, Signification, and Desire
Patrick Fuery

Pretending and Meaning: Toward a Pragmatic Theory of Fictional Discourse
Richard Henry

Inventing Nations: Justifications of Authority in the Modern World
Terry H. Pickett

Classical Cynicism: A Critical Study
Luis E. Navia

Rewriting the History of Ancient Greek Philosophy
Victorino Tejera

Freedom over Servitude: Montaigne, La Boétie, and *On Voluntary Servitude*
*Daniel Martin and David Lewis Schaefer, with Michael Platt, Randolph Paul Runyon,
and Régine Reynolds-Cornell, editors*

Understanding Confucian Philosophy: Classical and Sung-Ming
Shu-hsien Liu

Myths of Freedom: Equality, Modern Thought, and Philosophical Radicalism
Stephen L. Gardner

Platonic Errors: Plato, a Kind of Poet
Gene Fendt and David Rozema

Asian and Jungian Views of Ethics
Carl B. Becker, editor

The Last Choice: Preemptive Suicide in Advanced Age, Second Edition
C. G. Prado

Self-Construction and the Formation of Human Values: Truth, Language, and Desire
Teodros Kiros

Lightning Source UK Ltd.
Milton Keynes UK
UKHW020230211219
355797UK00004B/246/P